stupid faces in stunning paintings

stupid faces in stunning paintings

a serious exploration of art history's silliest expressions

Matthijs Van Mierlo
Creator of The Gaze

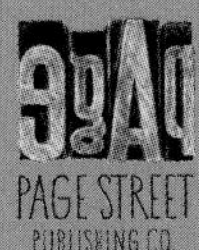

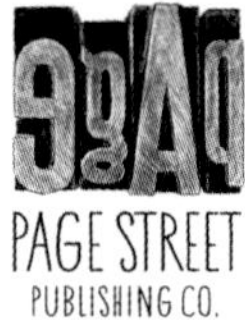

Originally published in Belgium "Stupid Faces in Stunning Paintings" 2025 by Borgerhoff & Lamberigts NV

Published in 2026 by
Page Street Publishing Co.
27 Congress Street, Suite 1511
Salem, MA 01970
www.pagestreetpublishing.com

Distributed by Macmillan, sales in Canada by The Canadian Manda Group.

30 29 28 27 26 2 3 4 5 6

ISBN-13: 979-8-89003-419-9

Library of Congress Control Number: 2025940442

Edited by Sadie Hofmeester

Book design by Gert Dooreman for Borgerhoff & Lamberigts NV

Printed and bound in the United States

Page Street Publishing protects our planet by donating to nonprofits like The Trustees, which focuses on local land conservation.

"the first
mistake of art
is to assume
that it's serious."

Lester Bangs

I love art history for three reasons: the beauty, the stories and the incredible amount of stupid faces. Along with hands and bicycles, faces are probably the most difficult thing to draw or paint, which might be one explanation why there are so many wacky faces in art. Some artists just weren't very good at rendering them.

introduction

Claude Monet, for example, was a master of light, color and landscapes. But faces? Not so much. And he knew it. So he didn't paint them that often, and when he did, they were usually hazy and lacking in detail. In other words, they were impressionist. Take *Woman with a Parasol,* a stunning painting with two very hazy faces. It's lovely, because it just works in this style.

Claude Monet, *Woman with a Parasol,* 1875.

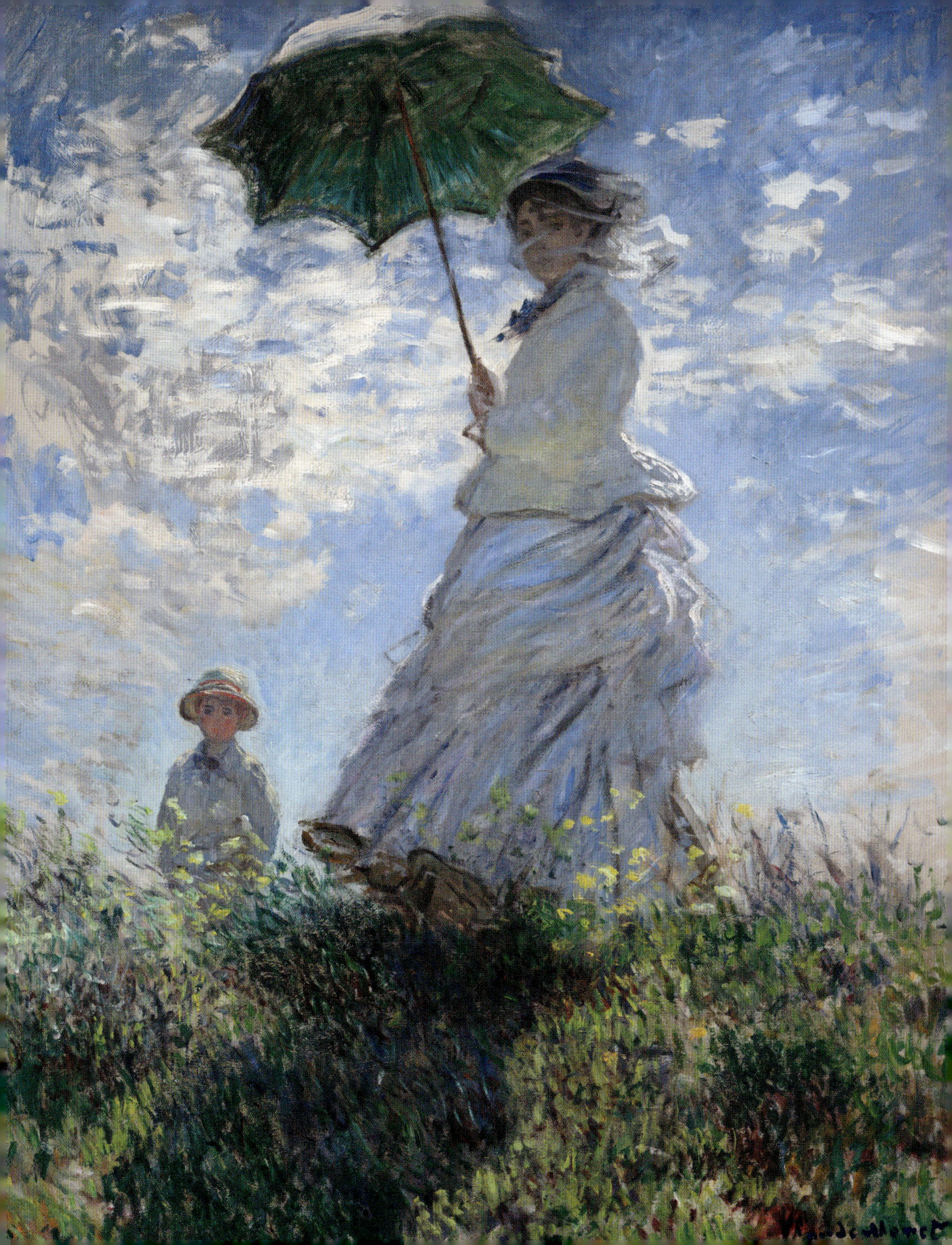

But sometimes, when Monet did venture to create a more detailed face, the results were just . . . weird. Granted, he got better at them later in his career, but at 22, he painted *Head of a Woman*. A wonderful example of a stupid face in a not-so-stunning painting.

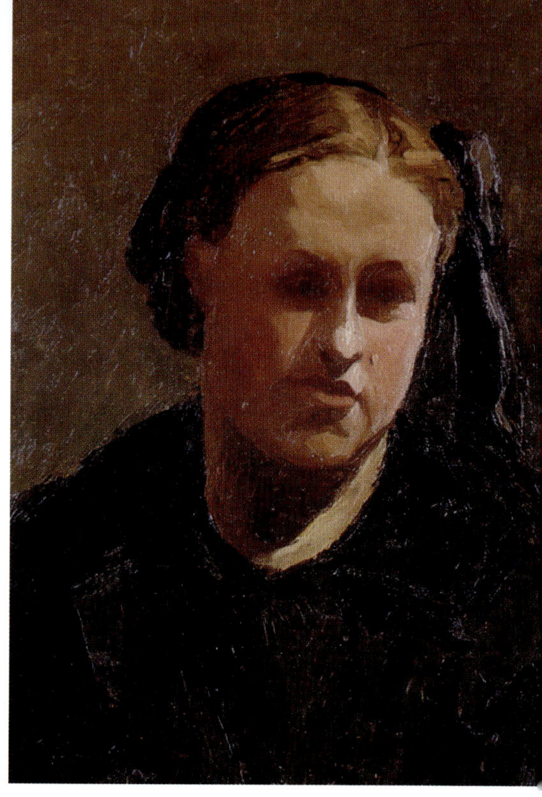

Claude Monet, *Head of a Woman*, c. 1862–1863.

But honestly, struggling with painting faces is perfectly fine—especially if you're talented enough to pivot toward an art movement that is not centered around faces and manage to become the godfather of that movement along the way. Kudos to Claude for that.

But what I like most is when a face looks stupid, not because the artist was bad at painting it, but because they *want* the face to look stupid. Or weird. Or goofy. Or whatever word you want to use to describe a face that's out of the ordinary. That's when you get *stupid faces in stunning paintings*. And these are the paintings we will explore in this book.

what is a stupid face?

But what exactly is a stupid face? Well, it certainly isn't the same as a stupid person. Someone who is considered stupid shows a lack of intelligence—whatever "intelligence" may mean—but that's not the kind of stupid we'll be talking about here.

No, we will be having a very close look at stupid *faces*, which has nothing to do with the intelligence of the person who owns the face. Anyone can make a stupid face. Albert Einstein for one was great at it. Arthur Sasse's famous photo portrait of Einstein shows an incredibly stupid face belonging to an incredibly smart man.

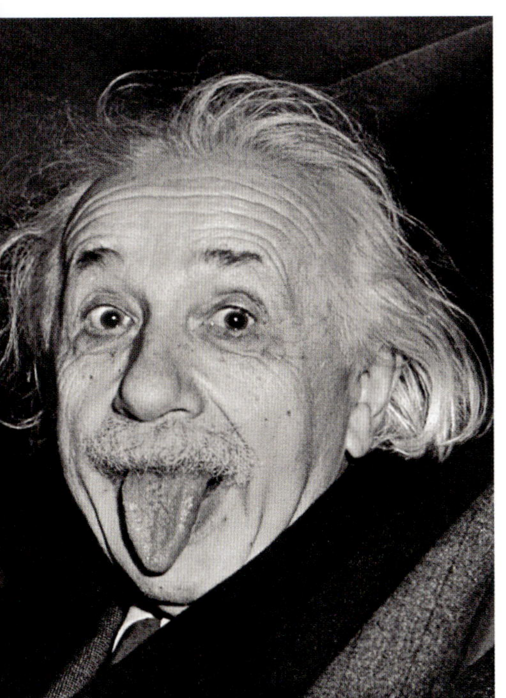

So when I call a face stupid, it has nothing to do with intelligence. It's all about the silliness of the facial expression or the unusual way in which an artist has rendered a face. Or a combination of both. Those are the faces we'll be focusing on. And most importantly, we will explore the stories behind those faces and their paintings. Because why exactly are they so wacky? Which emotions are hidden behind the weirdness? And how does the face relate to the painting it is part of?

Welcome to the wonderful world of stupid faces in stunning paintings. Let's dig in.

Arthur Sasse, *Albert Einstein*, 1951.

13th-century man-child

Apparently, if you dig deep enough into art history and meticulously study 13th-century Italian iconography, you might just stumble upon early depictions of the American director and screenwriter Quentin Tarantino. Because seriously, the resemblance here is uncanny.

Maybe it's one of Tarantino's long-lost Italian ancestors. Maybe it's a medieval doppelgänger.

Or maybe it's none of the above, because in reality, our very first face belongs to the most depicted man in art history, which isn't Quentin Tarantino, but that of another great storyteller called Jesus Christ of Nazareth. But isn't Jesus usually depicted with long hair and a beard? Well, it depends. Turning the page will give you a clue as to why he looks so . . . well-shaven.

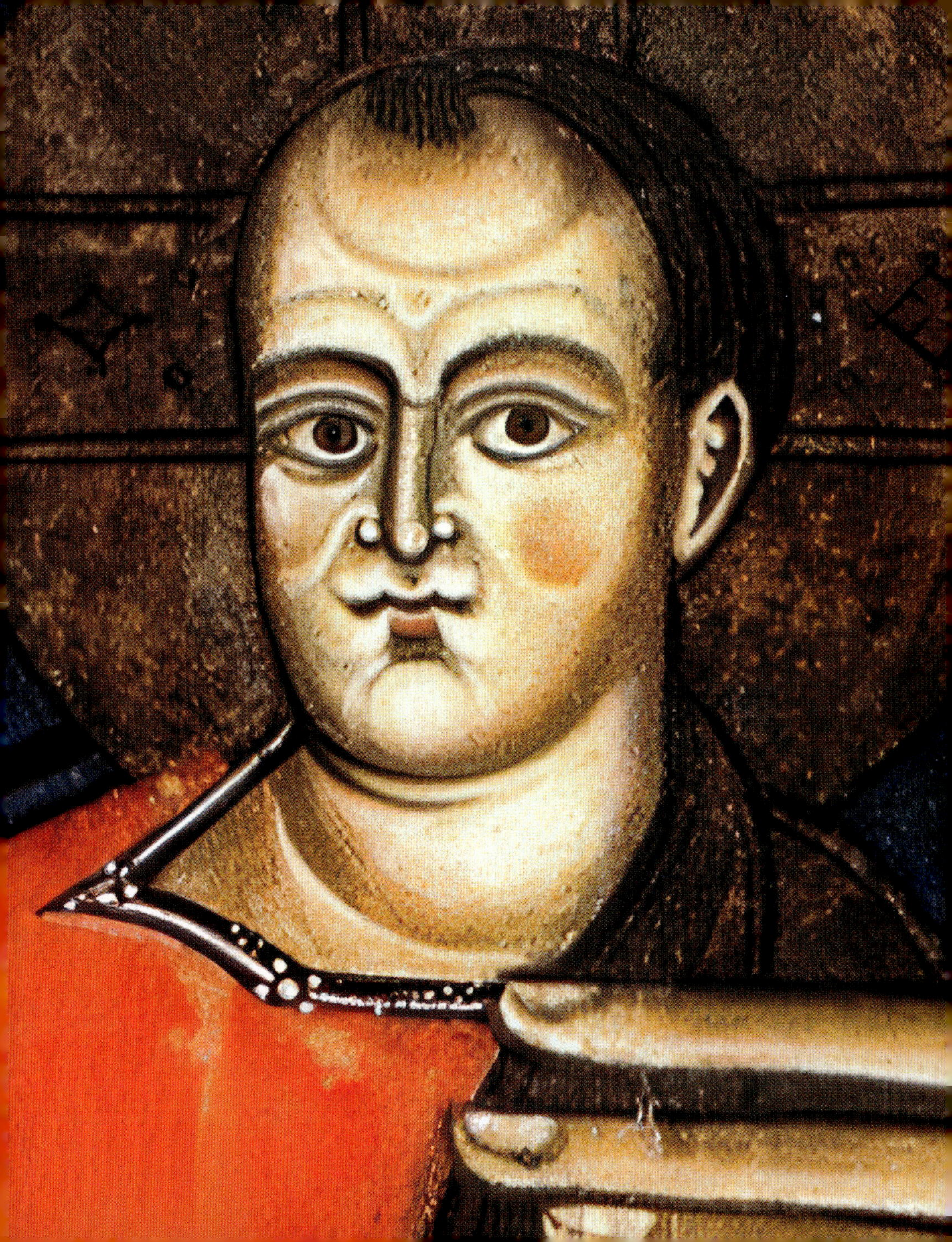

The reason why this particular Jesus doesn't have a beard is simple: He's still a baby. And babies don't have beards. But then again, most babies don't have the receding hairline of a middle-aged accountant either. So why does he look this way?

Well, it's certainly not because the artist didn't know what babies look like. No, depicting baby Jesus as a middle-aged man was a very deliberate choice, quite common in medieval Christian iconography. It's meant to emphasize that Jesus wasn't just your average drooling baby. He was a wise and divine baby, fully aware of his mission, even as an infant. Because while the baby Messiah might look like he's about to order two Budweisers after a long week of working in accounting, in reality, this man-child is raising his hand to bless us all. And all the while, his mother, Mary, stares ahead with a vacant gaze, as if silently wondering what on Earth she's holding.

With these kinds of depictions, the artists of the time weren't aiming for a lifelike resemblance—they were prioritizing theology over realism. What mattered wasn't what Jesus looked like, but what he *meant*. Leaving us with just one unresolved question: If it's okay to make baby Jesus look like a seasoned, wise man, why not give him a beard, too? Well, apparently, that was the line medieval artists wouldn't cross, because after all, a baby with a beard? Now *that* would be weird.

Bigallo Master, *The Madonna of the Fiesole Cathedral*, c. 1225–1250.

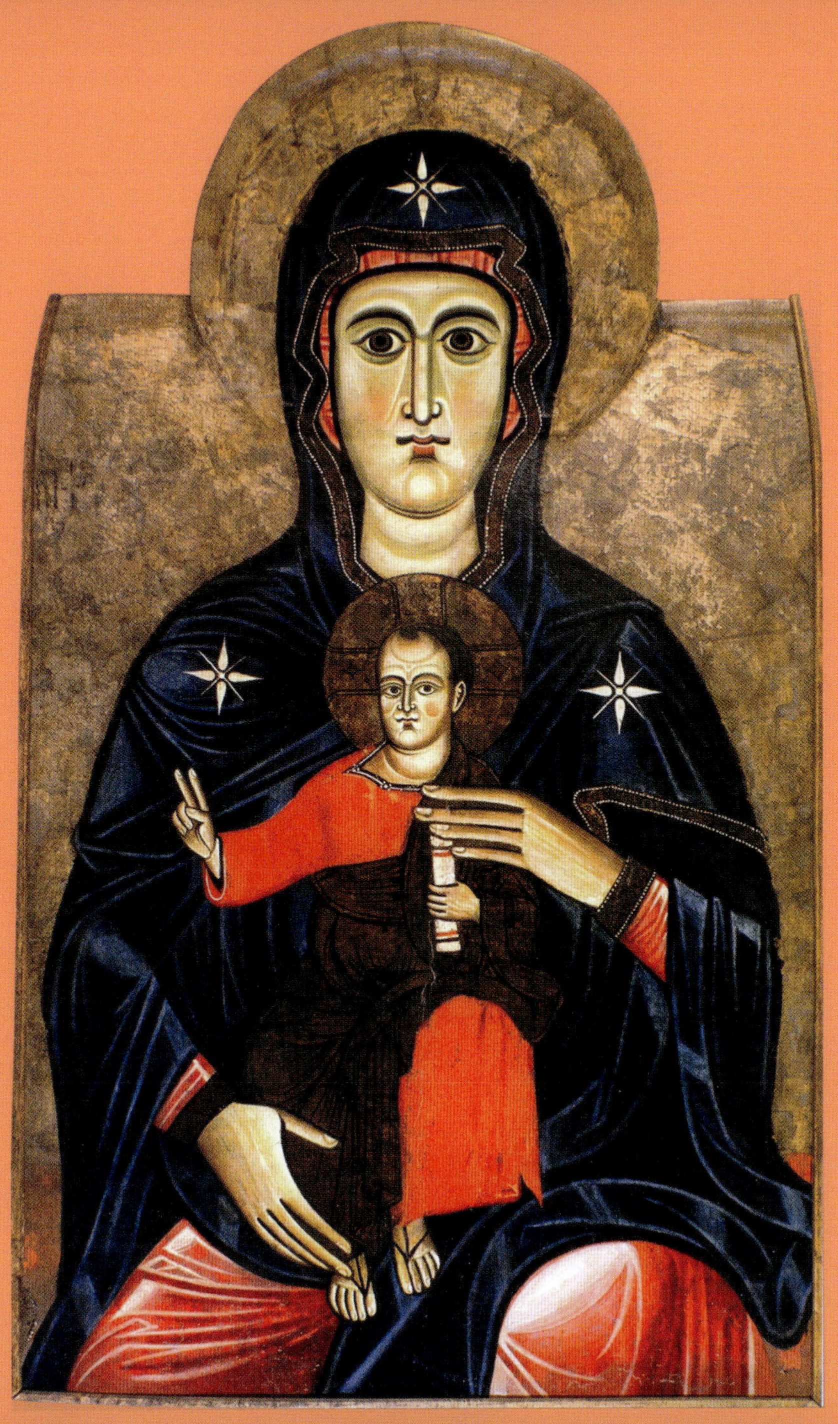

If paintings could move, this man's eyebrows would be bouncing up and down. He's clearly enjoying himself, wearing a slightly arrogant, self-satisfied smirk. He looks as if he just folded his entire laundry without having any leftover socks. Which, in fact, would be an acceptable excuse for carrying such a smug face. Bravo!

However, despite the smugness, he does look fabulous. Just look at that perfectly trimmed gray beard, his broad neck and pouting underlip. Or his rosy cheeks and slightly squinted green eyes. And topping it all off is his wild gray hair, serving as a cushion for a royal crown of laurels. Sure, this man looks way too pleased with himself, but honestly, he's earned it—because he's been through some crazy stuff.

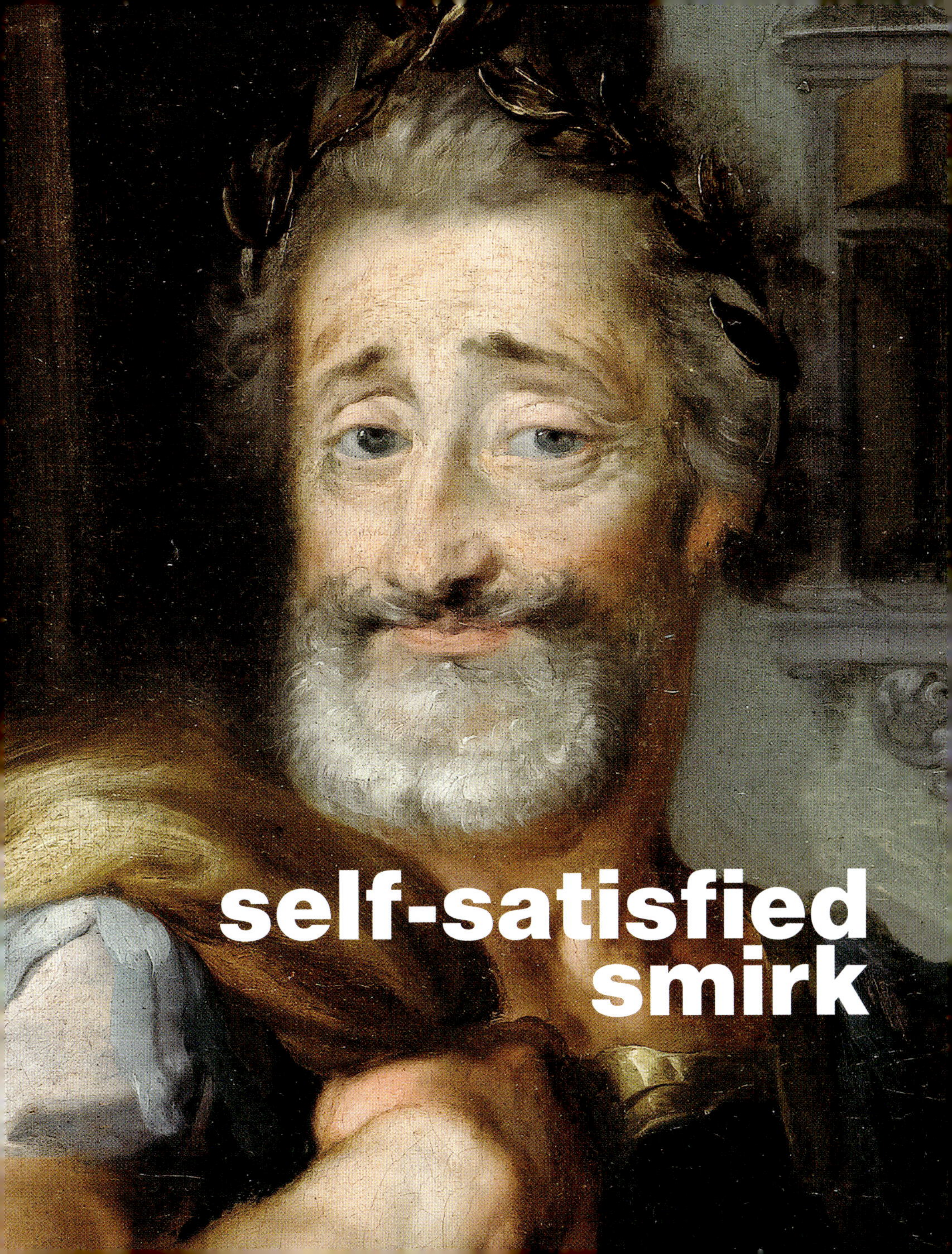
self-satisfied
smirk

There are two ways of looking at this painting, and the first one involves some insane mythology. Maybe you've heard of Hercules, the mythological hero who was tasked with completing 12 impossibly difficult labors. Folding a monumental mountain of laundry without ending up with leftover socks could've been one of them, but in reality, these labors were slightly less mundane. Take killing a nine-headed serpentine monster, for example, which is depicted here. It wasn't a simple chore, because every time Hercules chopped off one of the monster's heads, two new ones grew back. Luckily, Hercules called on the help of his nephew Iolaus, and his problem-solving abilities managed to save the day. "Maybe," Iolaus suggested, "we should scorch the neck-stumps to prevent the heads from growing back." The plan worked like a charm. Together they slayed the monster so Hercules could go back to shaving his insanely beautiful legs.

So that's the mythology behind the portrait, but the smug face in this stunning painting doesn't belong to Hercules—it belongs to Henry IV of France. And his proverbial nine-headed sea monster was called the French Wars of Religion. You see, Henry was a Protestant, which made him pretty unpopular with French Catholics. They didn't want him as king, so they fought long and hard to stop him. During his lifetime, Henry survived at least 12 assassination attempts.

Despite all the anger pointed against him, Henry remained a pragmatic guy. Because to secure his throne, he decided to convert to Catholicism, supposedly saying, "Paris is well worth a mass." Five years after his conversion, in 1598, he also signed the Edict of Nantes, which guaranteed religious freedoms to Protestants. In doing so, cheeky Henry managed to balance the interests of both Catholics and Protestants. The result? The French Wars of Religion finally came to an end, which is well worth a glorious portrait.

However, the painting got a bit ahead of itself, because in 1610, some 10 years after this portrait was painted, Henry finally met his end. He wasn't killed by a nine-

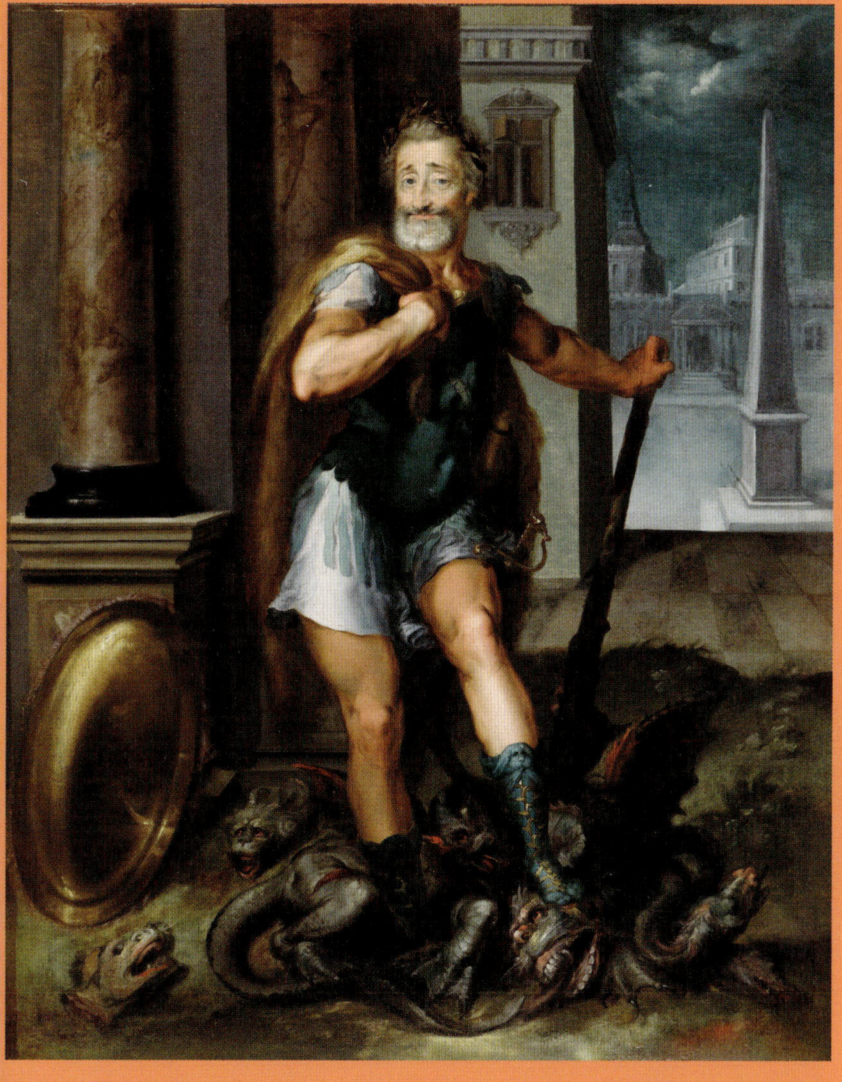

Toussaint Dubreuil, *Henry IV as Hercules Slaying the Lernaean Hydra*, c. 1600.

headed sea monster, but by a dissatisfied Catholic zealot. He stabbed him to death, wiping that smug smile off Henry's face for good. Lucky for us, we still have the painting.

deliciously dark secrets

This is a face of absolute astonishment. Judging by the man's location, you might think he's just been caught in a game of hide-and-seek, but his surprise has a much more intriguing source. This man is one of three main characters in a playful rococo masterpiece hiding some deliciously dark secrets. The first secret? It's hovering directly above our astonished gentleman.

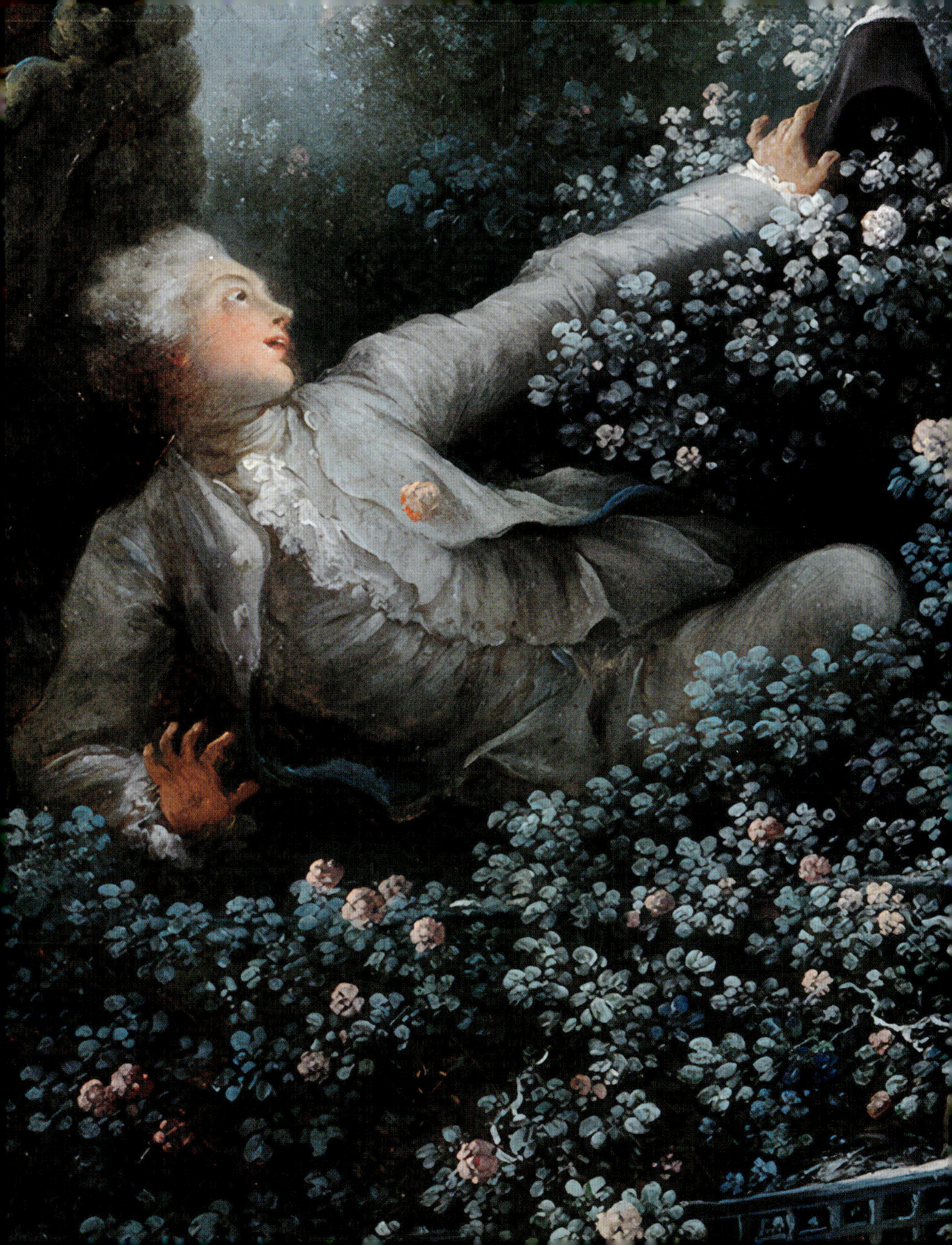

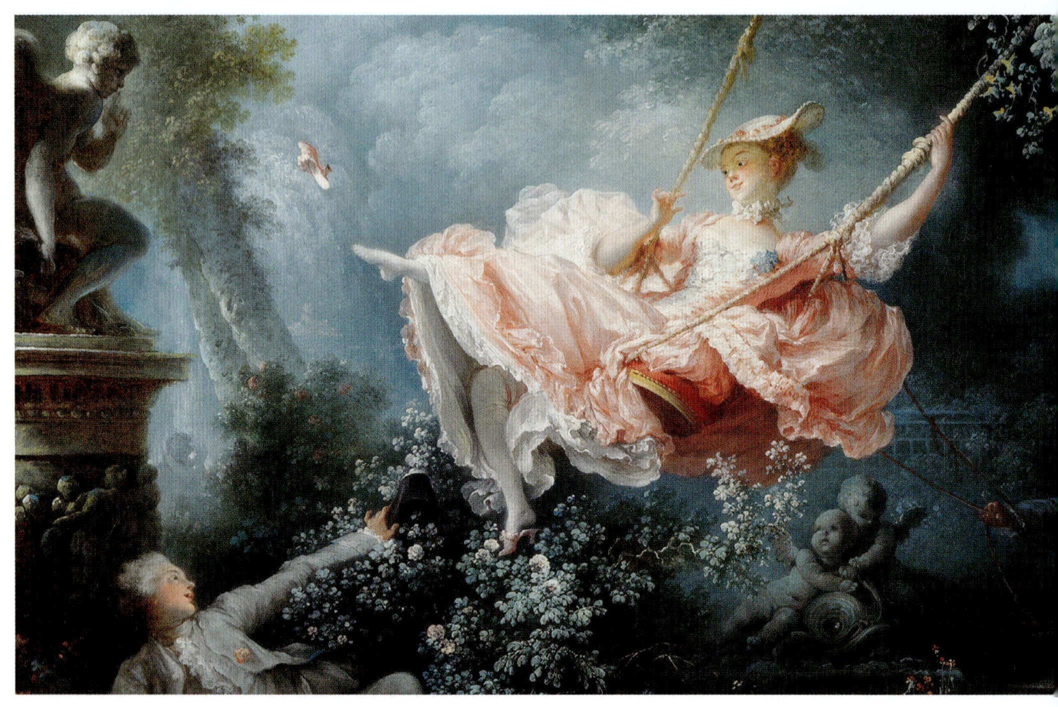

Behold our second protagonist, who is simply gorgeous. The blushing lady is swinging gracefully on a fancy, cushioned swing. She's mid-flight, playfully kicking her little pink slipper into the air, leaving her skirt wide open to anyone who happens to be in the right position to look underneath.

It's also worth noting that 18th-century women didn't wear underpants as we know them today.

They wore shifts, loose underdresses that—if you would hypothetically open up your legs at a certain height and a certain angle to a person in the right spot at the right time—did not conceal much.

Considering all this, I think we've discovered the source of our bush dweller's awe. But the story doesn't end here.

You're looking at *The Swing* by Jean-Honoré Fragonard, or as the French like to call it: *The Happy Accidents of the Swing* (*Les hasards heureux de l'escarpolette*). But let's be honest—losing that slipper wasn't an accident at all. This girl looks like she's deliberately teasing her peeping lover. And it gets even more intriguing when you notice the third character: an older man covered by darkness at the bottom right, tightly gripping the ropes of the swing.

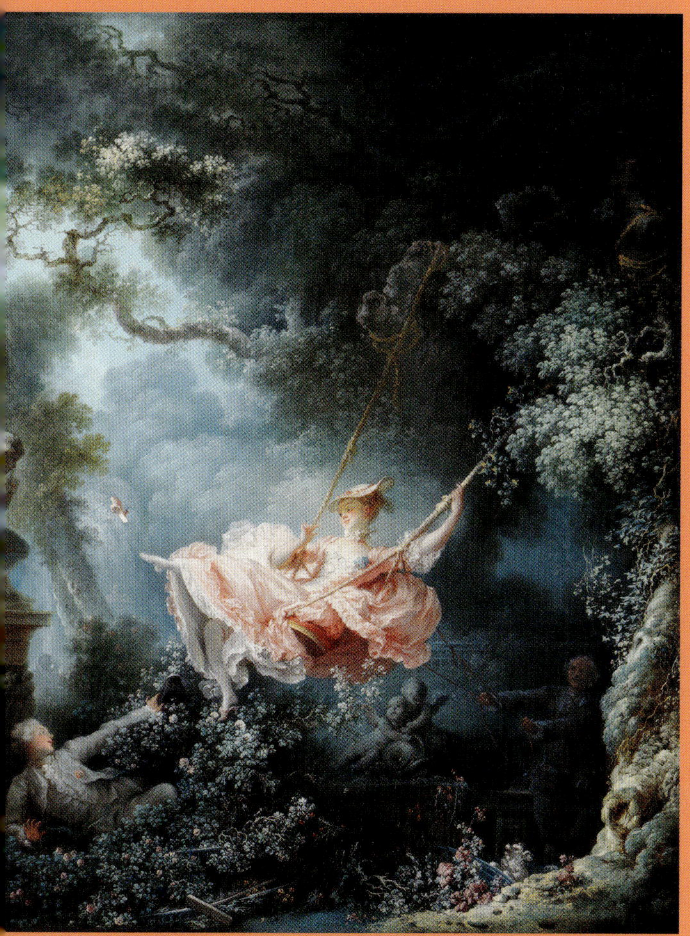

Is this shadowy figure the girl's deceived husband, and is she swinging from him to her lover and back? Or is he just an innocent bystander, unaware of the games being played? One thing is certain: He has a tight grip on those ropes.

Speaking of ropes, the swinging lady better watch out. Because if you look closely, the rope above her head is fraying, as if it could snap at any moment. And then the only question that remains might be the most important one of all: Which man will catch her?

Jean-Honoré Fragonard, *The Swing*, 1767.

baker man is baking heads

A head of cabbage? Don't get me wrong, I love absurdity, but I didn't expect this kind of extravaganza in a 400-year-old artwork. The green head you're looking at belongs to an upper-class lady who—despite her situation—seems to be completely at ease. She sits pensively with her fingertips pressed together, as if she's wondering, "Should I have gone for cauliflower instead?"

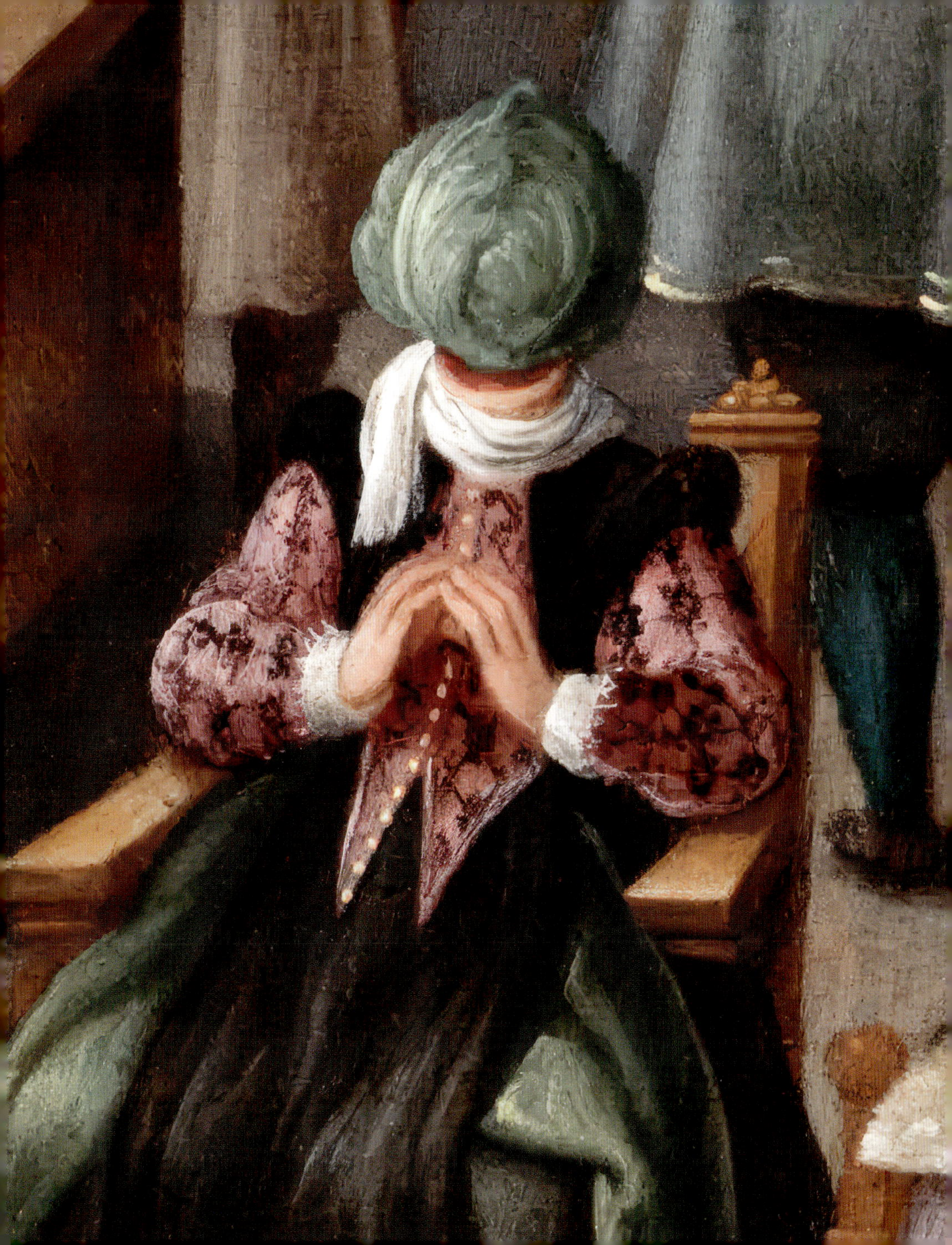

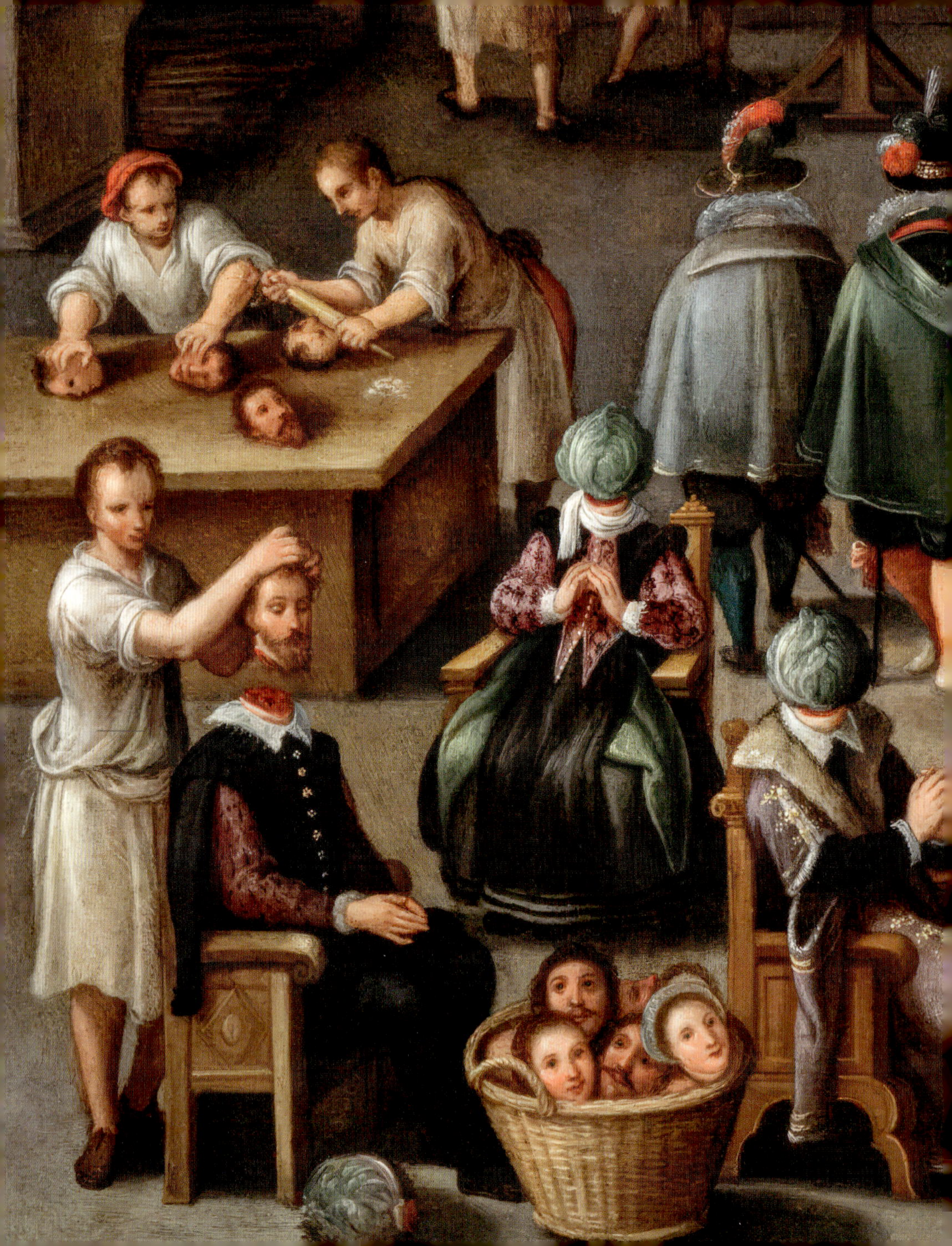

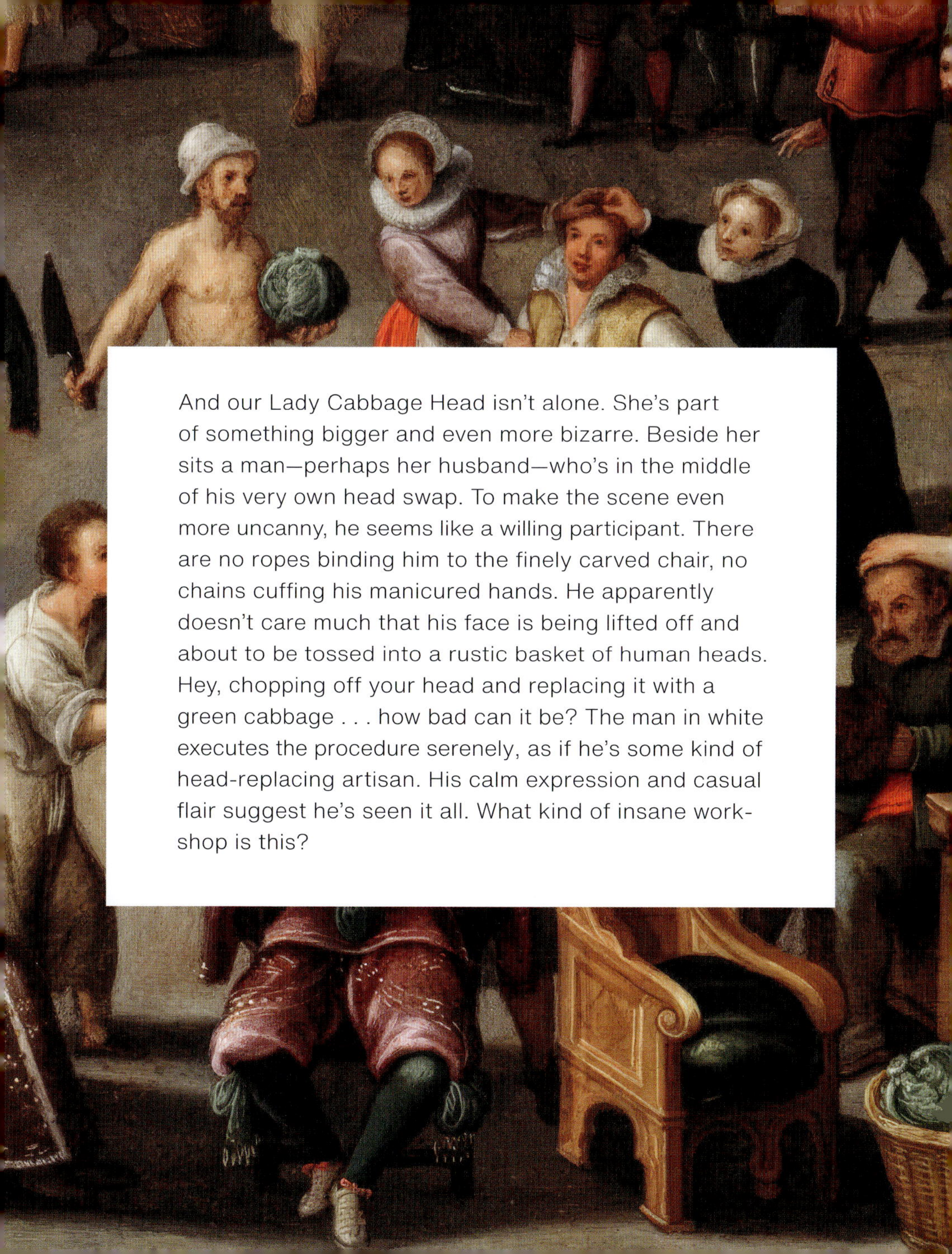

And our Lady Cabbage Head isn't alone. She's part of something bigger and even more bizarre. Beside her sits a man—perhaps her husband—who's in the middle of his very own head swap. To make the scene even more uncanny, he seems like a willing participant. There are no ropes binding him to the finely carved chair, no chains cuffing his manicured hands. He apparently doesn't care much that his face is being lifted off and about to be tossed into a rustic basket of human heads. Hey, chopping off your head and replacing it with a green cabbage . . . how bad can it be? The man in white executes the procedure serenely, as if he's some kind of head-replacing artisan. His calm expression and casual flair suggest he's seen it all. What kind of insane workshop is this?

It's a bakery—the kind where they chop off your head, knead it into shape, slide it into an oven and shelve it after baking to cool. In the meantime, the customers of this particular bakery get a fresh cabbage to ease the waiting. The nonchalance and easy-going vibe of this painting is unsettling. Some people are casually carrying severed heads while having a little chat, and others are chopping away like it's just another day at the market.

This was surrealism long before surrealism was a thing. But scenes like these, where humans or body parts are baked in ovens, were pretty common back in the day. Ovens were often seen as symbols of healing and transformation, with fire acting as the magic catalyst of change.

Unknown artist, *Head-Baker*, c.1600–1630.

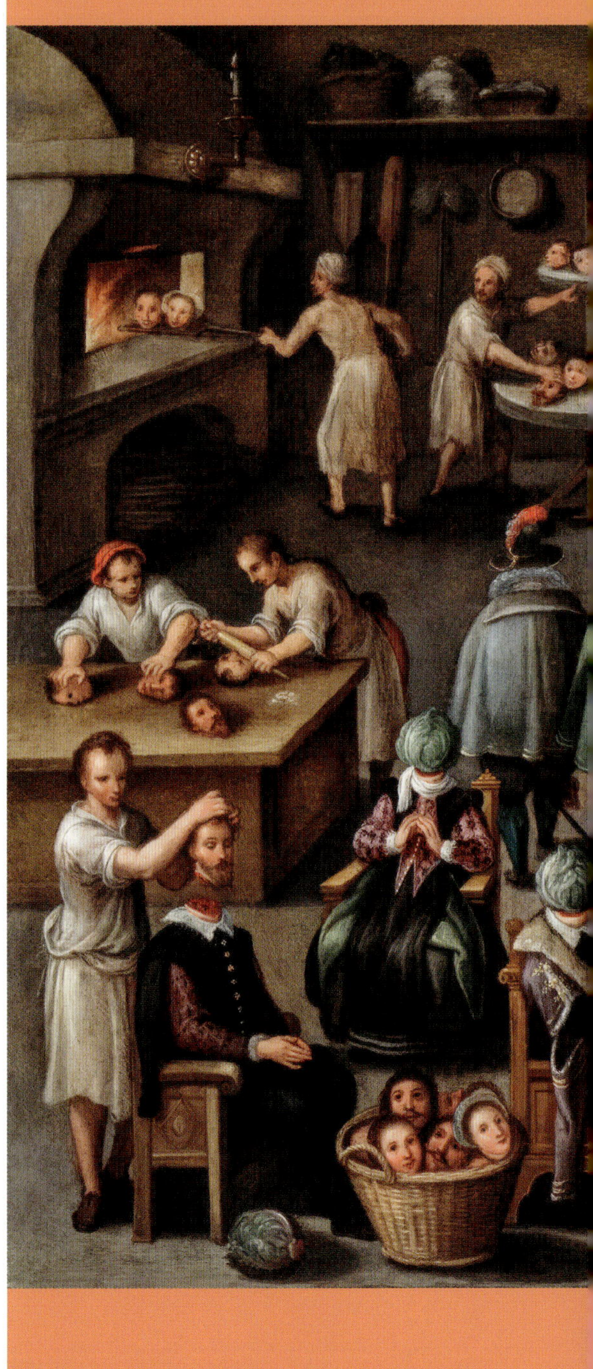

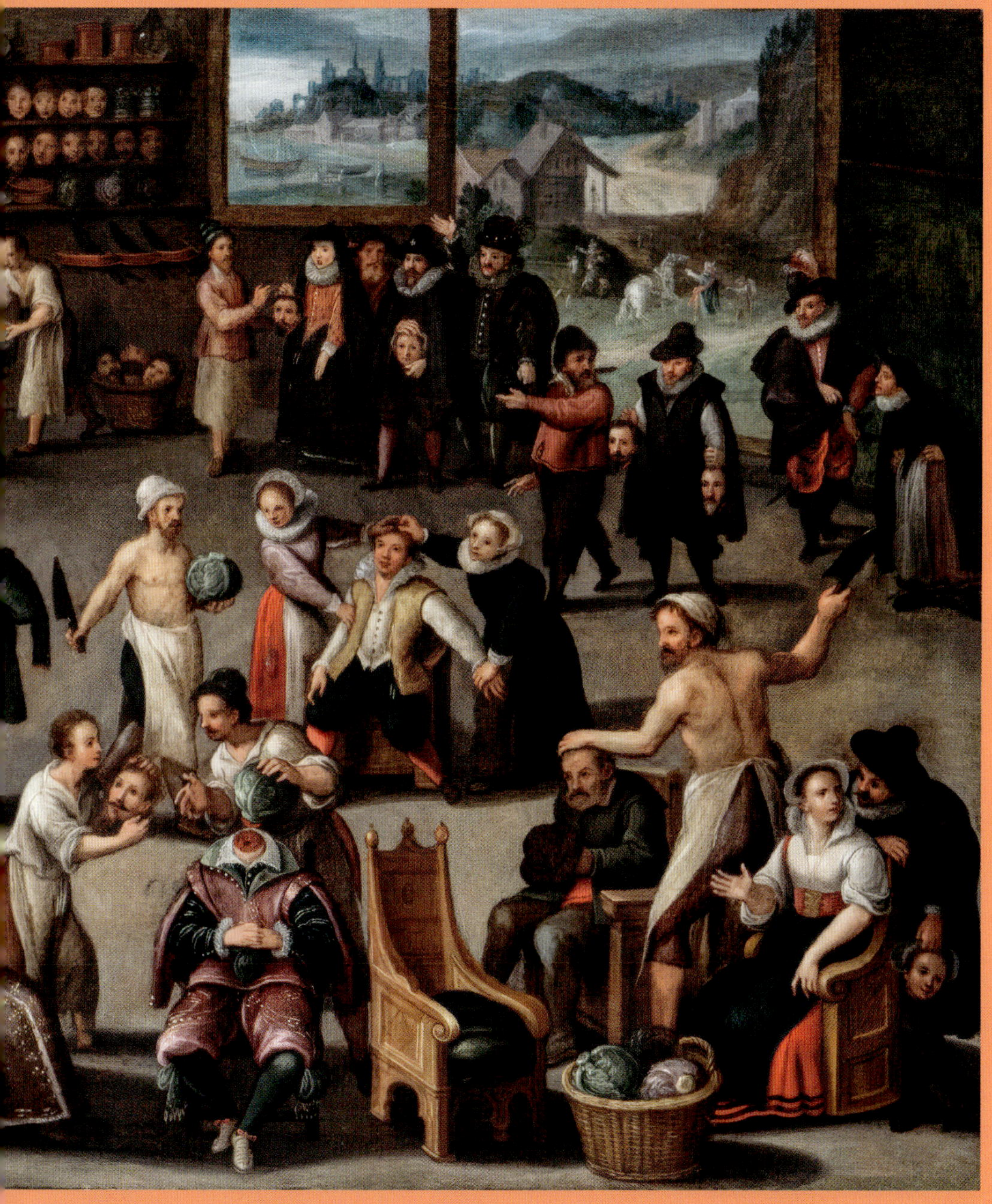

The people patiently waiting with their cabbage heads are probably clients paying good money to get treated. What exactly the head bakers are curing them from remains a mystery, as no one shows any signs of physical or mental illness.

As such, this crazy painting actually fits into a rather common 16th-century tradition of satirizing fictitious medical treatments. (We'll look at another example on page 46.) *Head-Baker* is most likely mocking rich people who think they can change their appearance or character by some sort of medical procedure. Which is a satisfying explanation, but still leaves us with one final question: Why cabbages? Well, in Dutch, *iemand een kool stoven* or "baking a cabbage for someone," is an old proverb meaning "to fool someone."

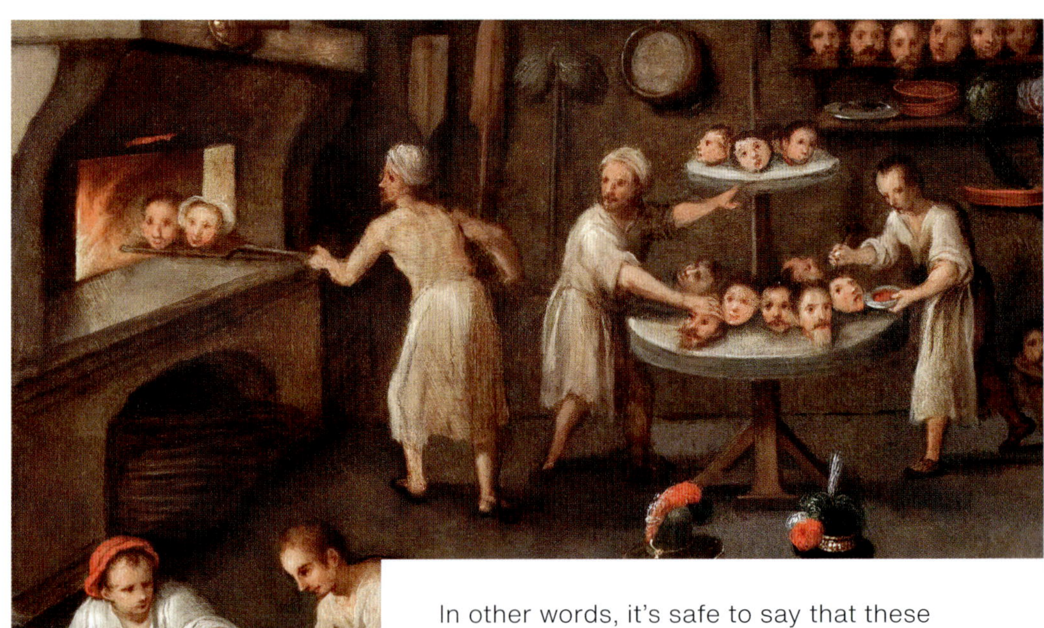

In other words, it's safe to say that these head bakers are just charlatans earning good money from rich people's vanity. Which, I think, is perfectly fine.

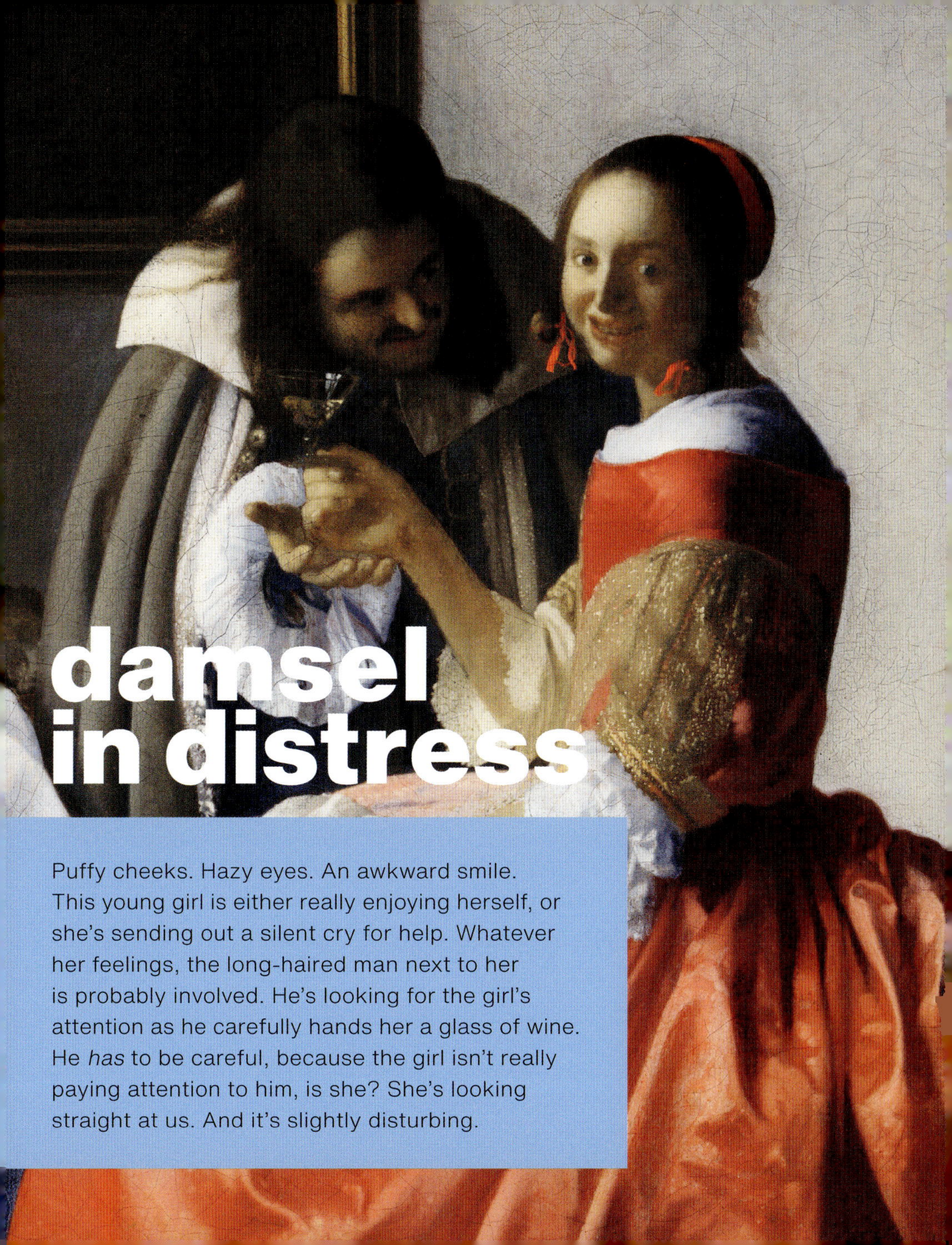

damsel in distress

Puffy cheeks. Hazy eyes. An awkward smile. This young girl is either really enjoying herself, or she's sending out a silent cry for help. Whatever her feelings, the long-haired man next to her is probably involved. He's looking for the girl's attention as he carefully hands her a glass of wine. He *has* to be careful, because the girl isn't really paying attention to him, is she? She's looking straight at us. And it's slightly disturbing.

What is the girl trying to tell us with her gaze? Is she silently screaming for help because a sleazeball is seducing her? Or is she beaming with satisfaction, because she's playing a clueless gentleman for free drinks and enjoying every moment of it?

Or, and this might be the most disturbing scenario, her strange gaze tells us nothing, because it's completely empty. She's flat out drunk. And if she's that far gone, perhaps we are dealing with a perverted predator who, with a subtle hand gesture, pushes her to drink even more. Is this poor girl about to be taken advantage of?

The full painting makes this scene even more complicated. In the dark corner of the room sits a third character, dozing off at the table. Is he a friend of the wine-feeding man? Or is he the girl's chaperone, knocked out because he's also drunk?

This unsettling painting was created by the Dutch master of light, Johannes Vermeer. Regardless of his intentions, the energy between this trio is unnerving. The girl in red might be in control of an entirely innocent situation, but at the same time, clues suggest that something bad is about to happen. We just don't know what the elephant in this fancy 17th-century room is.

And that's the magic of Vermeer. He creates scenes that feel slightly off. His paintings always tell a story, but those stories all have missing pieces. Fortunately, there's a way out, because neither the sleazy man nor the smiling girl controls this scene. *You* do. You're completely free to choose exactly what is happening in this bizarre puzzle by Vermeer. So go ahead and make your choice. But please, choose wisely.

Johannes Vermeer, *The Girl with the Wine Glass*, c. 1659.

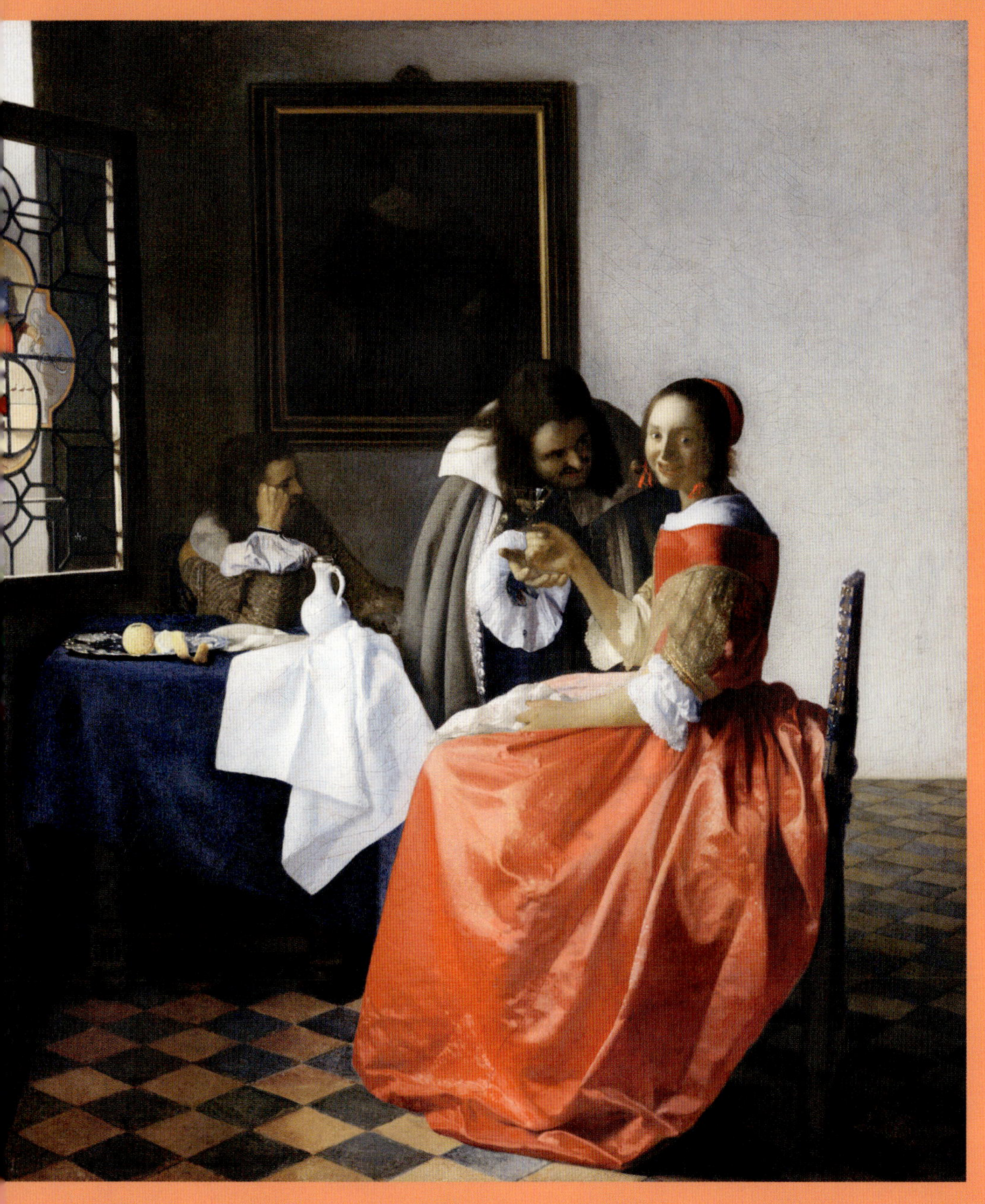

unicorn gone bad

According to art historians, unicorns symbolize purity, but this particular horny horse seems far from pure. The poor thing is worn and weary, with patches of paint fading and flaking after years of exposure. But the unicorn's rough condition isn't just due to age—it's also because it sits in the middle of three layers of oil paint, meaning it both covers an underlying image and was once concealed by an overlying one that has since been removed. Just to say: This painting has a history, and it shows. But before we dive into this layered past, let's take a look at the girl holding this mythical horsey.

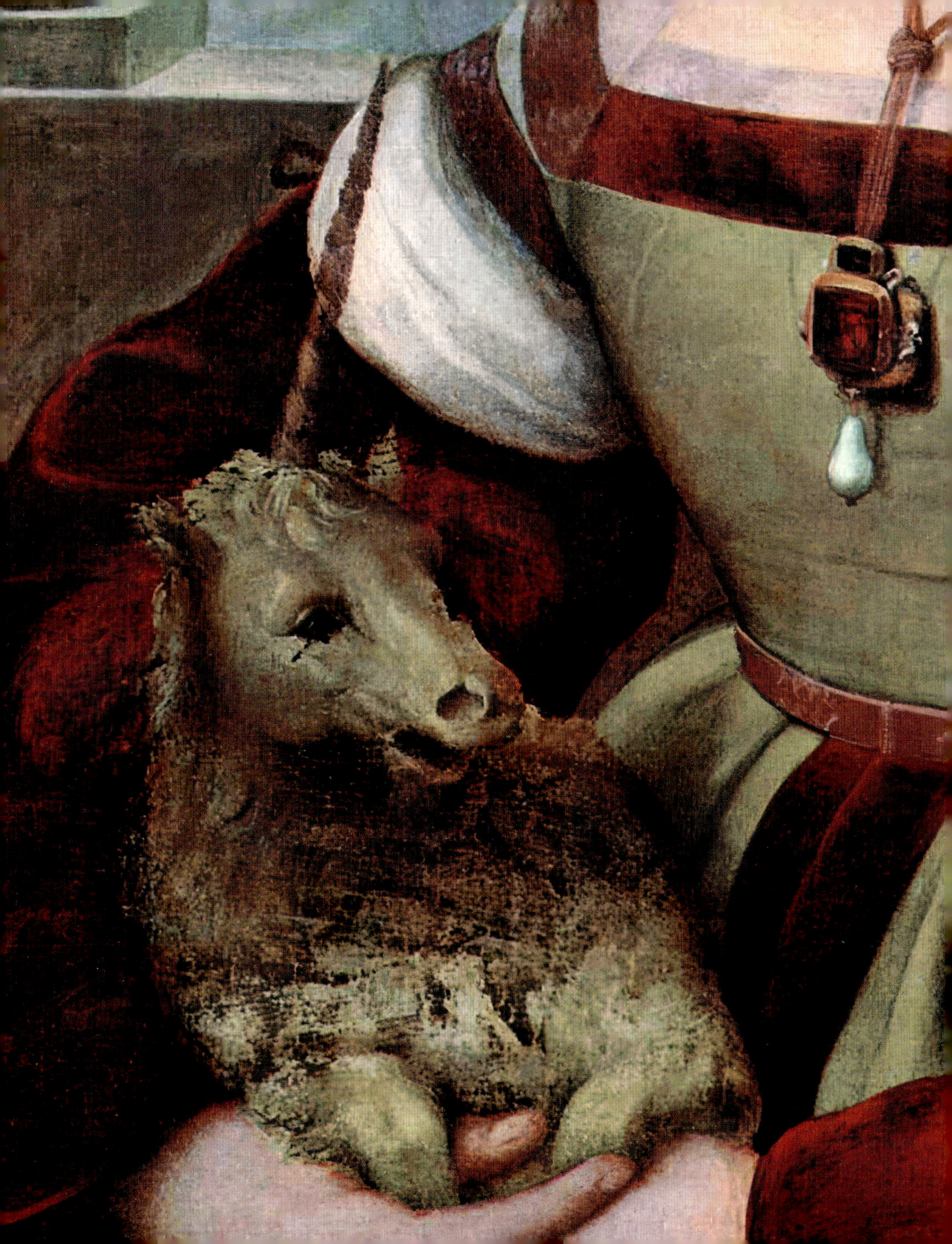

"Back off, this is *my* little pony." That's the vibe I'm getting from this lady. She's posing in front of a *loggia*—an open gallery or room that, in this case, overlooks the rolling Italian countryside. Combine this backdrop with the lady's enigmatic look and her slightly angled posture, and she brings to mind that other famous staring queen: the *Mona Lisa*. It's no secret that this classic by Leonardo da Vinci had a great impact on the 22-year-old Raphael, who painted this masterpiece.

But who is she? Well, back in the 1700s, she was identified as Saint Catherine of Alexandria, because at the time, this lady wasn't holding a unicorn, but an instrument of torture.

Raffaello Sanzio, *Portrait of Young Woman with Unicorn*, 1506.

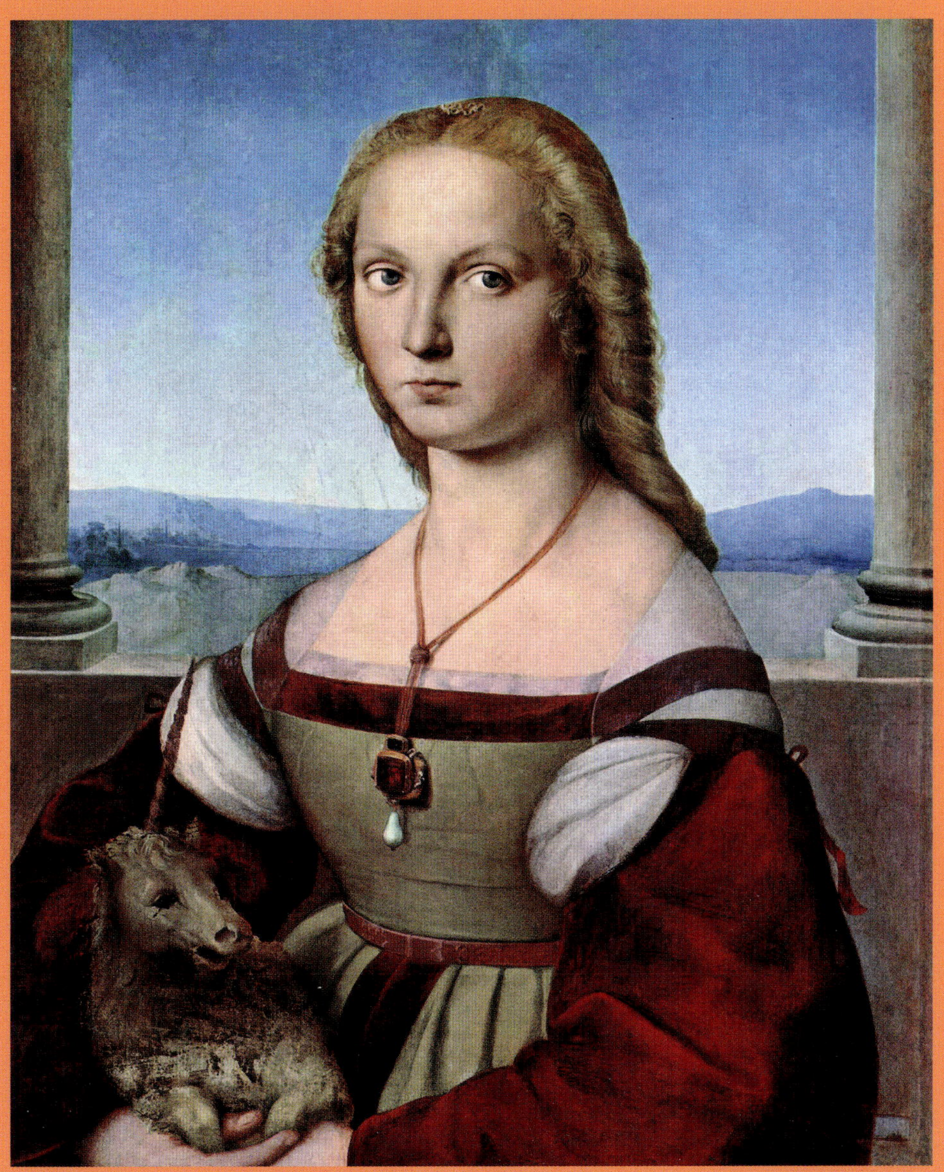

In the earlier version of the painting, our main character is holding a palm branch and a Catherine wheel, or breaking wheel—an instrument of torture used to break the bones of princesses who refused to renounce their Christian faith (Saint Catherine, to be precise).

So it seems that at one point, someone obviously didn't like the unicorn and replaced it with the second best thing: a torture wheel. And it took a few centuries before art historians figured out the strange switch. In the 1930s, during a restoration, the extra layer was discovered and removed. And voilà, the awkwardly adorable unicorn reappeared. *This* is the original version, experts claimed, and just like that, this was no longer a portrait of Saint Catherine. But then, whose was it?

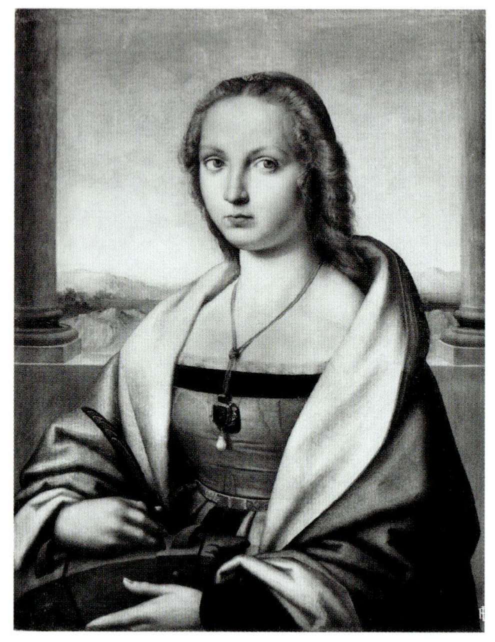

The painting prior to its 20th-century restoration, featuring Saint Catherine caressing her breaking wheel.

Unfortunately, the answer to that question remains a mystery. The painting might have been created as a wedding gift, with the unicorn symbolizing purity—a reasonable guess. But the story doesn't end here, as there is one final plot twist to uncover.

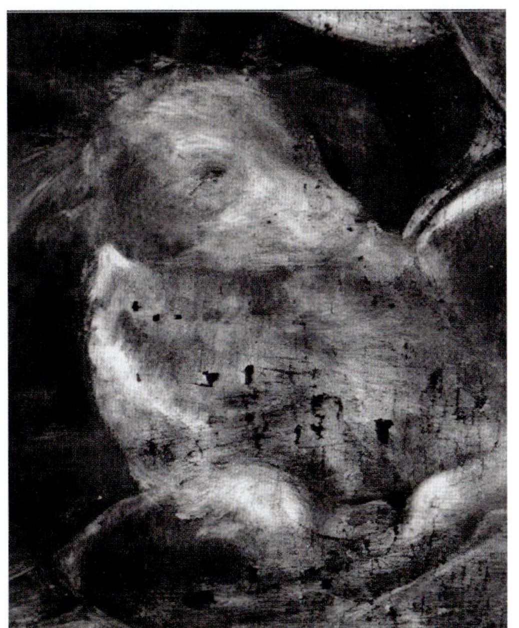

The little dog discovered after an X-ray scan.

Because apparently, before he painted the silly unicorn, Raphael had another animal in mind. During a new restoration in the 1950s, experts used X-rays to analyze the painting and discovered the image of a little dog. You can still make out the ghostly outline of the dog's ears in the final version of the painting.

So Raphael initially chose a dog as the lady's lap sitter, probably as a symbol of fidelity. But somewhere along the way, he changed his mind and decided on a unicorn instead. And even though the poor little animal looks worn out and bad today, I still feel Raphael made an excellent choice.

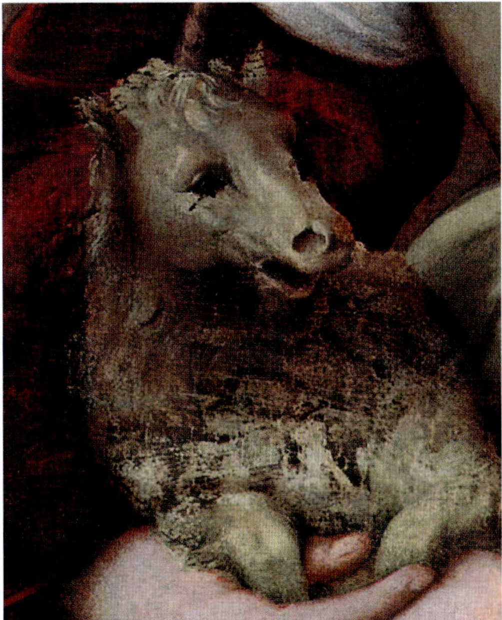

The restored version of the painting, with the dog's ears still visible.

a bored archangel

Raising a single eyebrow can mean several things. Maybe this man is skeptical. Maybe he's curious. Or maybe he's just a slightly bored archangel, fed up with his task of protecting the Holy Virgin and Baby Jesus from devilish harm day in and day out. Whatever his mood, this odd face is both uncanny and beautiful.

The combination of vibrant colors, bold black lines and two slightly misaligned eyes creates an image that feels unusual, especially in Western art. But, of course, that's because this isn't Western art.

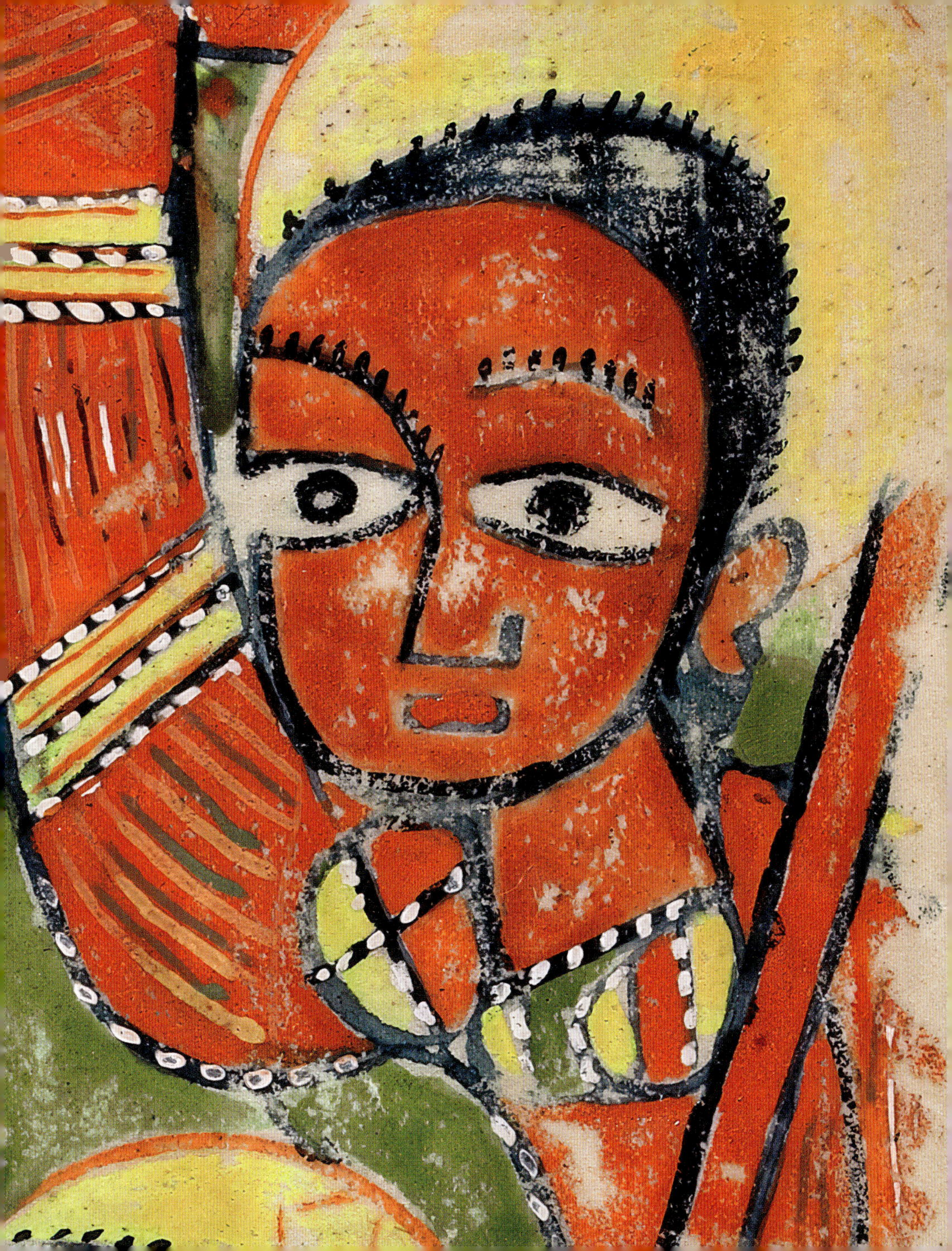

This color bomb is part of a 16th-century Ethiopian gospel book. It might come as a surprise, but Ethiopia was one of the earliest regions in the world to fully adopt Christianity. A mere 300 years after Jesus's life, death and resurrection, the religion reached the East African kingdom. The result? A country dotted with ancient monasteries and churches, filled with countless Christian artifacts and gospel books adorned with gorgeous illustrations like this one.

Unknown Artist, *Virgin and Child with the Archangels Michael and Gabriel*, 1504–1505.

If this image of the Virgin Mary and Jesus looks unusual to you, it's probably because you're used to European depictions of the holy duo, where Mary is dressed in robes of blue and red, showing off her serene and idealized face and usually holding a perfectly proportioned angelic infant.

Forget all those Western paintings with their fancy details, realistic shading and idealized depictions of the holy pair, because this Ethiopian painting flips that approach on its head. It chooses style over realism. So much so that it almost has an abstract quality. The Virgin Mary and Child are depicted in bright and bold colors without any shading. Thick black lines form stylized shapes and patterns, and their simplified faces are painted with a warm, orange hue along with big, almond-shaped eyes—all typical hallmarks of the Gunda Gunde style.

And then there are the two archangels, Michael and Gabriel. Michael holds his hand to his chest, looking charmed by the baby he is sworn to protect. Meanwhile, Gabriel appears slightly bored, seemingly unimpressed by the immaculate conception of his newborn boss. But hey, that's just one interpretation, because honestly, I think he looks just perfect. Even though this image is over 500 years old, to me, it feels very refreshing.

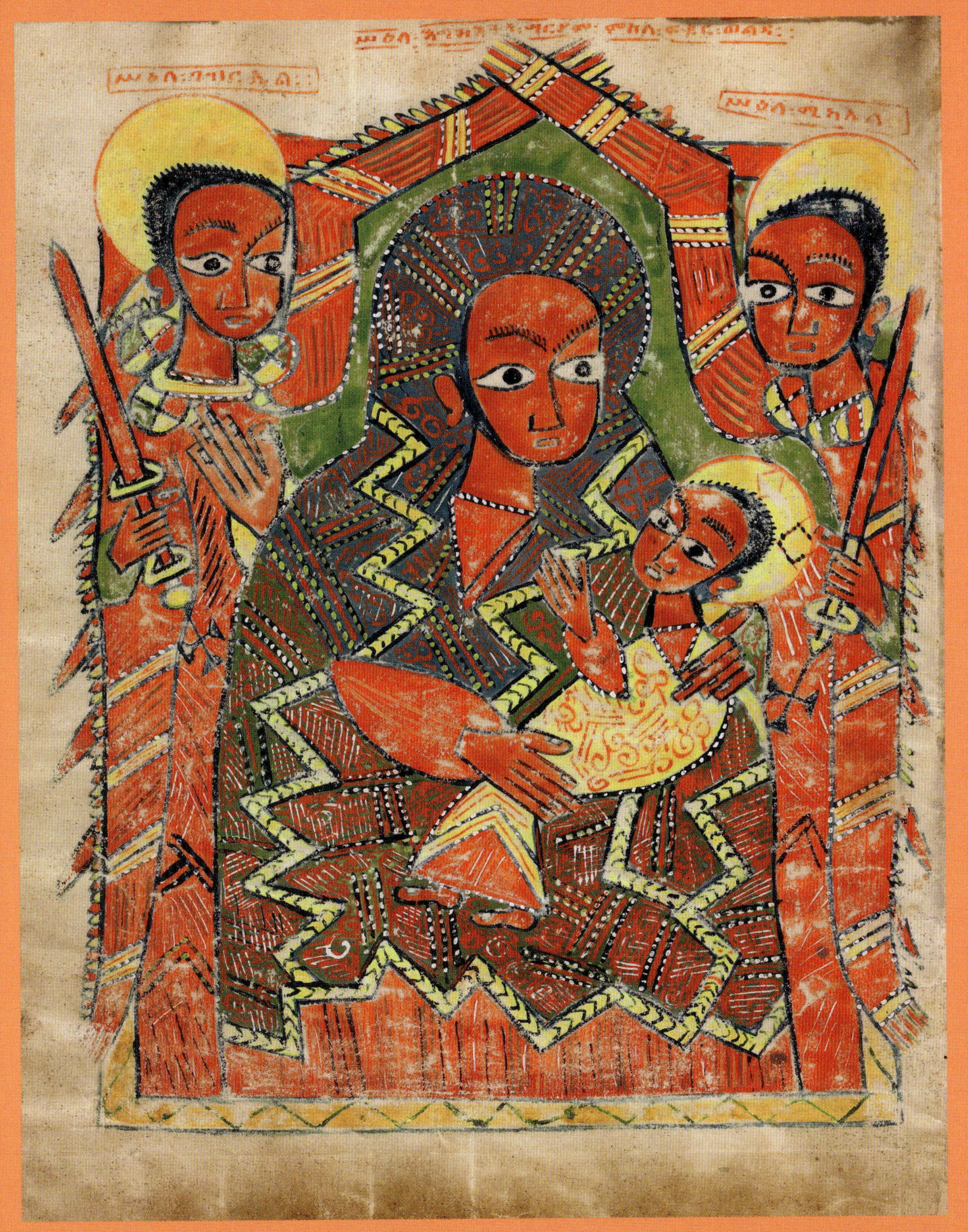
ሥዕለ፡ እግዝእትነ፡ ማርያም፡ ምስለ፡ ፍቁር፡ ወልዳ፡
ሥዕለ፡ ገብርኤል፡
ሥዕለ፡ ሚካኤል

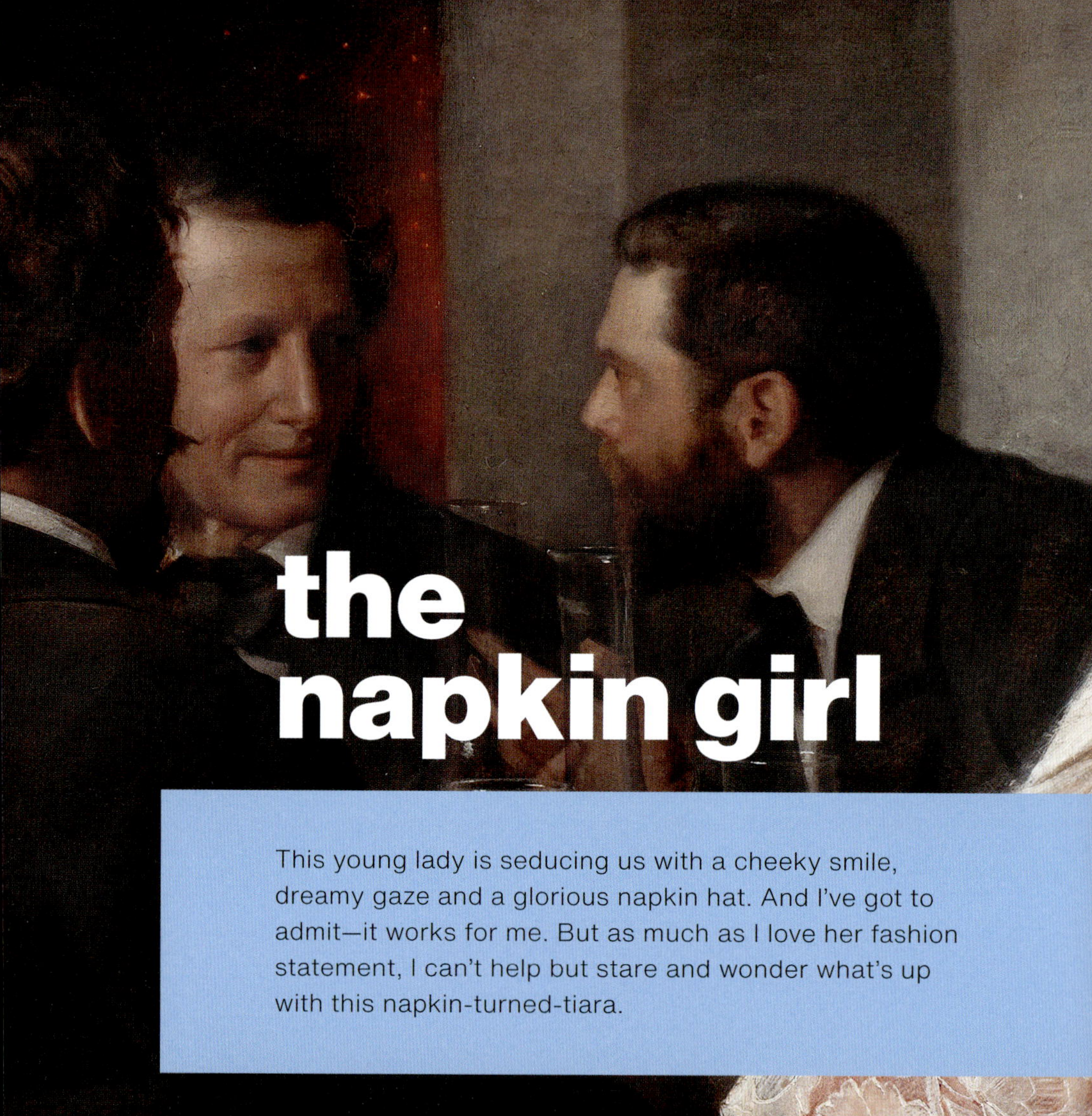

the napkin girl

This young lady is seducing us with a cheeky smile, dreamy gaze and a glorious napkin hat. And I've got to admit—it works for me. But as much as I love her fashion statement, I can't help but stare and wonder what's up with this napkin-turned-tiara.

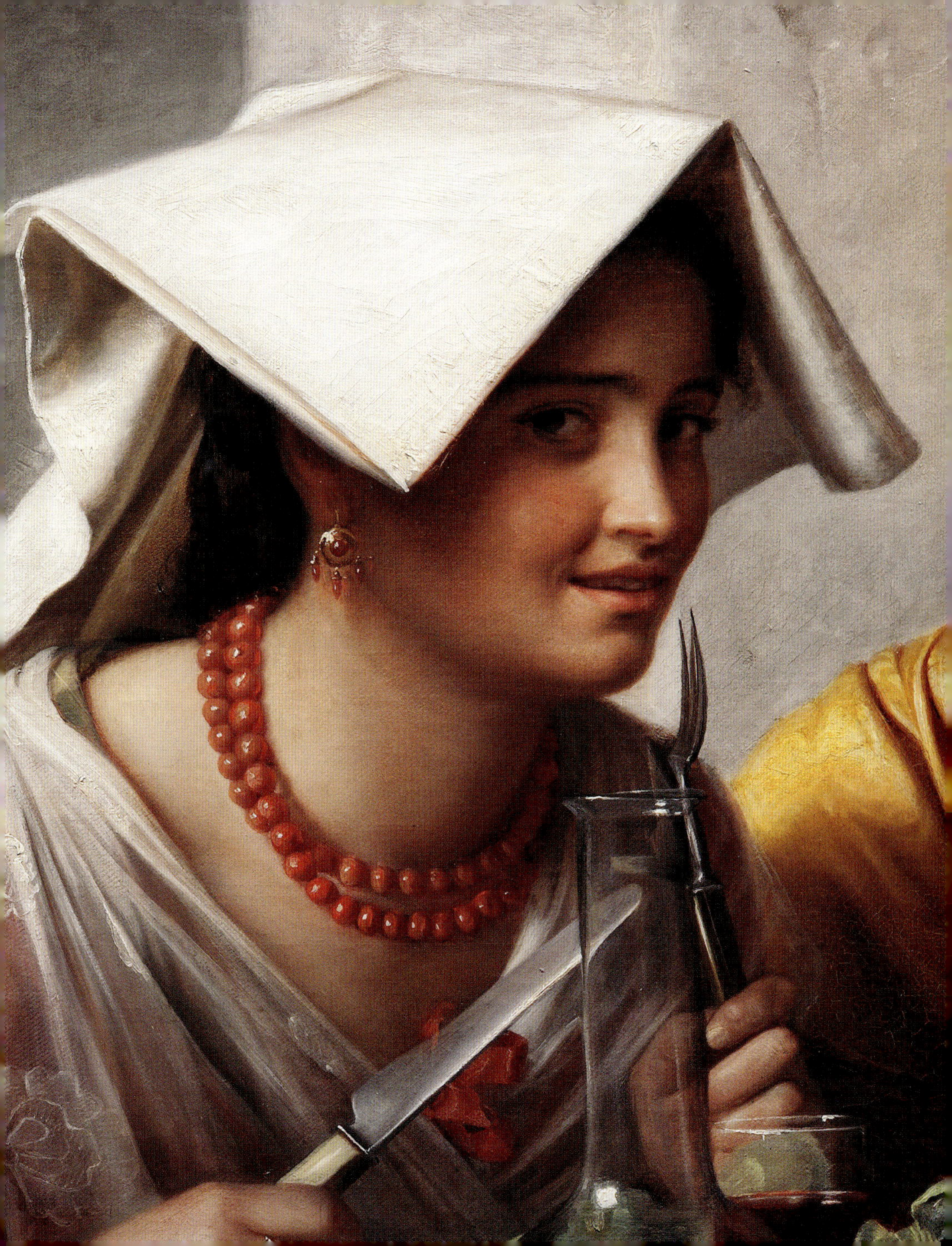

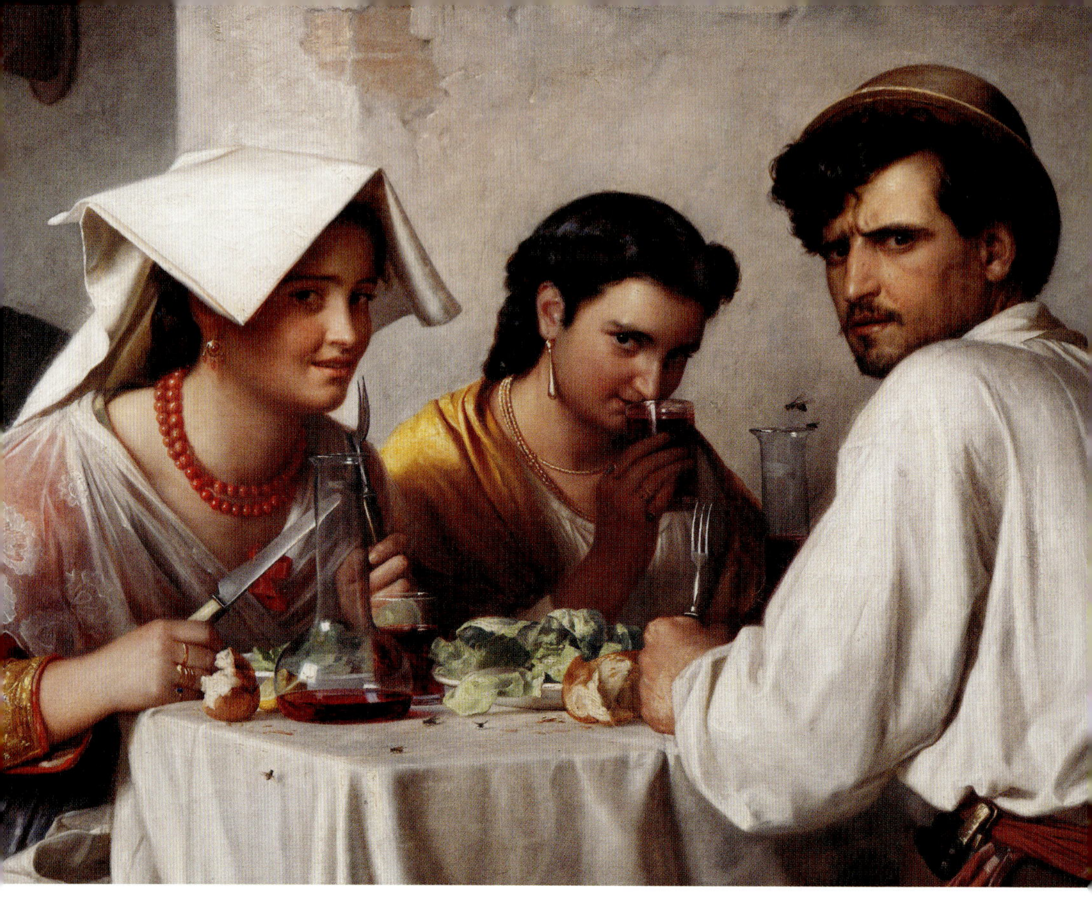

Maybe we should stop staring, because her companion isn't amused. Is he her boyfriend? A protective brother, perhaps? Whoever he is, his fork-clenching fist and the blade in his pocket are ready for action, so we should probably proceed with care. But let's keep looking, because this staring contest isn't over yet. Across from the disgruntled man sits a third pair of gazing eyes, belonging to a woman that clearly doesn't like her glass half-empty. Her glance is as sharp as the wasp hovering over the wine flask. Or is that just her way of flirting?

Anyway, we can't leave without solving the big question: Why on earth is our protagonist wearing a napkin? Maybe we'll find some clues as we zoom out to the full painting.

Nope, no clues, just more judging eyes, this time belonging to a grumpy cat. Our presence really isn't appreciated. So what now? Politely nod and return to our meal, or grab a knife and start a classic Italian bar fight? Maybe it's best to leave them to their meal and move on to the next painting.

Oh yes, I almost forgot. *In a Roman Osteria* was painted in 1866 by the Danish painter Carl Bloch, and the unusual headwear isn't actually a napkin but a *mantilla*, a traditional headdress worn in the 19th century in central Italy. I'm disappointed, too.

Carl Bloch, *In a Roman Osteria*, 1866.

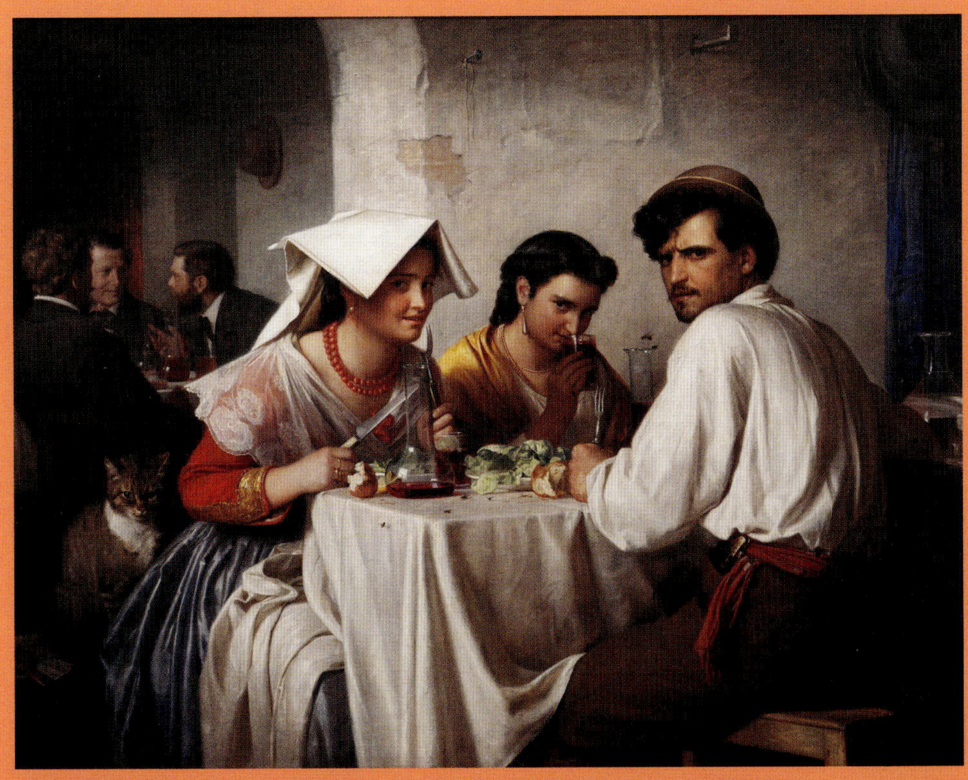

medieval

General anesthesia is a blessing, especially if you're having brain surgery. But this man didn't get to enjoy such a medical luxury. Considering his droopy eyes and slack jaw, there are a few possible explanations for his stupid face: He's either drunk, in excruciating pain or dead. Whichever it is, you have to wonder what exactly they are pulling out of this poor man's skull.

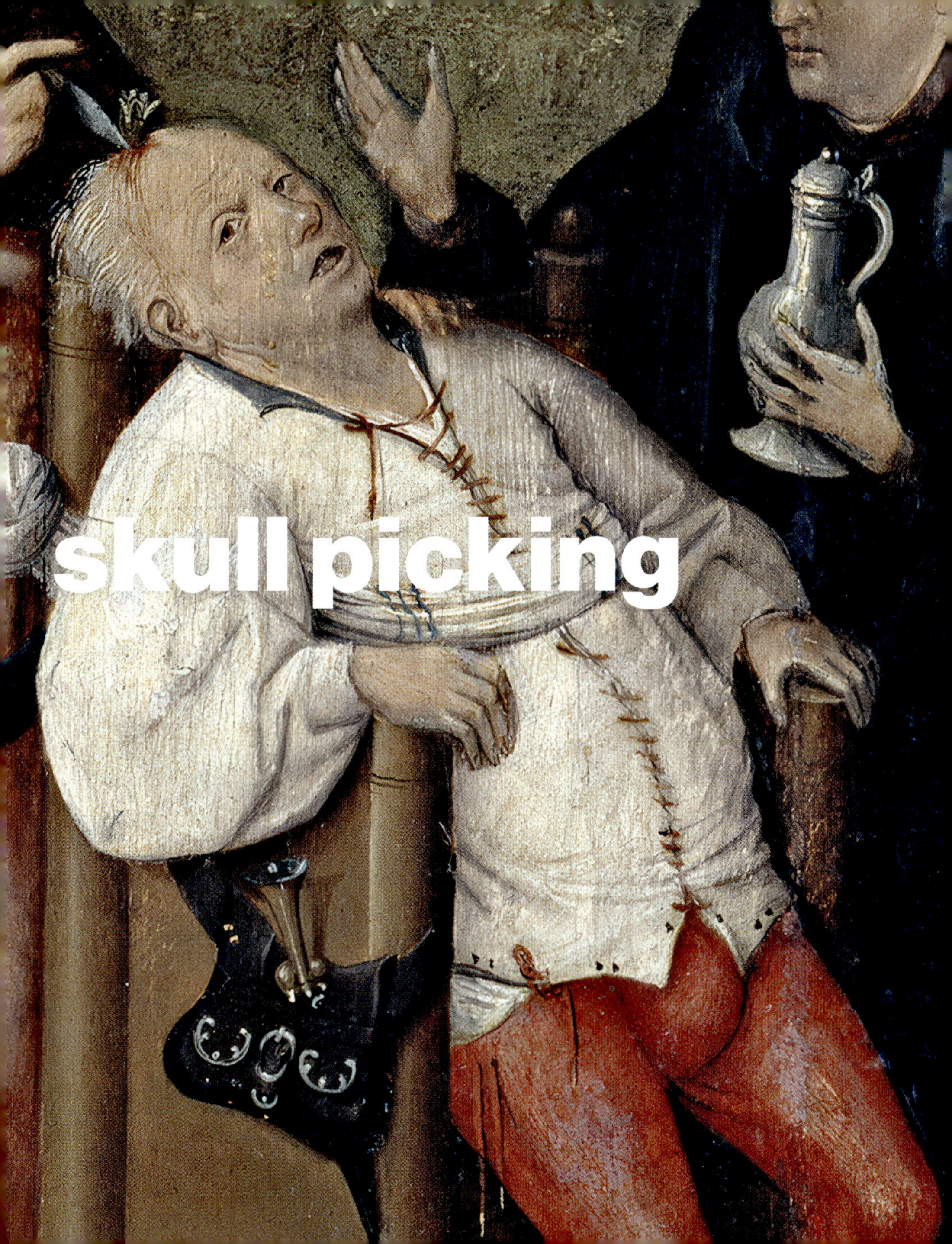

skull picking

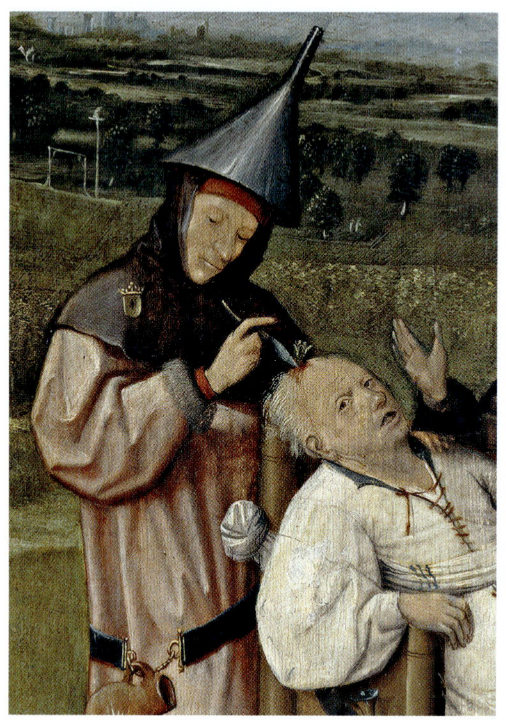

This bizarre little scene is part of a painting called *Cutting the Stone*, probably created by the 15th-century master of the bizarre, Hieronymus Bosch, or one of his followers. True to his style, it's filled with riddles and strange imagery.

Here's what we know for sure: The so-called doctor poking the skull is curing this man of his madness. According to a dubious late medieval theory, insanity was caused by a stone lodged in the head (obviously), which had to be removed in order to be cured.

Whether people really believed this and really went looking for stones in skulls remains a question mark, but the theory does explain the painting's title. By the way, the surgeon performing the operation is wearing a funnel hat, which is a pretty good indicator that we're not dealing with a licensed physician here, but with a quack. It also tells us that this painting doesn't take the stone theory seriously.

Considering all this, the first safe conclusion we can draw is that this work is seriously weird. And the full picture only adds to the madness.

There's a lot to unpack here, but let's start with the fancy golden lettering. If you're fluent in Old Dutch, you probably know it says, *Meester snijt die keye ras. Mijne name Is Lubbert Das.* This translates into, "Master, cut the stone out, fast. My name is Lubbert Das."

Apparently, the poor patient's name is Lubbert Das, and he wants to be cured of his insanity. In fact, Lubbert Das was a foolish character in old Dutch literature, so the painting might depict a scene from a play or a story. Anyway, the stone-in-the-head-that-causes-insanity theory is confirmed by the curly text, but there's a catch. The quack isn't removing a stone, but a flower—specifically a columbine flower. The explanation is simple: The columbine used to be a symbol of foolishness, because its shape resembles the hat of a jester.

To sum it up, the surgeon is cutting out a stone that's actually a flower that represents folly. Complicated, I know. And it's not like the other two characters help to clear things up. The surprised monk is clutching a bottle, which suggests he might be drunk. So we probably can't take him seriously, either. And then there's the confused lady throwing a WTF-like gesture while casually wearing a book for a hat. The fact that she doesn't read her books, but instead prefers to use them in a balancing act, suggests that she isn't really interested in gaining knowledge. So, she might be a fool as well. But honestly, your guess is as good as mine.

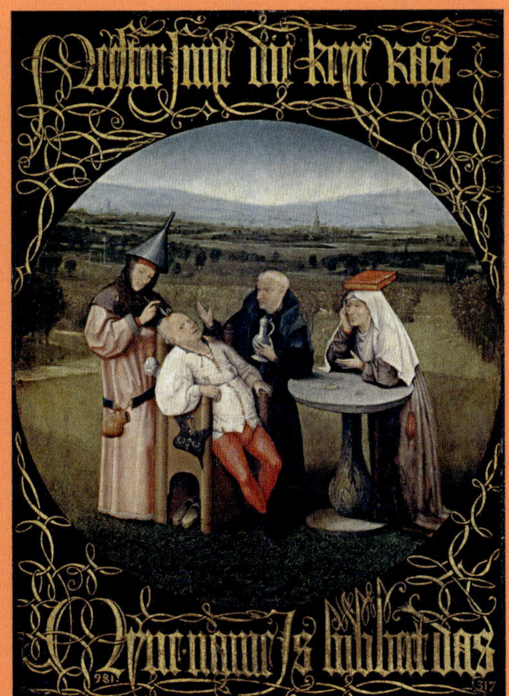

Hieronymus Bosch, *Cutting the Stone*, 1501–1505.

The best guess from art historians is that this painting is poking fun at quack doctors and dubious medical theories. But whatever it means, one thing is certain: This painting is absolutely bonkers.

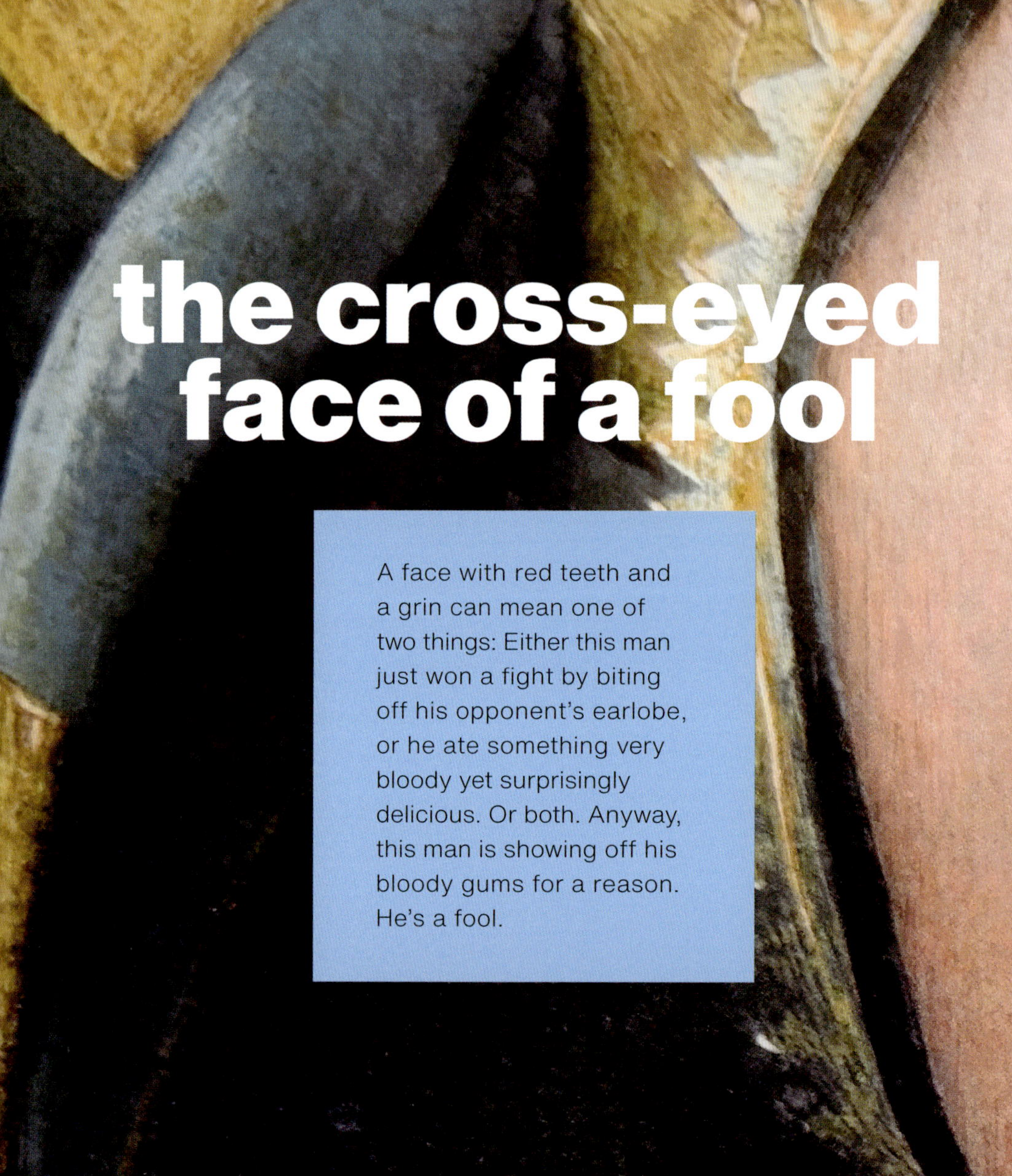

the cross-eyed face of a fool

A face with red teeth and a grin can mean one of two things: Either this man just won a fight by biting off his opponent's earlobe, or he ate something very bloody yet surprisingly delicious. Or both. Anyway, this man is showing off his bloody gums for a reason. He's a fool.

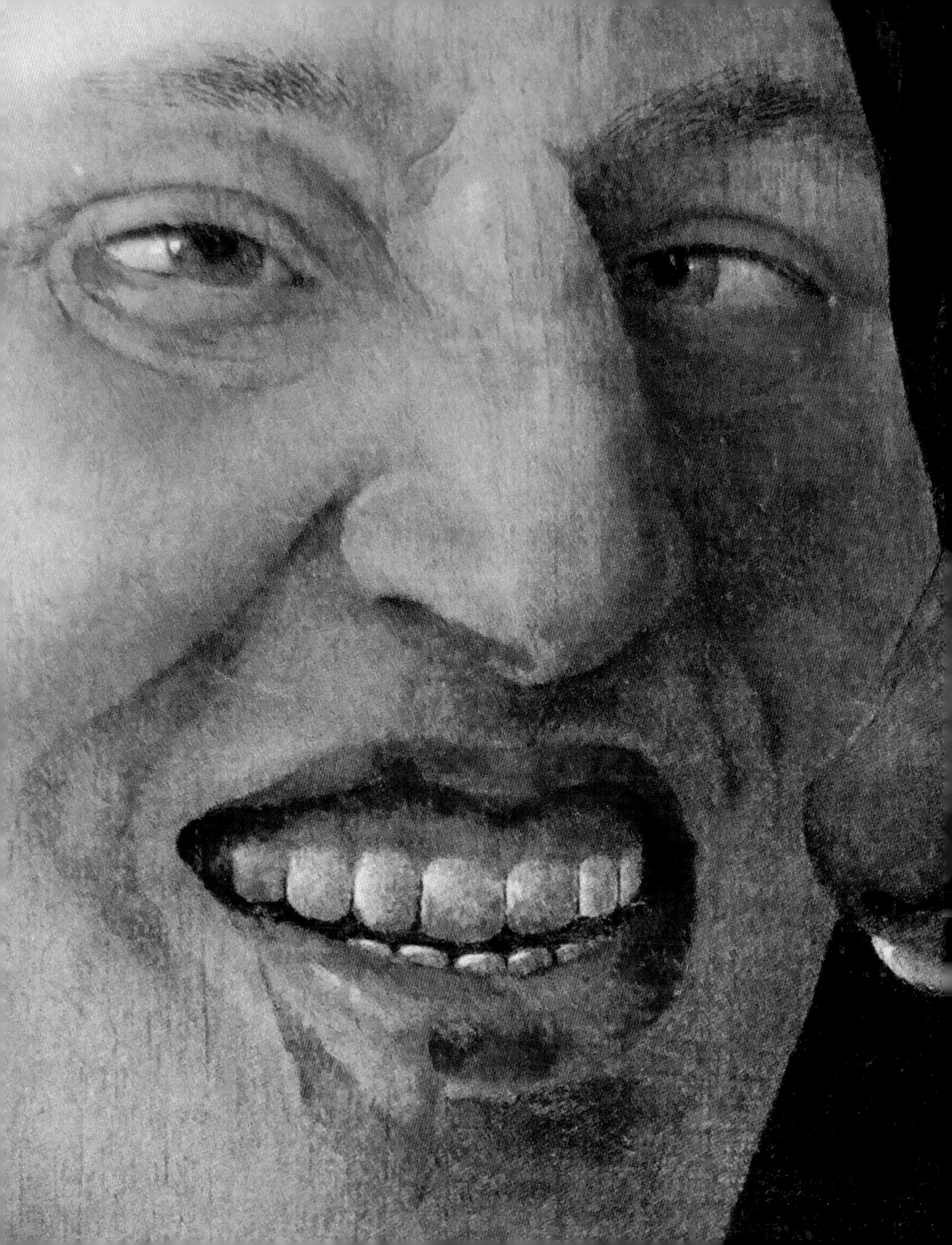

In fact, he's a jester. During the medieval and Renaissance eras, a jester was someone who performed for noble and royal households, entertaining guests through storytelling, juggling, telling jokes and pulling stupid faces, while also sometimes subtly criticizing their patrons in ways that other members of court wouldn't dare. This particular jester is wearing the classic fool's hat with little bells and dangling donkey ears. He's also carrying a baton, called a bauble, that mirrors his own head. He's the real deal.

A little puppy is snuggling up to him. He might be interested in the red goo running from the jester's mouth and fingers. It's not blood, but egg yolk, as the fool is eating the white of what seems to be a softly boiled egg.

But really, what exactly are we looking at? What are we supposed to think of this man? Is he *really* stupid? Or is he just a professional performing his foolish act? He very well could be, but there's no definitive way to tell what all this means. Some art historians believe the cracked egg symbolizes the poor and simple mind of this cross-eyed fool—a man as innocent as a little puppy, yet significantly less cute. Maybe he's an idiot. Maybe he's in on the joke. Or maybe, like all of us, he's just trying to get through the day, one stupid facial expression at a time.

Marx Reichlich, *A Jester*, c. 1520.

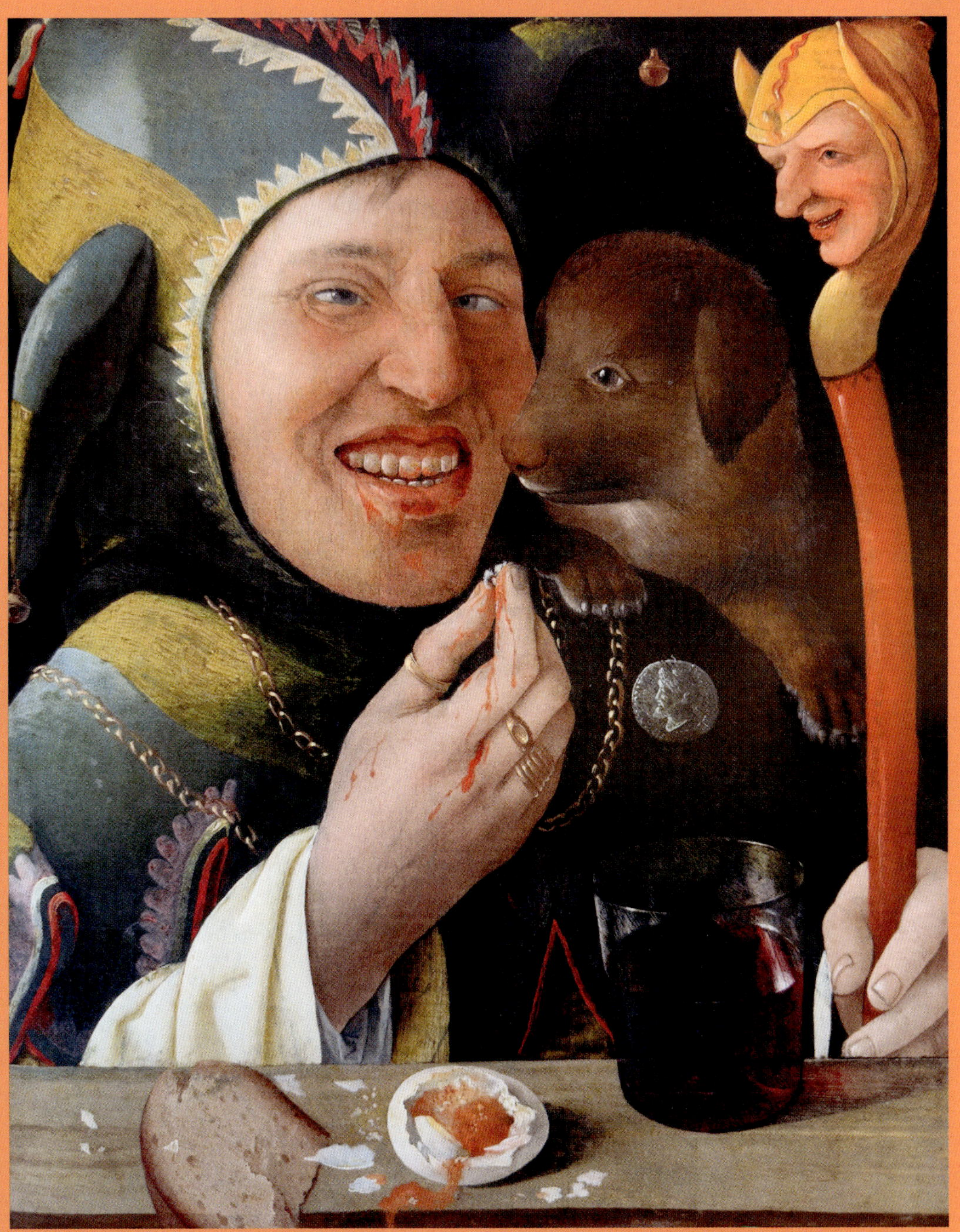

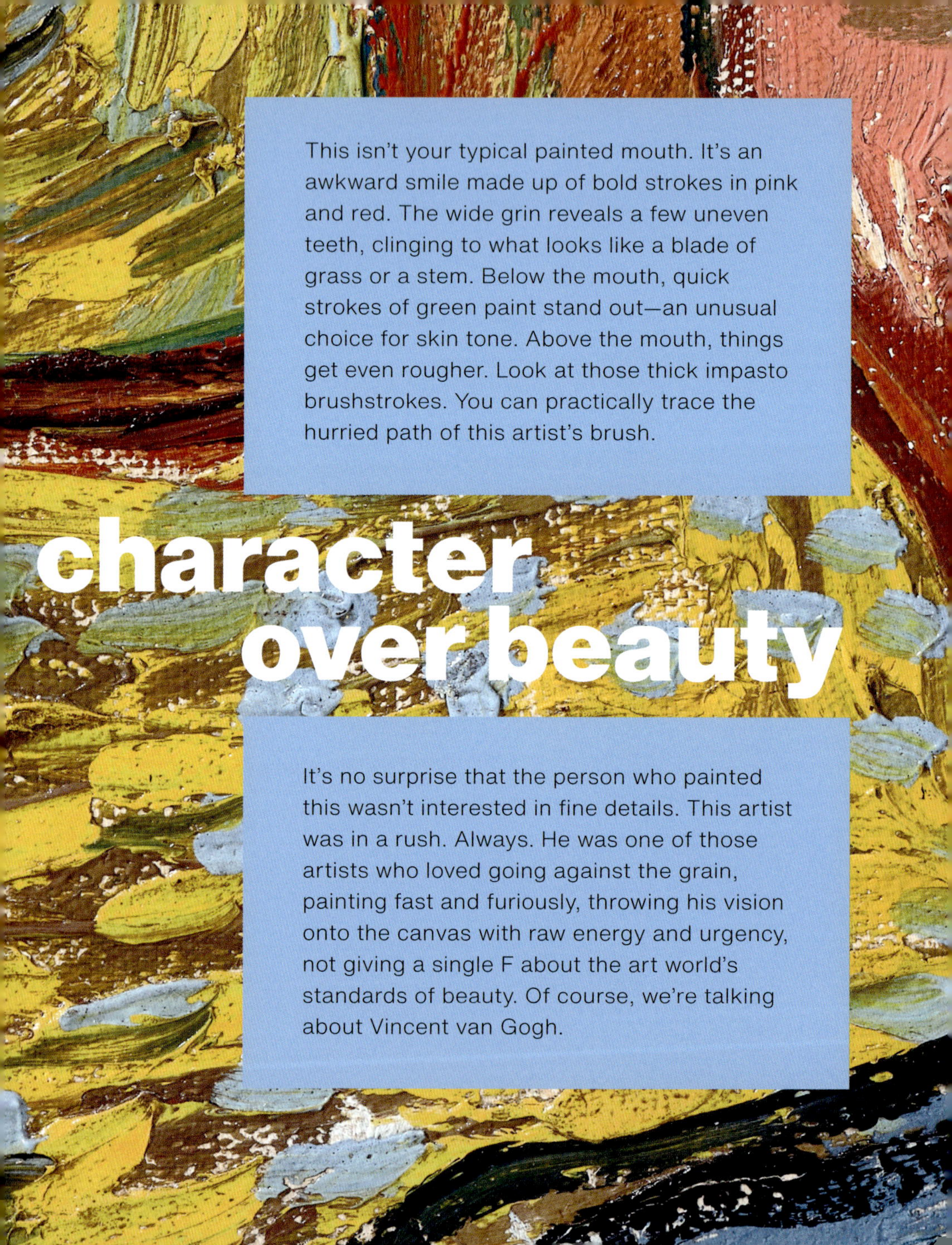

This isn't your typical painted mouth. It's an awkward smile made up of bold strokes in pink and red. The wide grin reveals a few uneven teeth, clinging to what looks like a blade of grass or a stem. Below the mouth, quick strokes of green paint stand out—an unusual choice for skin tone. Above the mouth, things get even rougher. Look at those thick impasto brushstrokes. You can practically trace the hurried path of this artist's brush.

character over beauty

It's no surprise that the person who painted this wasn't interested in fine details. This artist was in a rush. Always. He was one of those artists who loved going against the grain, painting fast and furiously, throwing his vision onto the canvas with raw energy and urgency, not giving a single F about the art world's standards of beauty. Of course, we're talking about Vincent van Gogh.

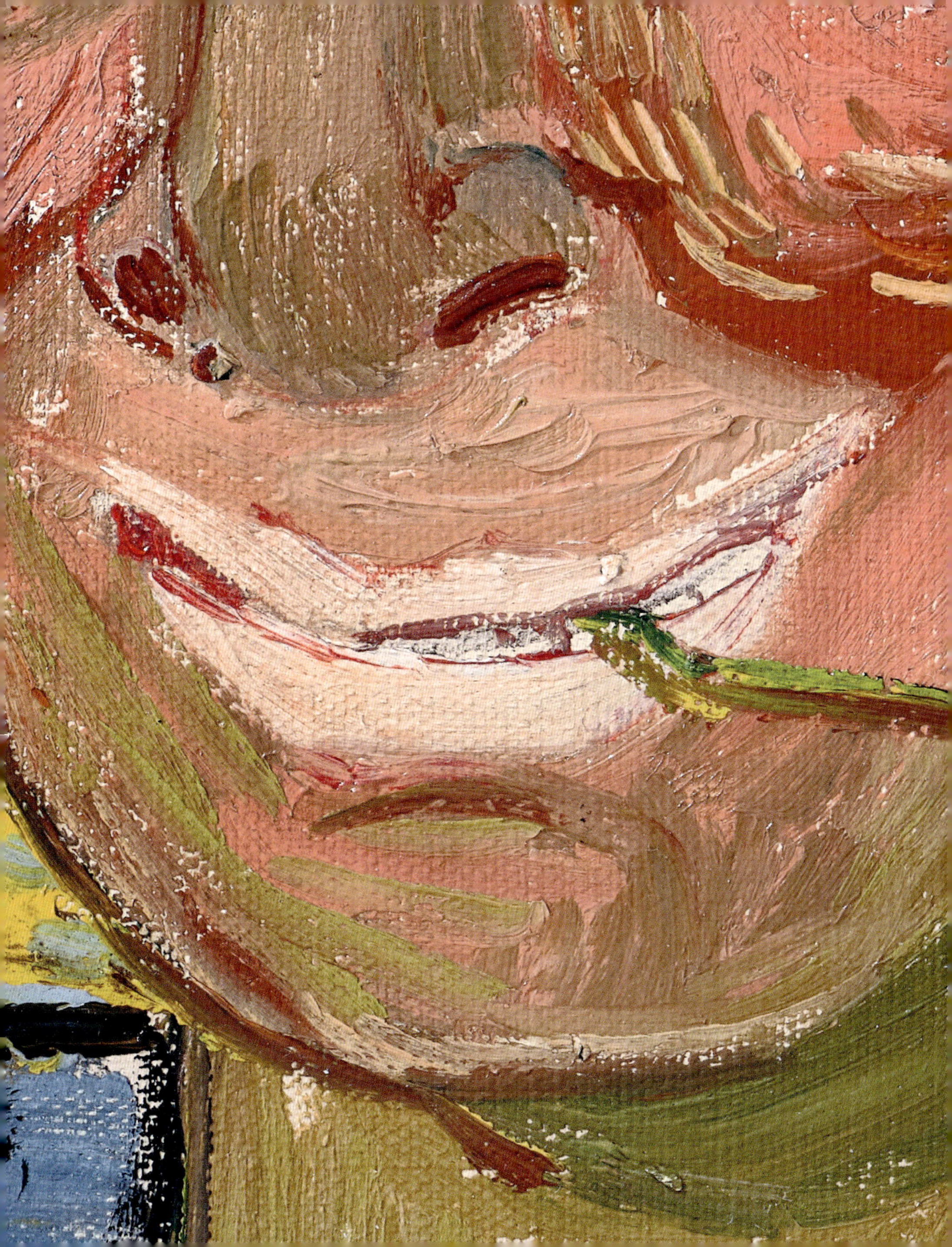

You might know Van Gogh for his bright landscapes, his swirling starry skies, or his vivid yellow sunflowers—but maybe not for his ugly faces. Don't get me wrong, Van Gogh created some amazing portraits, but this kid's face looks like it's been run over by a horse and carriage. There's an explanation, though. Van Gogh painted this portrait in June 1890, just weeks before he shot himself in a field near Auvers-sur-Oise, north of Paris. It's a time when Vincent's urgency and fury reached a boiling point. In just 70 days, he painted no fewer than 74 landscapes, still lifes, and portraits—many of which are now considered his finest. But with all that energy, sometimes his art turned out . . . well, like this.

Frankly, it's off. This kid's face looks flat, the whites of his eyes are actually green, his neck seems unhealthy and his thick hair is a chaotic mix of red and yellow. Even I, a huge admirer of Van Gogh, can't help but feel a bit unsettled by this face. But still, I love it, because this portrait isn't about beauty, it's about character.

I think it's a nice example of what Van Gogh called *the modern portrait*, a concept he was really excited about. For Van Gogh, a portrait should render a person's character, not by imitating their appearance, but by using bold lines and vibrant colors that express your feelings towards the person you're portraying. In this case, Van Gogh looked at this kid and probably saw a playful, wild little rascal. Maybe he caught sight of him darting through the golden wheat fields of Auvers. And perhaps the kid was so quick and so full of life, that even the brief time that Van Gogh usually needed to capture a person on canvas wasn't enough this time.

Vincent van Gogh, *Young Man with Cornflower*, 1890.

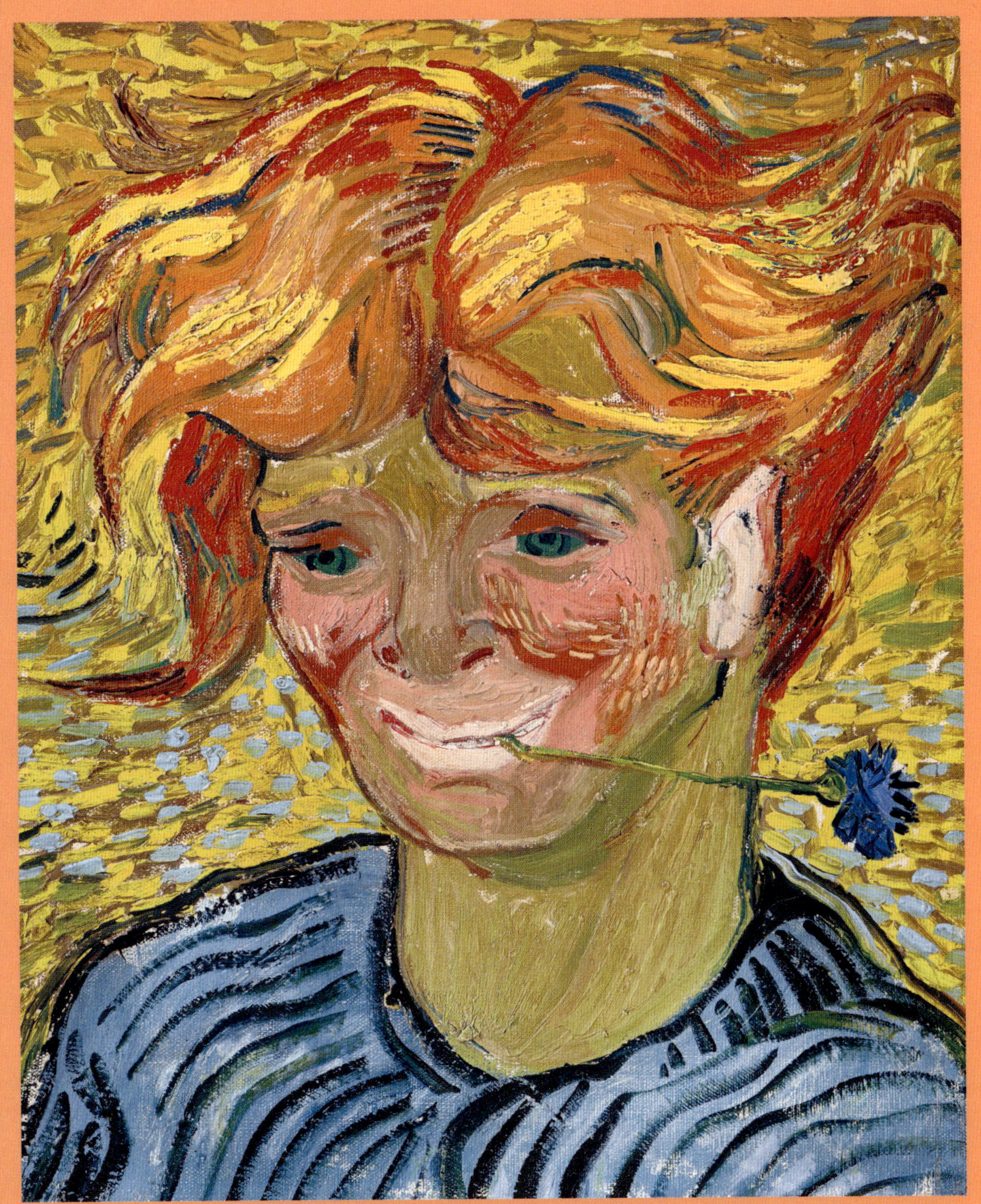

misery and marigolds

A golden crown, eyes half shut and a droopy facial expression. At first glance, this kid seems to be in a slumber—as if he's just woken up. But something isn't right, especially if you consider the small trickles of blood running from his nose and mouth.

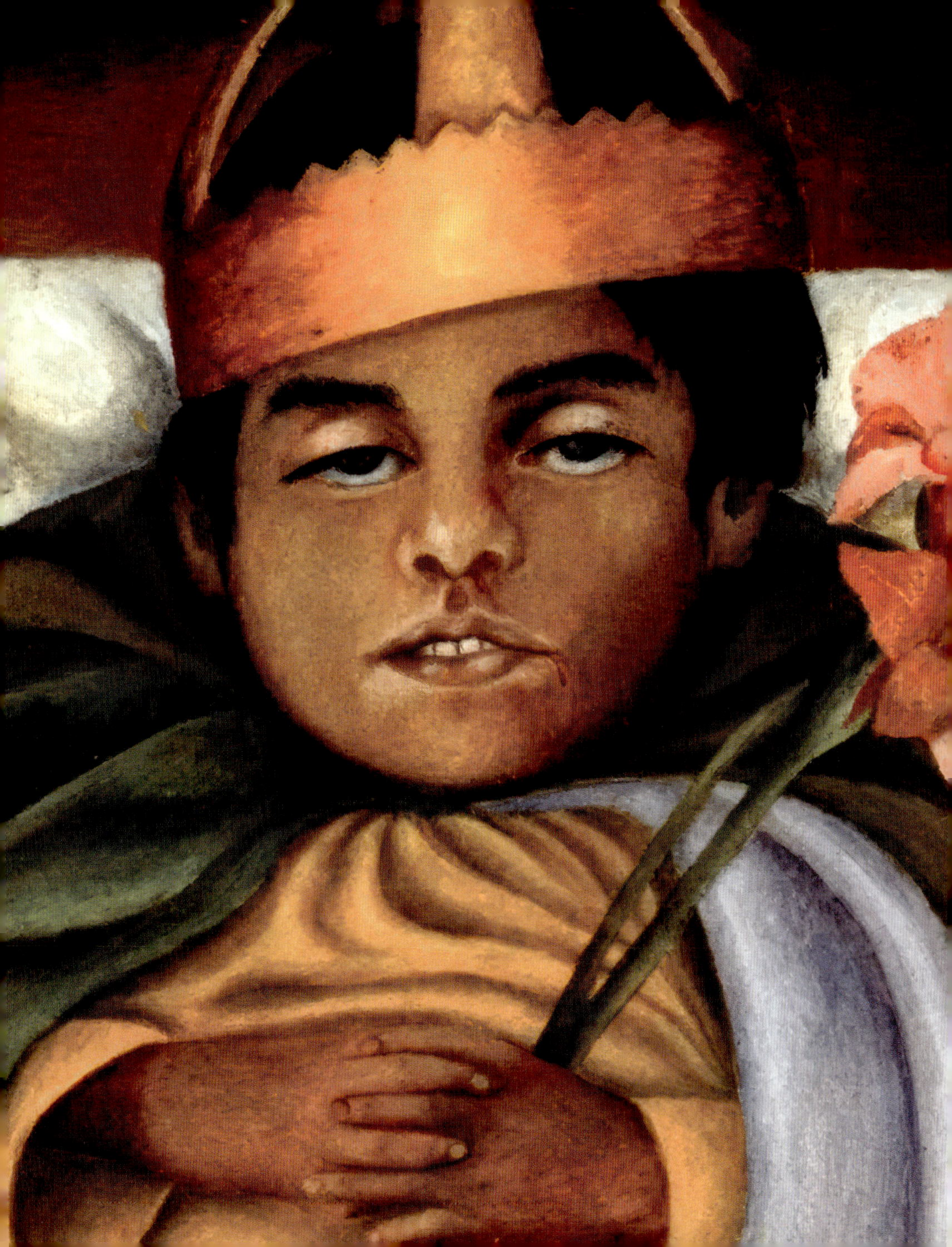

No, this isn't a peaceful slumber. Dimas, the three-year-old boy in the portrait, has passed away. The renowned Mexican artist Frida Kahlo, who knew tragedy well, painted this heartbreaking piece for her friend Delfina, Dimas's mother. In Mexican culture, death is viewed as a natural part of life, and there's a long-standing tradition of honoring the dead through art. The story behind this boy's death is tragic, but let's look at the painting first.

Kahlo titled this work *Dressed Up for Paradise*, because Dimas is dressed as a little St. Joseph, with a crown on his head to assure he is admitted to the kingdom of heaven. The boy is holding beautiful pink gladiolus, symbolizing remembrance. Scattered around the little body are orange marigolds, the iconic flower of the *Día de los Muertos* or Day of the Dead, the Mexican holiday celebrating the dead. On this day, the spirits of the deceased are believed to visit their family homes, and the flower's fragrance and bright color is supposed to lead them there.

On the pillow next to the boy's head sits a picture of Christ tied up to a column, before his crucifixion, which probably points to the boy's innocence. At his feet there is a note that reads, "The Deceased Dimas Rosas at 3 years old."

Creating these kinds of portraits wasn't uncommon in Mexican culture, as it is part of a tradition called *la muerte niña* or "the child death." During vigils, families or parents would often hire painters or photographers to capture their children's final, glorious image, as a way to celebrate their memory.

The little Dimas died due to illness, after his family refused to go to a medical doctor and chose a village witch doctor instead. The result of this choice can be seen in the painting. However, there's one important thing that the family did right: hiring Frida Kahlo to paint his final portrait.

Frida Kahlo, *Dressed Up for Paradise (The Deceased Dimas Rosas at Three Years of Age)*, 1937.

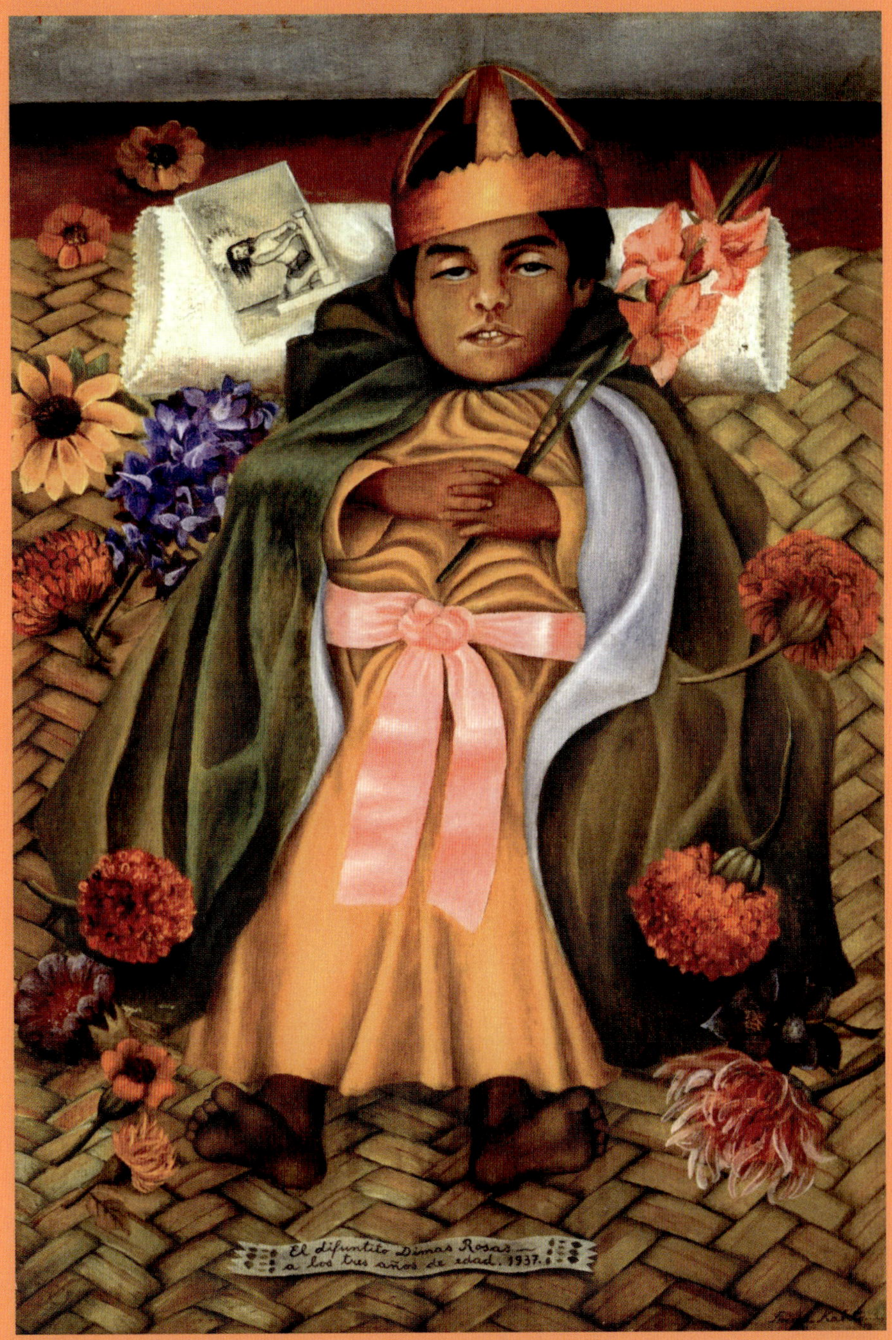
El difuntito Dimas Rosas —
a los tres años de edad. 1937.

hippopotamus in distress

Hippos are fabulous. They look like giant bath toys, they're always smiling and they can crush a small car with their jaws.

This one, though, is having a rough day. His tongue is twisting mid-scream, the eyes are pleading for mercy and there's a little trickle of blood dripping from one of those massive teeth.

But it's not just the stress that makes this face interesting. Something is off. That head looks too small for a hippo. His jaw should be bigger. And the lips shouldn't curl up like that. There's a good reason for this uncanny look: The hippo that modeled for this painting was dead.

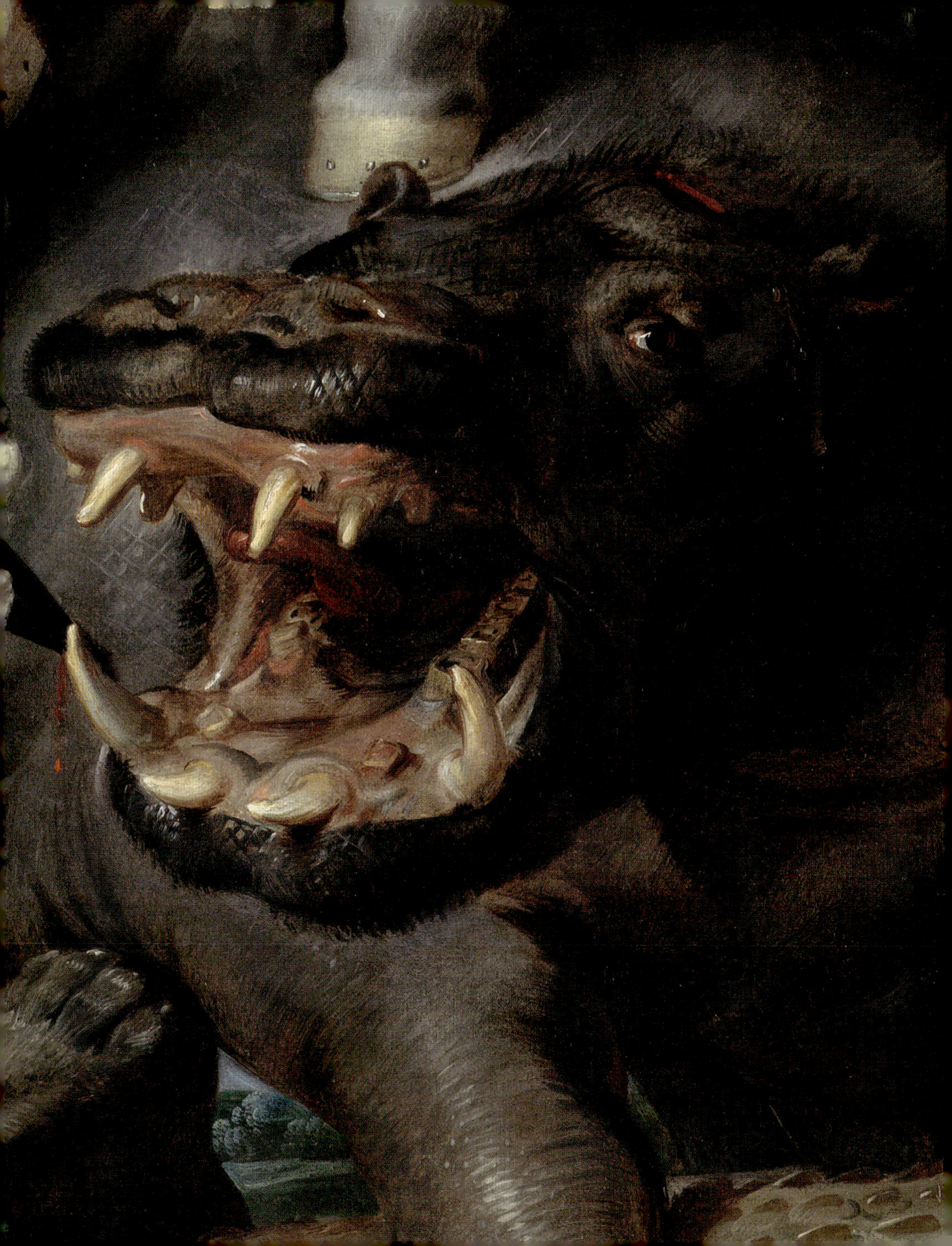

Well, this explains why our big friend is stressed. He's fighting for his life against a squad of professional killers. It's an unfair fight. The hippo and his crocodile sidekick are up against armed men, three ferocious dogs and three war-ready horses. One of the horses is even biting the hippo in the back, which isn't something you see in your average nature documentary.

This insane scene was put to canvas by the king of baroque, Peter Paul Rubens. It was commissioned by the Bavarian Duke Maximilian I to decorate his huge hunting lodge and glorify the questionable thrill of killing exotic animals. But there was one small problem: Rubens had never actually seen a hippo in real life. So how did he manage to paint one that looks both impressive and . . . not quite right?

The answer: taxidermy. A few years before painting this, Rubens was working in Italy, at the court of Duke Vincenzo Gonzaga—a man with a deep love for dead animals. And among his collection of stuffed creatures was a hippo. The poor animal was shot in Egypt, dunked in a brine bath to stop it from rotting and finally stuffed into its final form. The result? A dried-out, shriveled husk that looked nothing like a healthy hippo. And this is what Rubens used as his model, explaining the hippo's slightly uncanny features.

Poor thing. Imagine being killed on the banks of the Nile, getting submerged in brine, then being stuffed and brought back to life on canvas, only to be brutally murdered *again* at those same river banks. No wonder he's screaming for help.

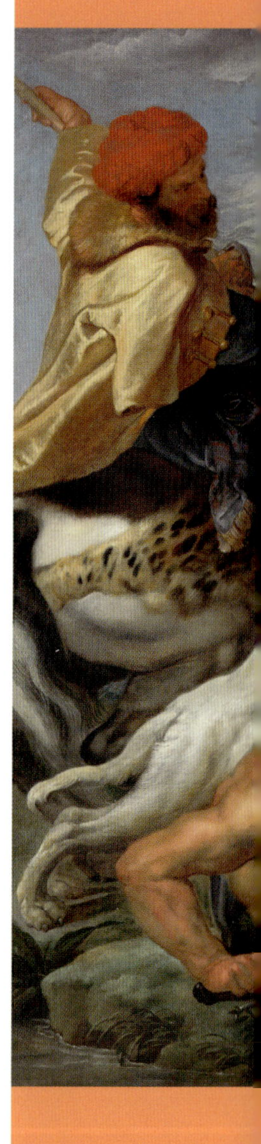

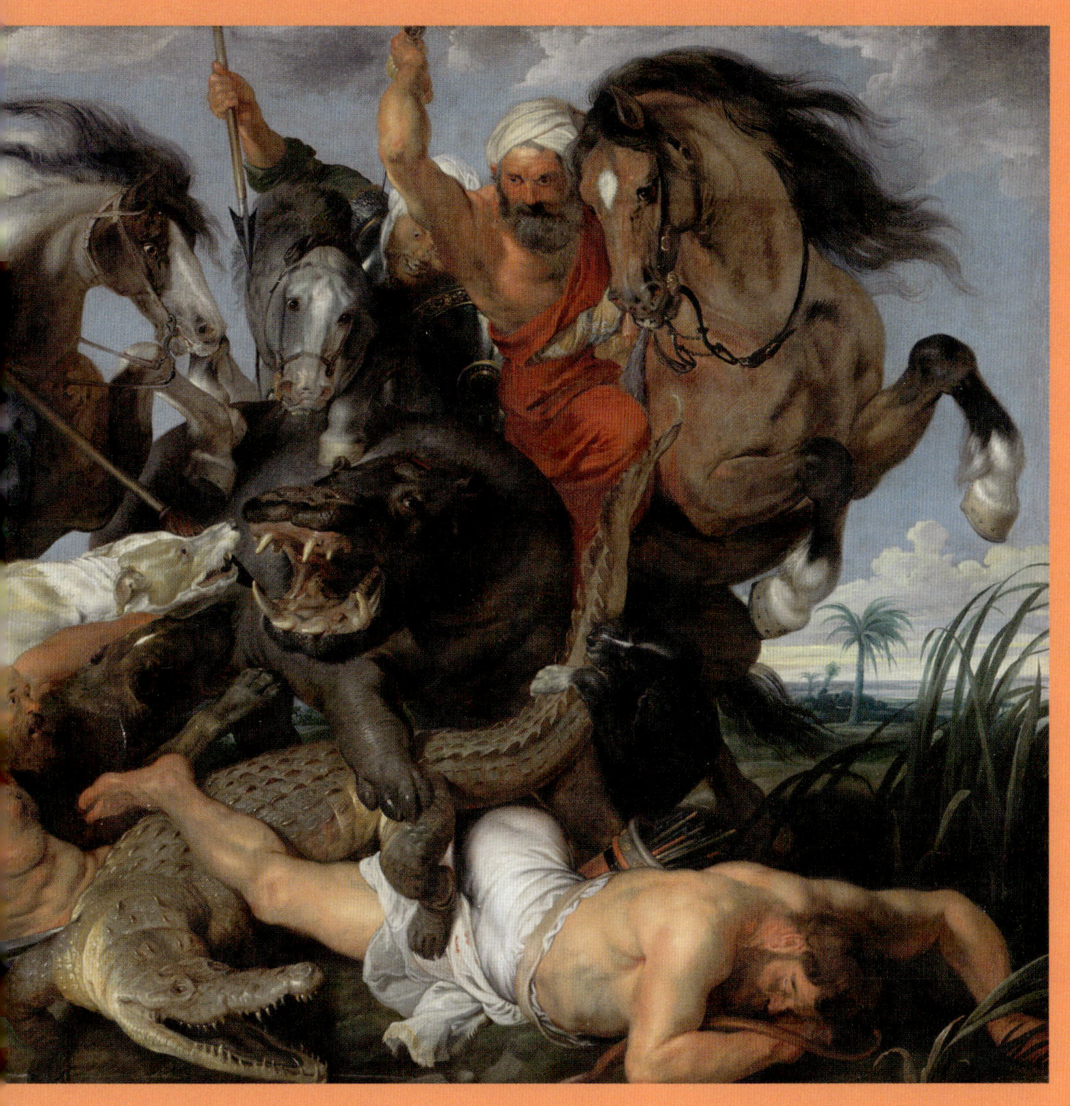

Peter Paul Rubens, *The Hippopotamus and Crocodile Hunt*, c. 1615–1616.

This dainty mole, with its cute little bouquet of wiggly hairs, belongs to one of my all-time favorite faces in art history. This 16th-century masterpiece features a proud nose, a grand pair of ears and a cute constellation of shiny pimples, just waiting to be popped. Let's see who owns this spectacular set of features.

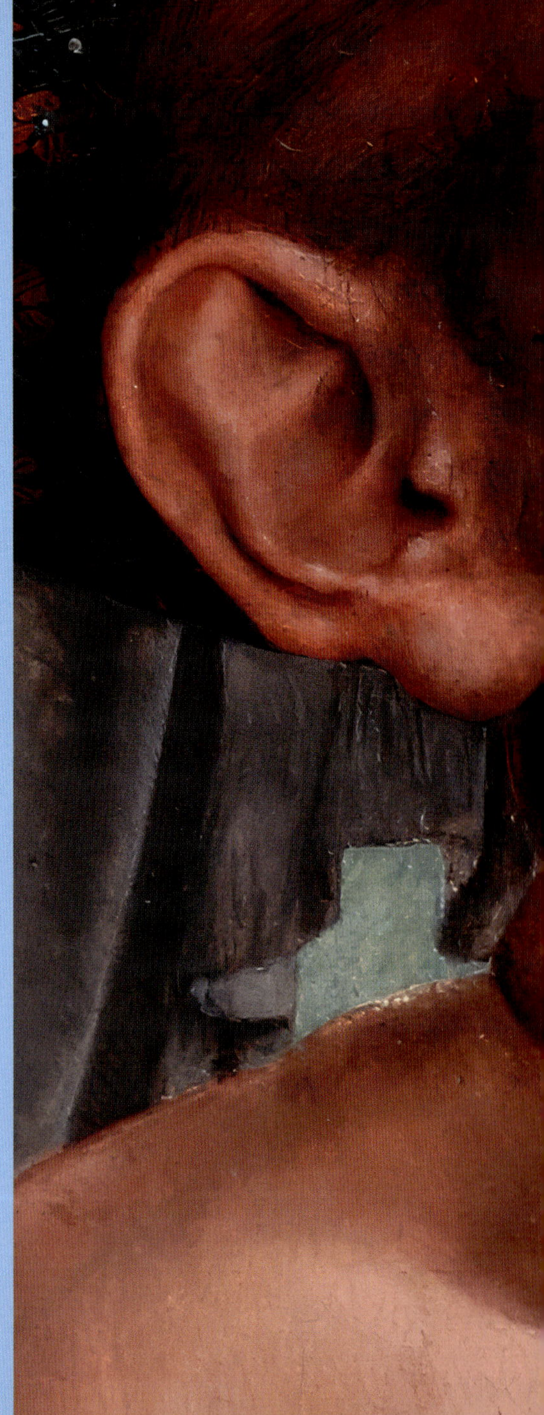

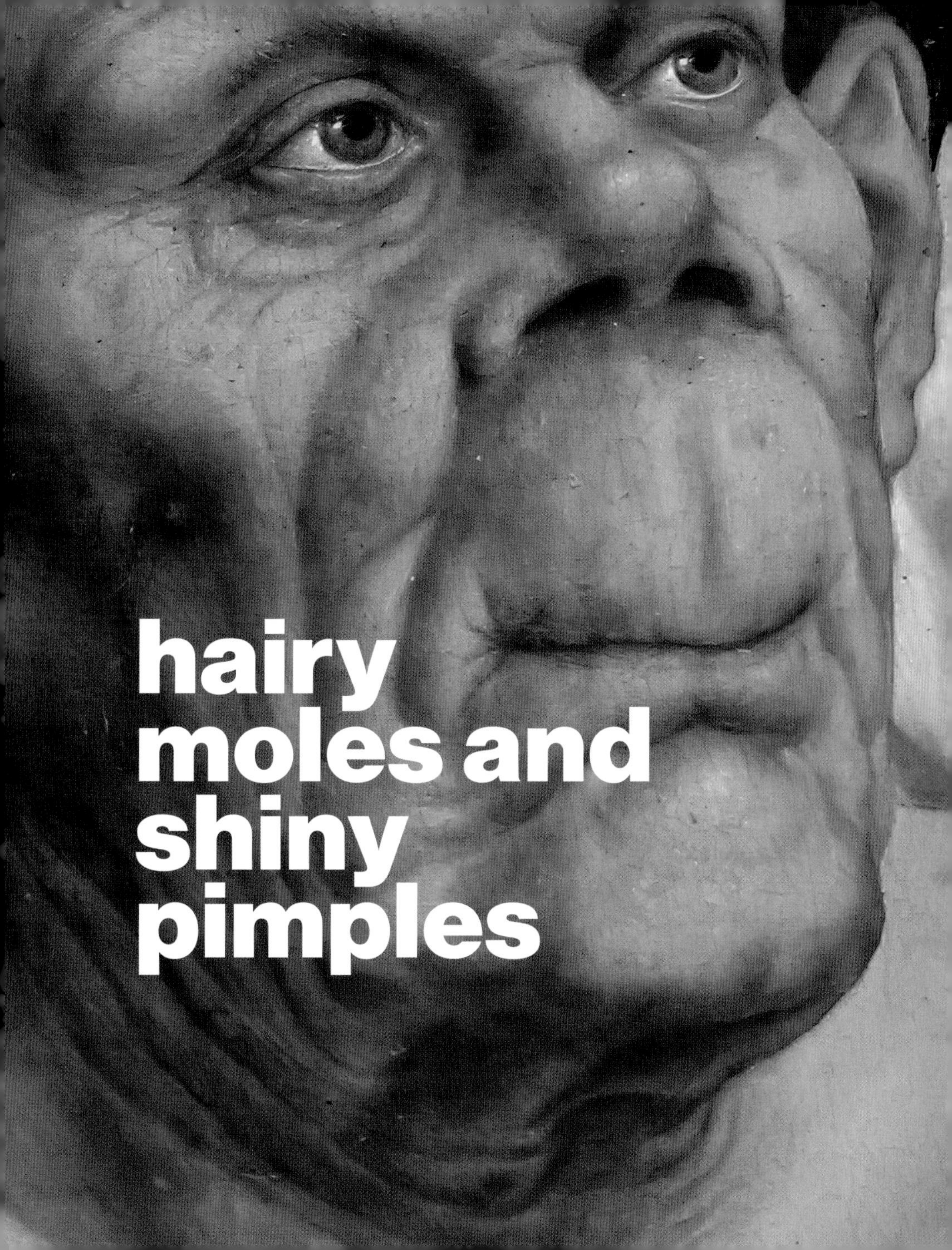

hairy moles and shiny pimples

Quinten Massys, *The Ugly Duchess*, c. 1513.

There she is: *An Old Woman* by Quinten Massys, more commonly known as *The Ugly Duchess*. But honestly, I don't really agree with that title. Sure, this lady is aesthetically challenged, but Massys transforms her so-called ugliness into something remarkably fascinating. Beautiful, even.

Let's start with her outfit. Our lady's hair is neatly tucked beneath a wonderful, heart-shaped headdress. Her impressive forehead is crowned by a pearly brooch, holding a veil that only just manages to cover her broad shoulders. And then there's her chest, with two determined breasts, desperately struggling to escape the tightly laced bodice.

For a long time, art historians figured that this portrait was by the hand of Leonardo da Vinci, because this face looked a lot like the grotesque faces in some of Da Vinci's sketches. But apparently, Leo was just a big fan of Massys. The two wrote to each other and loved to exchange drawings.

Massys's intentions with this portrait are unknown. Maybe it's a satire on vanity or material obsession, or perhaps it pokes fun at elderly people desperately clinging to a youthful appearance. Personally, I see someone boldly being themselves, not giving a care in the world about the conventions of their day. And in that sense, this 500-year-old painting is still incredibly relevant today. But then again, that's just how I see it. What do you think?

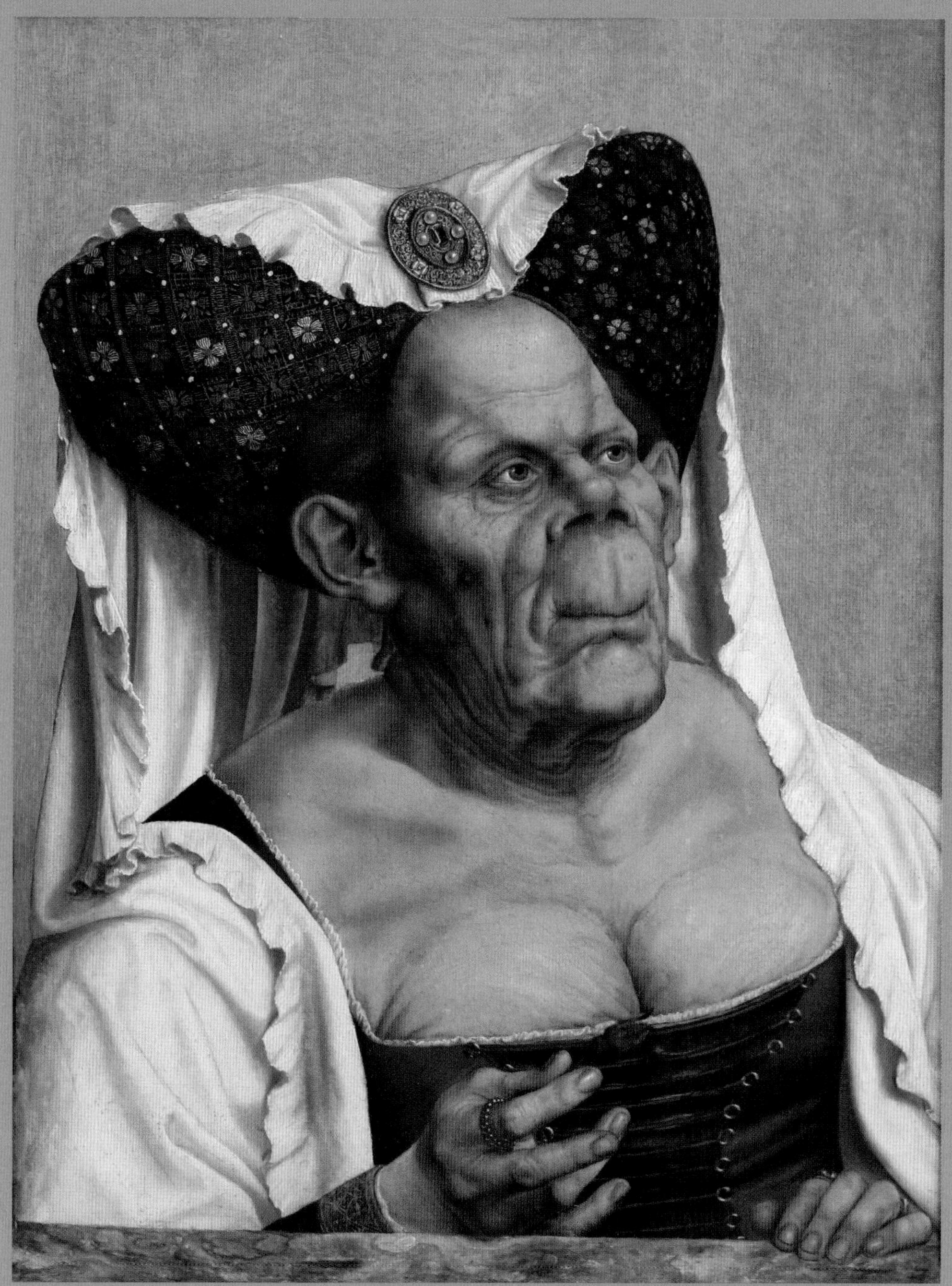

the facial buffet

Shiny grapes and golden wheat, some spring onions and a colorful garland of flowers. These three images are all part of the same painting, and it looks like we're dealing with a very elaborate still life. Or maybe we're looking at details of a 19th-century market stall. Or maybe it's a royal feast prepared for a devoted vegetarian. Whatever it is, it's vibrant, detailed and straightforward. But there's no stupid face in sight. So, why are we looking at this? Well, because it *is* a face.

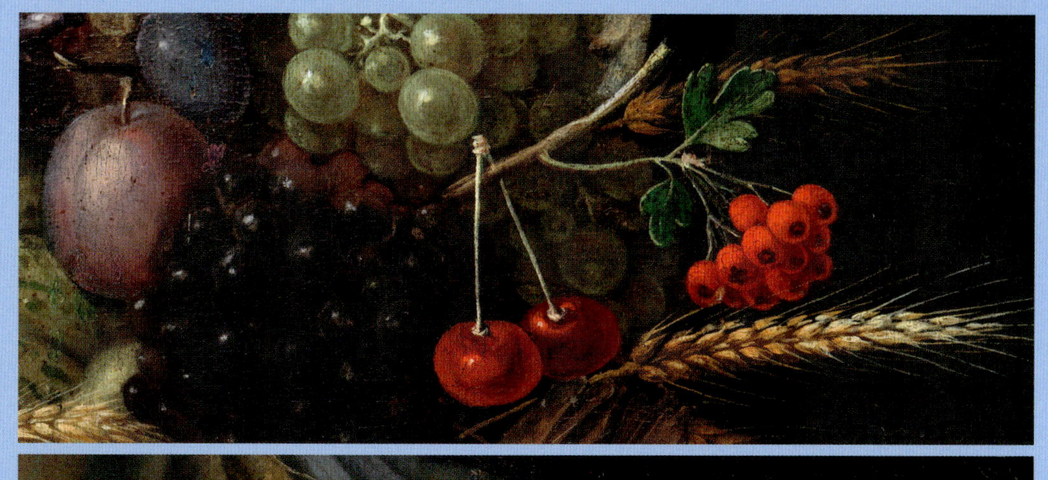
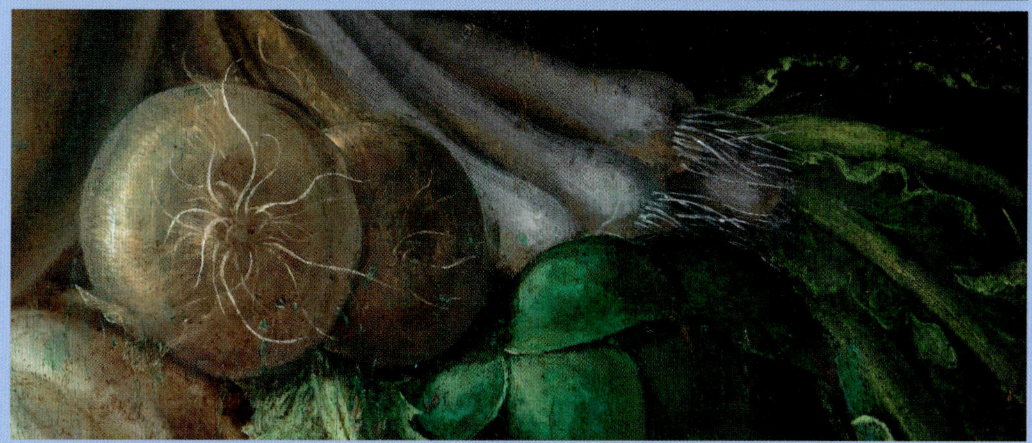
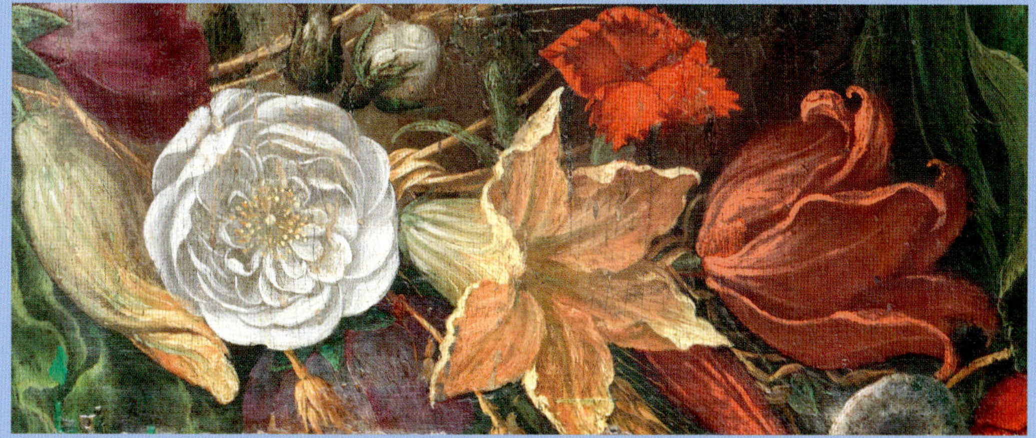

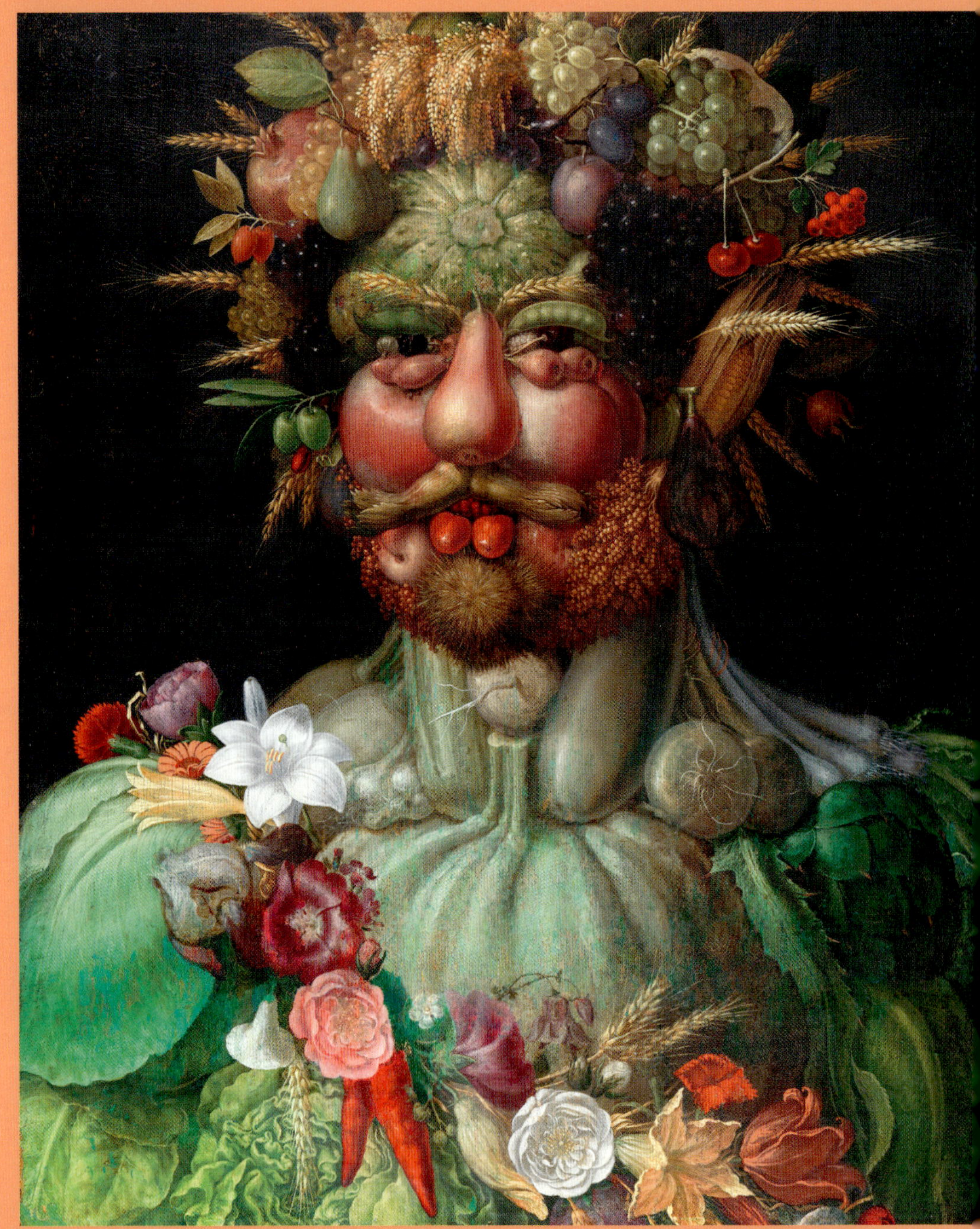

This is a portrait of Vertumnus, the Roman god of seasons, gardens and fruit trees—and he seems to be taking his job very seriously. He really looks the part as well, with the face of an orchard and suit of a salad bar. When it comes to greens, this man means business.

Giuseppe Arcimboldo, *Vertumnus*, 1590–1591.

At first glance, this wild portrait might seem like some surreal masterpiece, but it was actually painted in 1591. Because Renaissance masters weren't just interested in linear perspective, human anatomy and fancy shadows, some of them also just liked to paint fruit faces. Like Giuseppe Arcimboldo, the 16th-century king of composite images. He created a series of bizarre portraits where human heads were made entirely of themed objects: seasons, elements, professions. You name it. There's a man made of fish, a librarian built from books and even a person composed of fire and smoke. It was strange, clever, and incredibly popular.

But this particular puzzle is more than just a portrait of Vertumnus; it's also an allegorical representation of Emperor Rudolf II of the Holy Roman Empire. It's supposed to symbolize the golden era that blossomed under Rudolf's rule. And it also harbors a little added bonus, because in reality, the emperor's nose was so big that it *actually* looked like a pear.

And while Arcimboldo's paintings might look whimsical or crazy today, art scholars also believe that they simply catered to the tastes of his time—because Renaissance people were fascinated by puzzles and riddles and by the grotesque and the bizarre. So Arcimboldo probably wasn't a madman; he was the ultimate vegetable virtuoso of his era.

the heavy metal tronie

This guy looks like he's belting "Highway to Hell." Long greasy hair, a brown schoolboy cap and a face distorted in mid-yell . . . this *must* be an AC/DC fan, right? Wrong. This isn't an Angus Young fan screaming his way to hell; this is a 17th-century peasant screaming in disgust. Two kinds of people that, apparently, have more than one thing in common. His eyes and brows are scrunched in sheer revolt, and his mouth seems to be unleashing the foulest of curses. But what's causing all this disgust? Let's have a look.

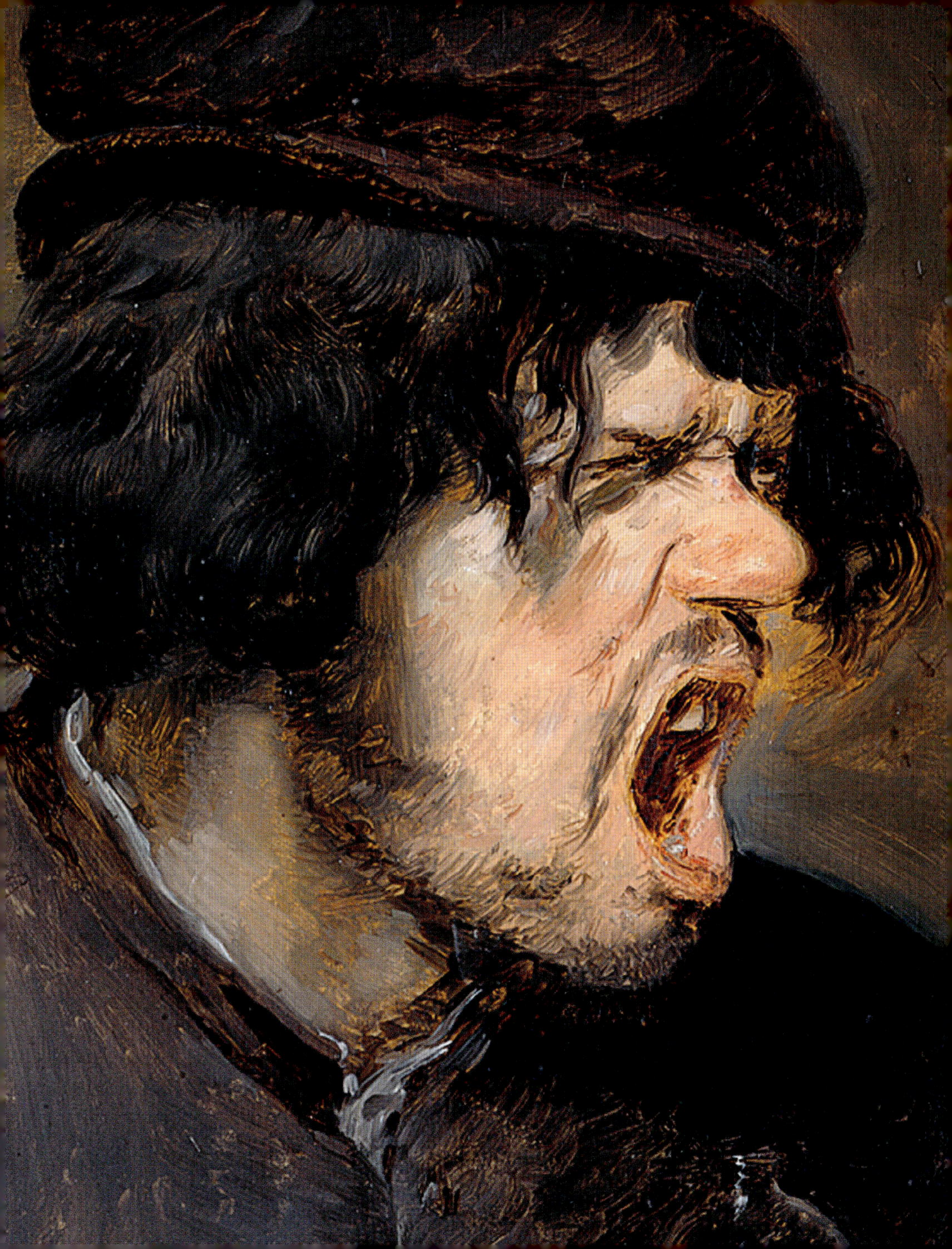

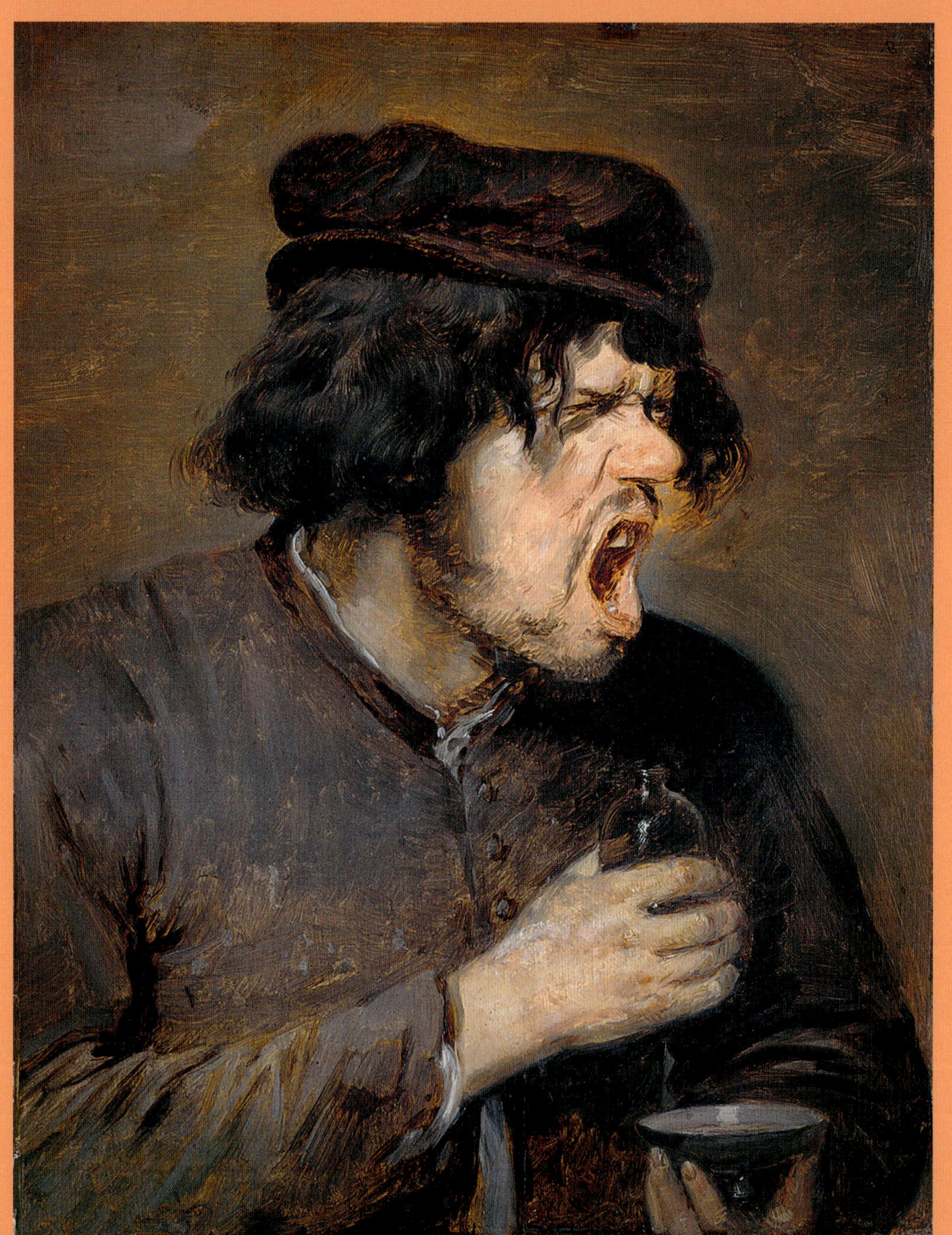

Aha! Our peasant is holding a metal cup and a small glass flask. He's clearly just taken a sip of what must be a gut-wrenching concoction. This is *The Bitter Potion* by Adriaen Brouwer, a 17th-century Flemish master who excelled in painting vivid facial expressions. He loved capturing the faces of peasants, soldiers and other so-called lower-class people as they smoked, fought, played music or—like this guy—drank something awful.

Adriaen Brouwer, *The Bitter Potion*, c. 1636–1638.

This kind of face is known as a *tronie*, a depiction of a fictional character with a very vivid expression, designed to convey a powerful emotion. In this case, revulsion. Artists like Brouwer created these tronies to make a living by selling them and to showcase their technical skills. And Brouwer really knew how to show off. With just a few quick brushstrokes, he created a wonderful facial drama that pulls you in and makes you wonder what on earth is in that flask.

Well, it's probably a medicinal drink made from tree bark, intended to combat malaria. Because even back in the 17th century, doctors knew that the bark of the tropical *Cinchona* tree contained a component that kills malaria parasites: quinine—the super-bitter stuff you'll also find in tonic water. So, the next time you're enjoying a gin and tonic, maybe raise your glass to this poor man, take a big sip, and pull your best bitter face.

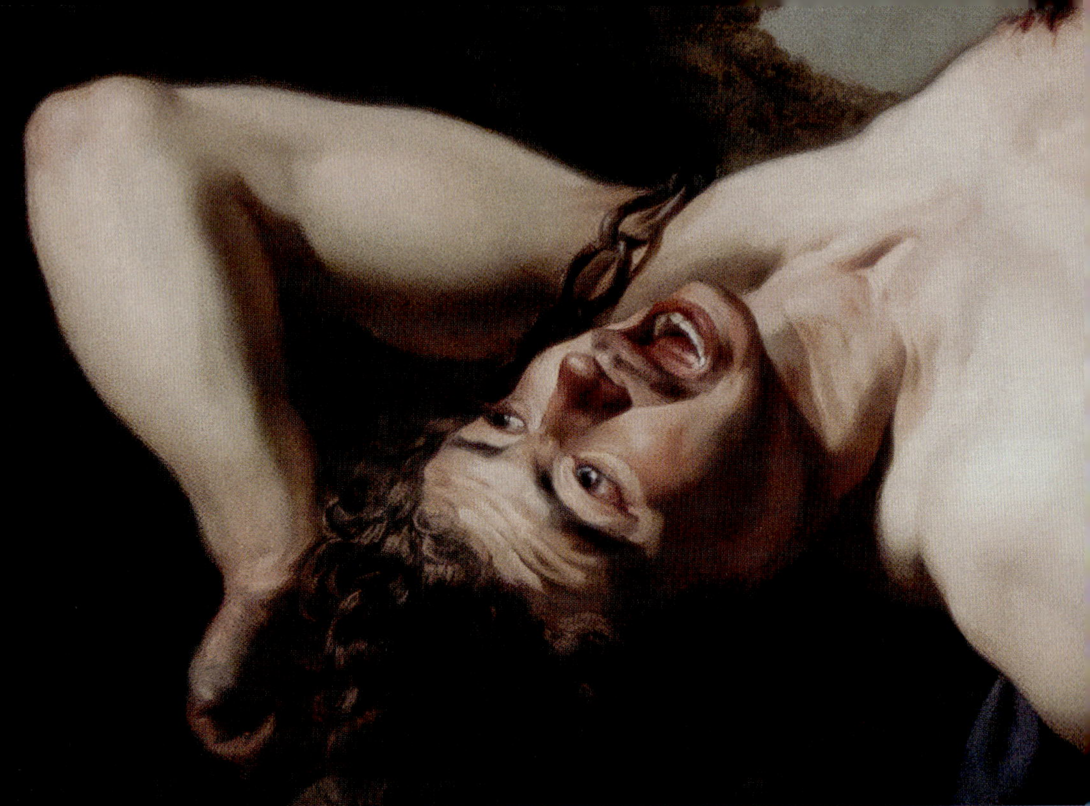

Zeus

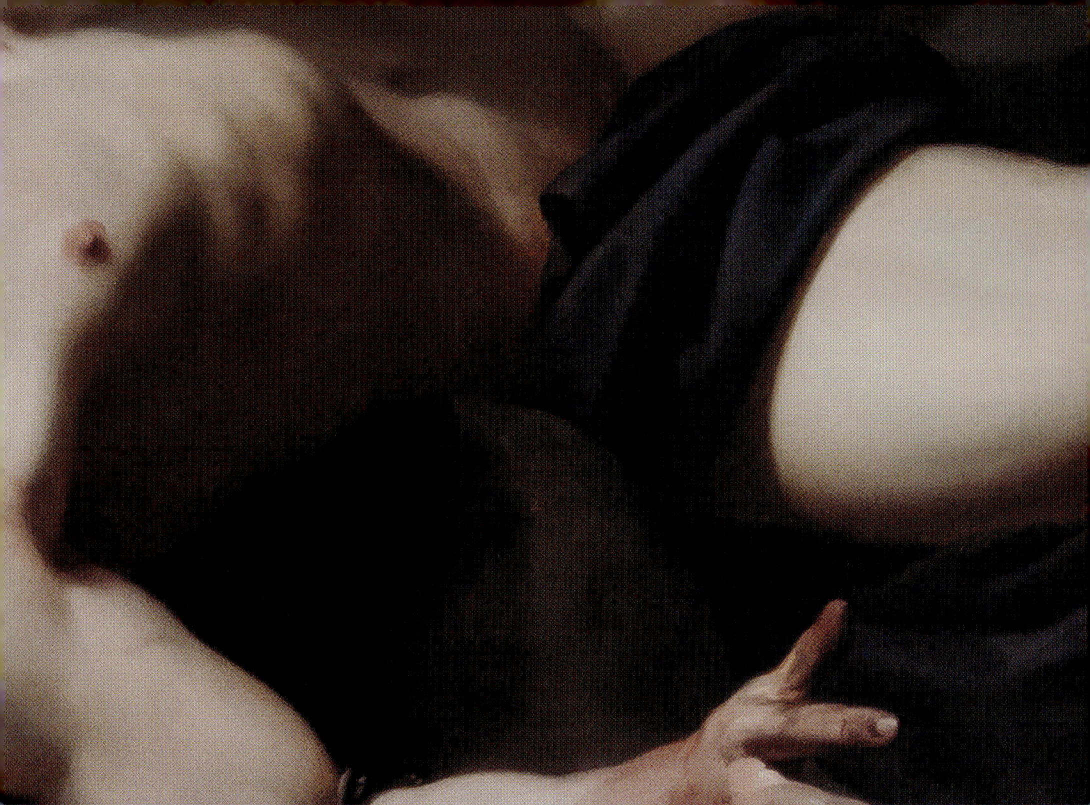

isn't amused

You can't spell "painting" without spelling "pain," and this painting looks *very* painful. The look on this man's face is remarkably similar to my own facial expression when my four-year-old switches on the bedroom lights at 5:00 a.m. on a Sunday. Bloodshot eyes, hands reaching for the scalp and a mouth screaming in agony. This is a look of pain and horror. But this painting isn't about my Sunday morning torment; it's about a mythical man suffering from eternal damnation. And we're about to find out why.

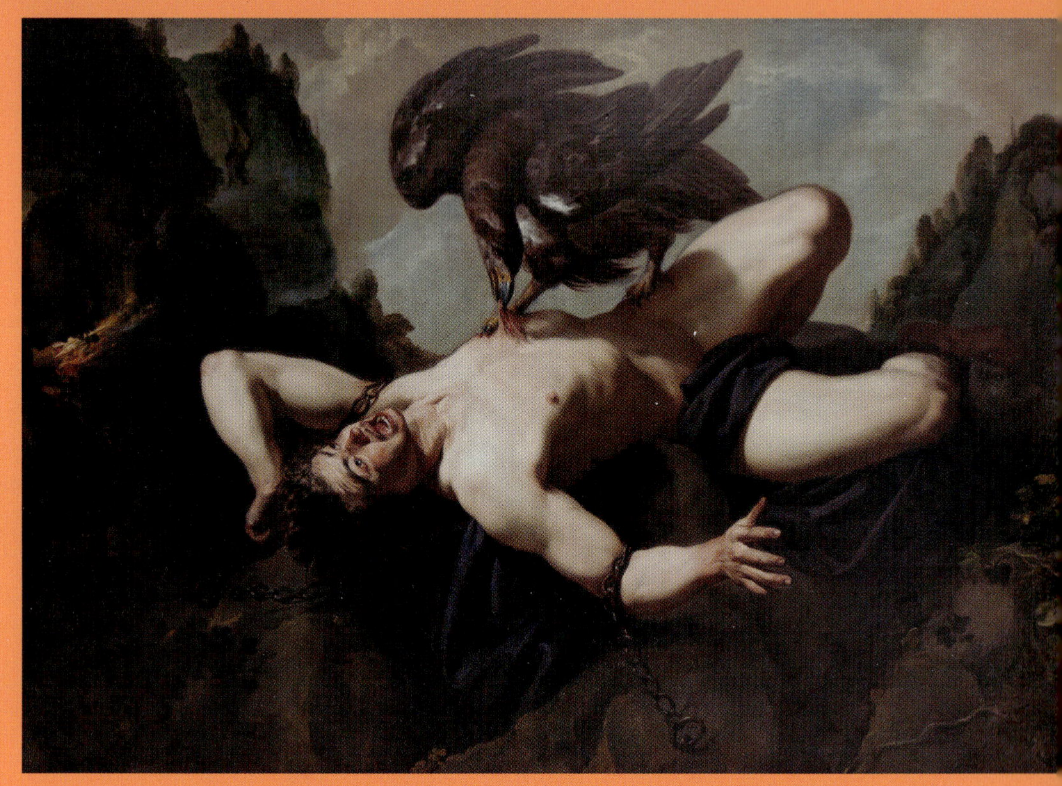

Theodoor Rombouts, *Prometheus*, 1623.

You're looking at *Prometheus* by Flemish Baroque master Theodoor Rombouts—a pretty intense portrayal of a Greek god in torment. As the myth goes, Prometheus is the one who stole fire from the heavens and gave it to humanity. A very nice gesture, because it allowed us mere mortals to survive. But it was also a reckless move, because Zeus—the king of the Olympian gods—wasn't amused.

This is the the result of Zeus's wrath. Prometheus is chained to a desolate mountainside, his arms pulled painfully back and his muscles straining against the iron shackles.

He isn't exactly comfortable, to say the least, and to add to the misery, Zeus has also arranged for an eagle to stop by and pick out his liver. Every single day. Because, as luck would have it, Prometheus's liver grows back overnight, so the bird can feast again. And again. And again. It's an unbreakable chain of pain.

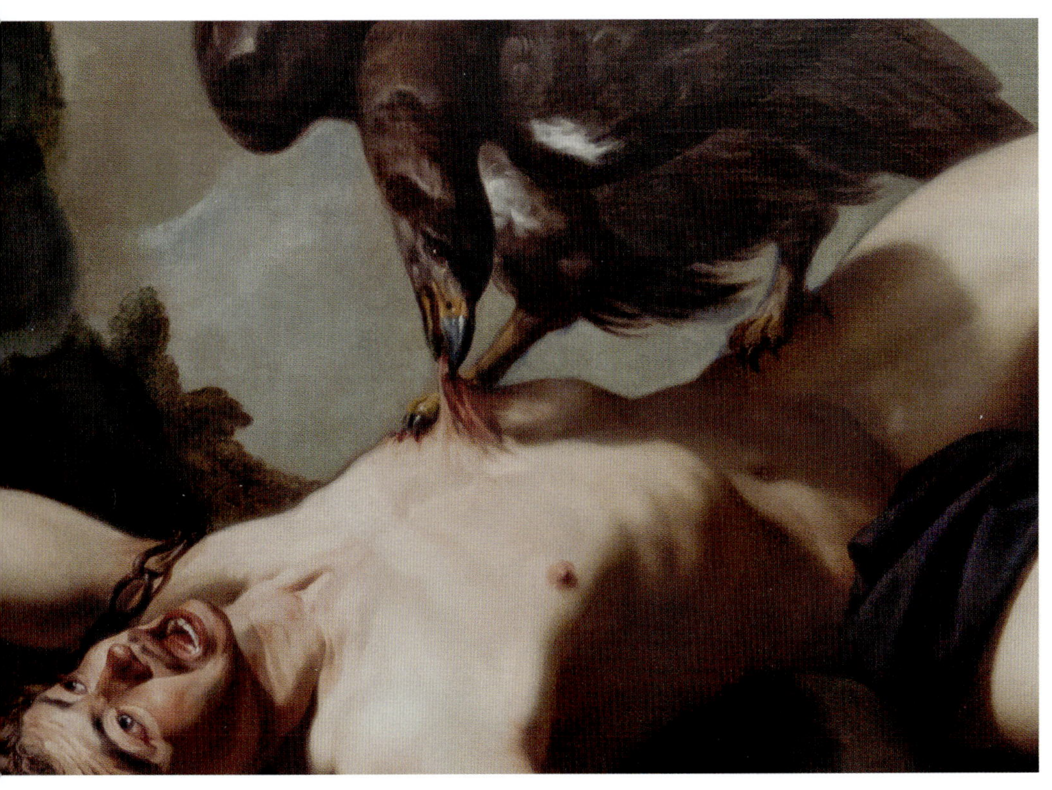

And to top it off, the eagle in Rombouts's painting is also picking the wrong nipple, because human livers are situated at the other side of the chest. So I guess the bird will soon have to start pulling the other nipple. Poor Prometheus. But then again, he isn't woken up by a four-year-old on a Sunday morning, so how bad can it really be?

They say a fish's memory only lasts a few seconds, but the catfish in this painting looks like he's experiencing a moment he will never forget. Mouth wide open, eyes bulging—he's clearly in shock, and for good reason: He got caught.

Fortunately, he's not facing this trauma alone. Our gasping fish is surrounded by crabs, eels and flatfish, all being pulled in by a strong pair of fisherman's arms. What a great haul. But the bearded fisherman didn't net all this by himself. He got crucial help from the man standing right beside him on the boat—barefoot and wearing a red robe. Let's see who we're dealing with.

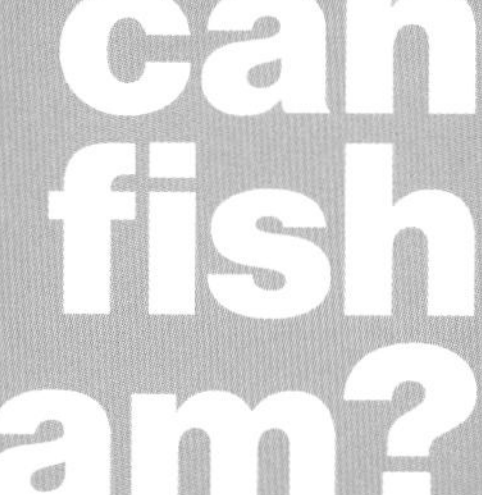

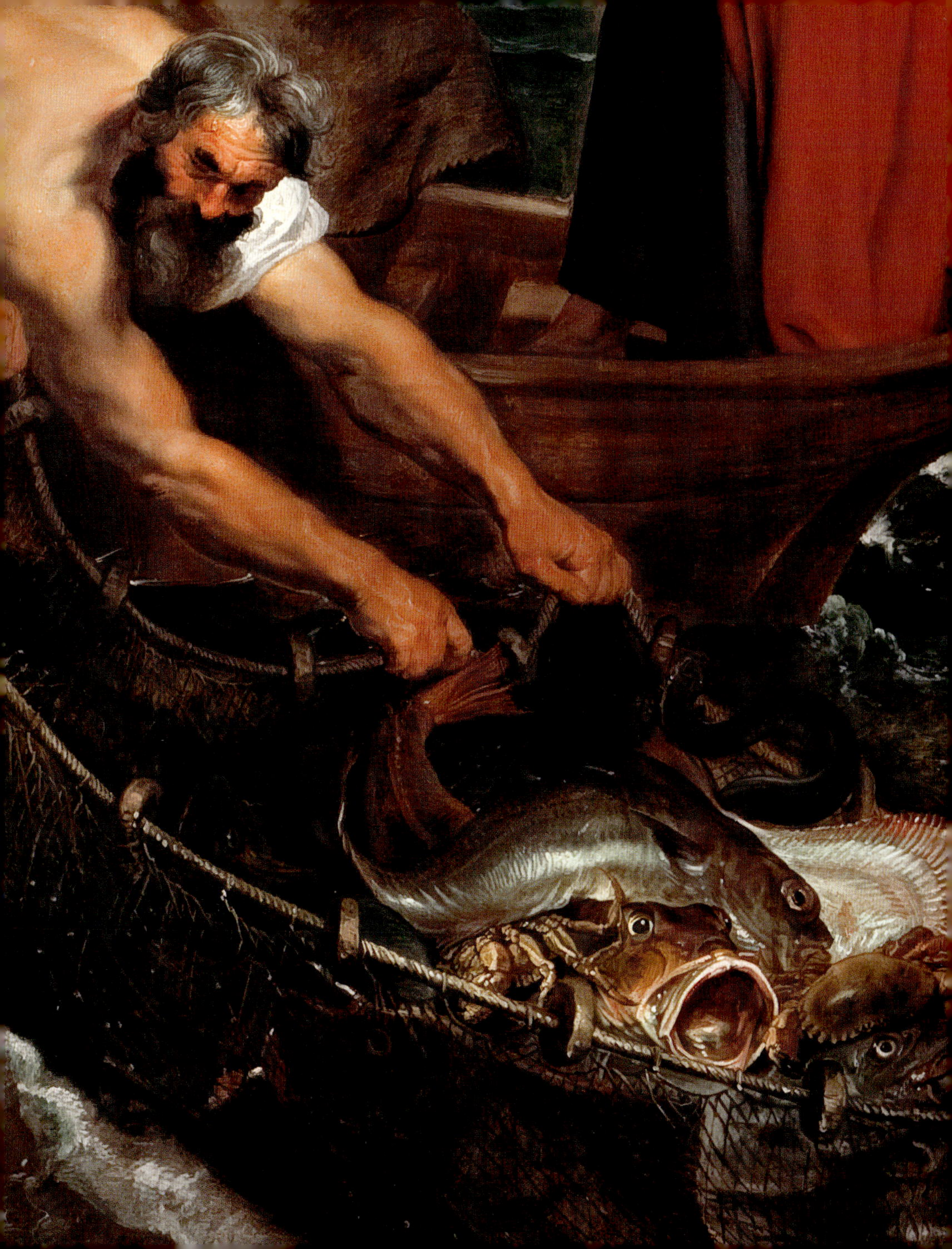

There he is, the most depicted man in art history: Jesus Christ. This vibrant altarpiece by Peter Paul Rubens is called *The Miraculous Draught of Fishes.* It was commissioned by a local fishmongers' guild, which might explain why the fishermen look incredibly ripped. Either the fishmongers asked for strong arms, or Rubens was simply pleasing his client. But as the title suggests, the big catch wasn't the result of these fishermen's strength or skill.

No, according to the Biblical story, these men had sailed the whole day and didn't even catch a single fish. They're exhausted and desperate, when an unshaven man in sandals appears and commands them to "Try one more time." After which the Lord performs his magic trick and fills their nets with all kinds of fish, which is a great way to impress and recruit a bunch of fishermen as your disciples.

The men are completely astonished, and then Jesus closes the deal with a brilliant catchphrase: "Do not be afraid, because henceforth you will be catching men." Mic drop. The fishermen leave everything behind—their nets, their boat, and yes, even our poor fish—and follow him. And so, using some amazing recruitment tactics, Jesus Christ caught himself an entourage for the ages, killing an incredible number of innocent fish along the way.

Peter Paul Rubens, *The Miraculous Draught of Fishes*, 1618.

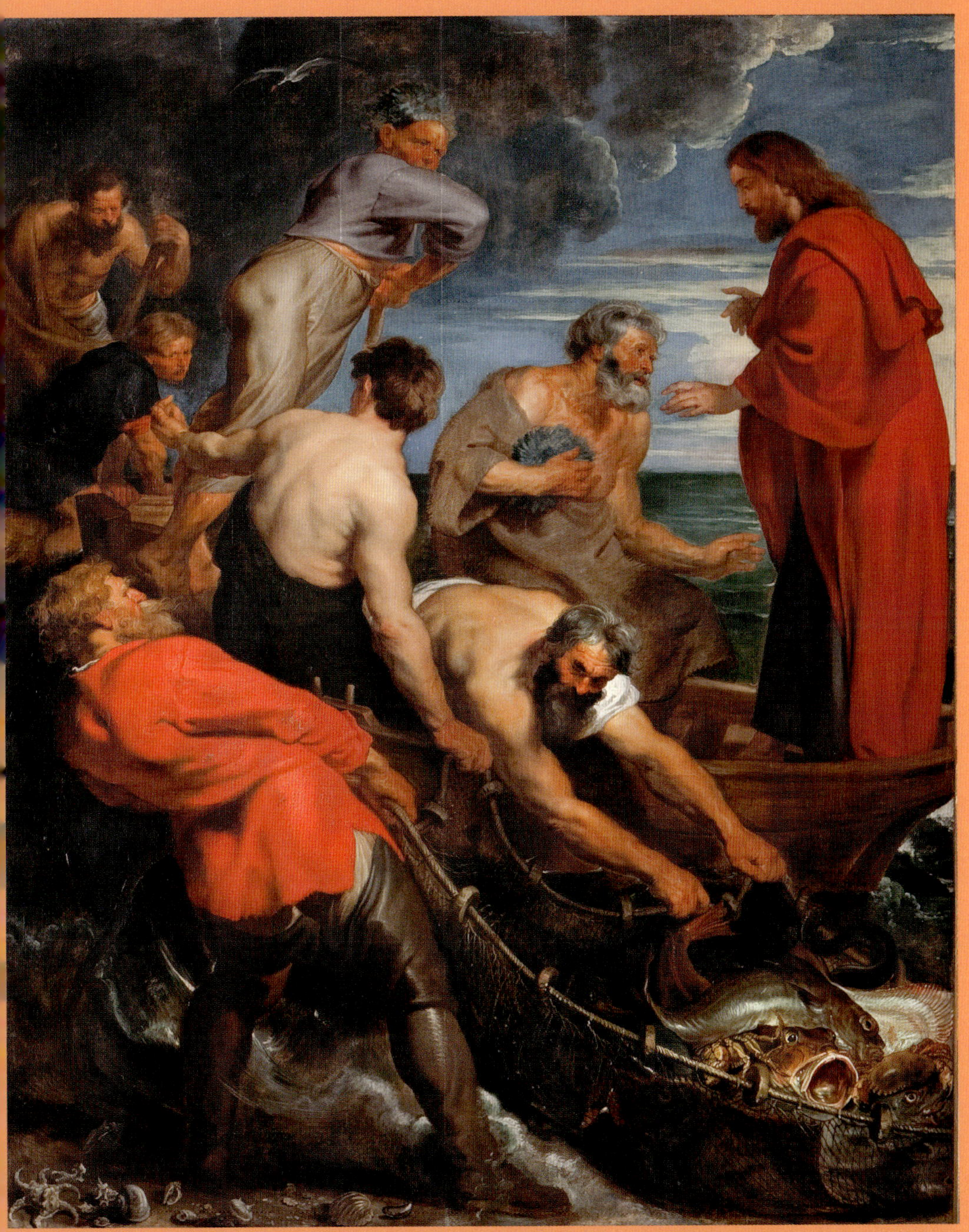

perfection is boring

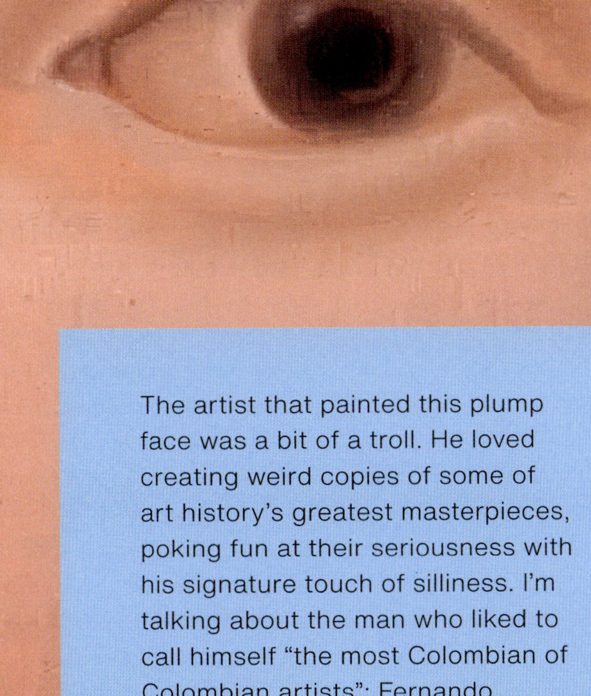

The artist that painted this plump face was a bit of a troll. He loved creating weird copies of some of art history's greatest masterpieces, poking fun at their seriousness with his signature touch of silliness. I'm talking about the man who liked to call himself "the most Colombian of Colombian artists": Fernando Botero.

Botero thought he was "the most Colombian artist living" because he considered himself isolated from international art trends, which is a fair point, given that his style is as weird as it gets. Weird, yet undeniably fascinating.

Just look at his quirky pastiche of Da Vinci's *Mona Lisa*. He transformed art history's most famous and gracious noblewoman into an inflated, pear-shaped lady. Like the original, this version has pursed lips, but they're comically tiny. She has those iconic gazing eyes, but they're slightly less enchanting and more concerningly wide set. The painting even has the same mountainous background, but Botero threw in a surprising detail: a little pear mountain.

Botero's balloon-like shapes are the hallmark of his style, known as *Boterismo*. Once you've seen one Botero, you'll recognize all of them. He actually developed this style by accident while creating his *Still Life with Mandolin*. As he was painting the instrument, he made its sound hole unusually small, which had the effect of making the mandolin look massive. The artist realized that adding tiny details—like a small nose or little pursed lips—make the surrounding shapes look incredibly bloated. Botero liked it, so he ran with it.

You could say Botero's *Monalisa* is a bit of a joke, but it's not a cheap one. What makes his artwork so special, I think, is that they're much more than chuckle-inducing caricatures. Just because the most famous painting in the world has the perfect face with the perfect smile and the perfect gaze, doesn't mean that these proportions are the gold standard of beauty. Sure, perfection might often be gorgeous, but sometimes it's also slightly boring—which Botero's swollen faces never are.

Fernando Botero, *Monalisa*, 1978.

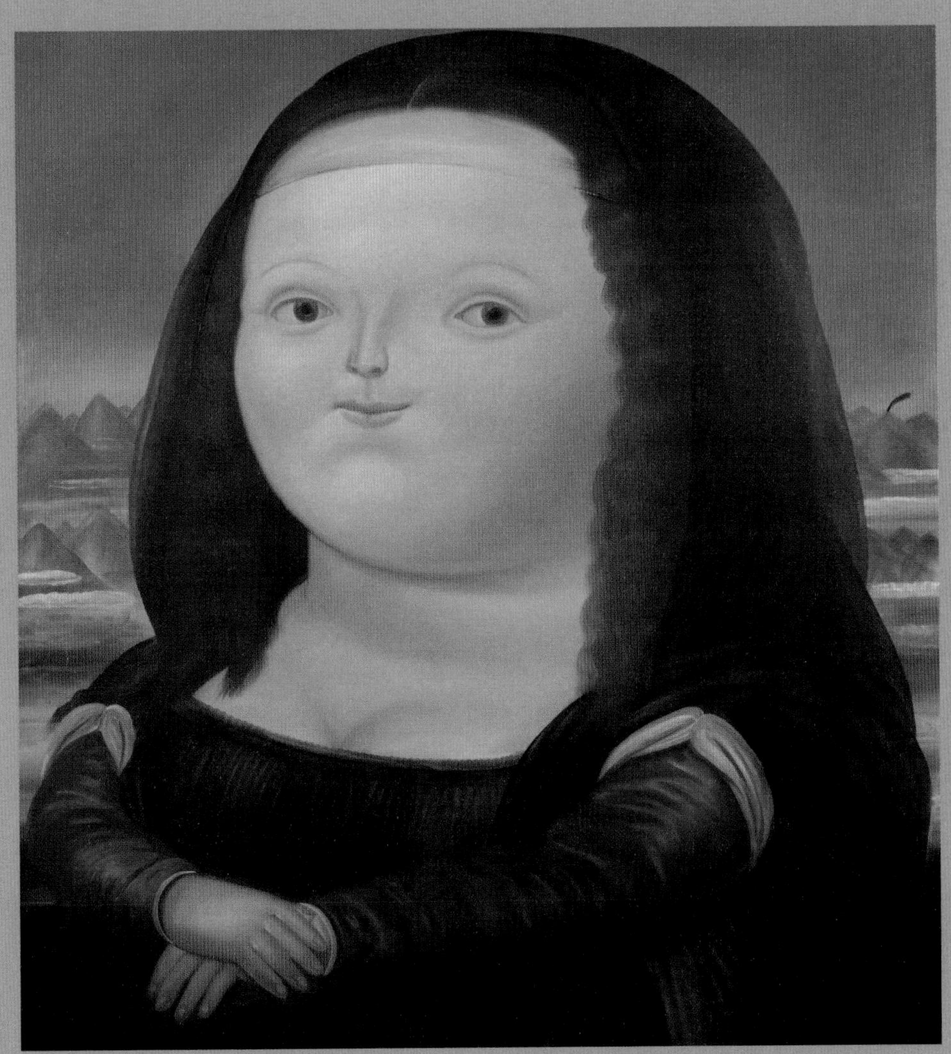

If faces were puzzles, this one would be missing a few pieces. But even though you'd never see a face like this in real life, we still recognize it as one. That's because our brains are always looking for meaning, finding patterns in shapes wherever we can.

the power of pareidolia

A random cloud can be an elephant. A rock formation can be a human profile. And a loosely arranged puzzle of lines, colors and geometrical shapes can easily be a face. We don't need much to recognize something. In psychology, this phenomenon is known as *pareidolia*, and the artist behind this masterpiece knew exactly how it worked. Let's have a look at some other tricks he had up his sleeve.

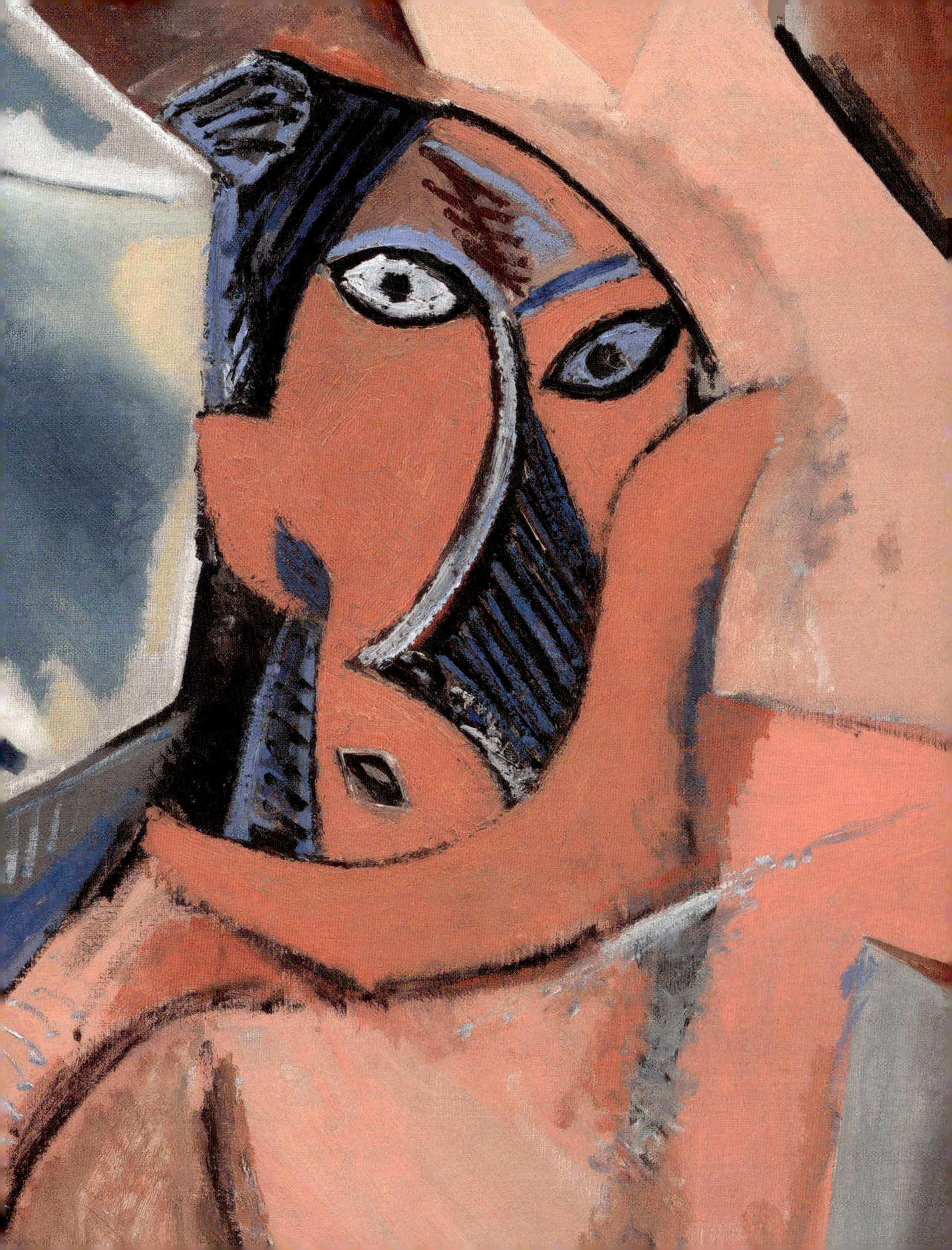

Zooming out, we discover another face puzzle, but also the human body attached to it. And even though the black-and-green face doesn't look particularly feminine, the shapes that make up the body do look like they belong to a woman, despite being very sharp and angular—thank you, *pareidolia*.

But let's focus back on the faces, because they're pretty intriguing. They've got long, crooked noses, misplaced eyes and an uncanny flatness. They're human, but they also look like objects, specifically masks. The artist, Pablo Picasso, was fascinated by African art and masks, and it shows in this painting. It's obvious he wasn't interested in Western ideals of beauty or realism. Instead, he plays with abstraction, creating faces that are both familiar and unnerving. And we're not done yet, because there are three more faces in this work. So, let's take a step farther back and look at the full picture.

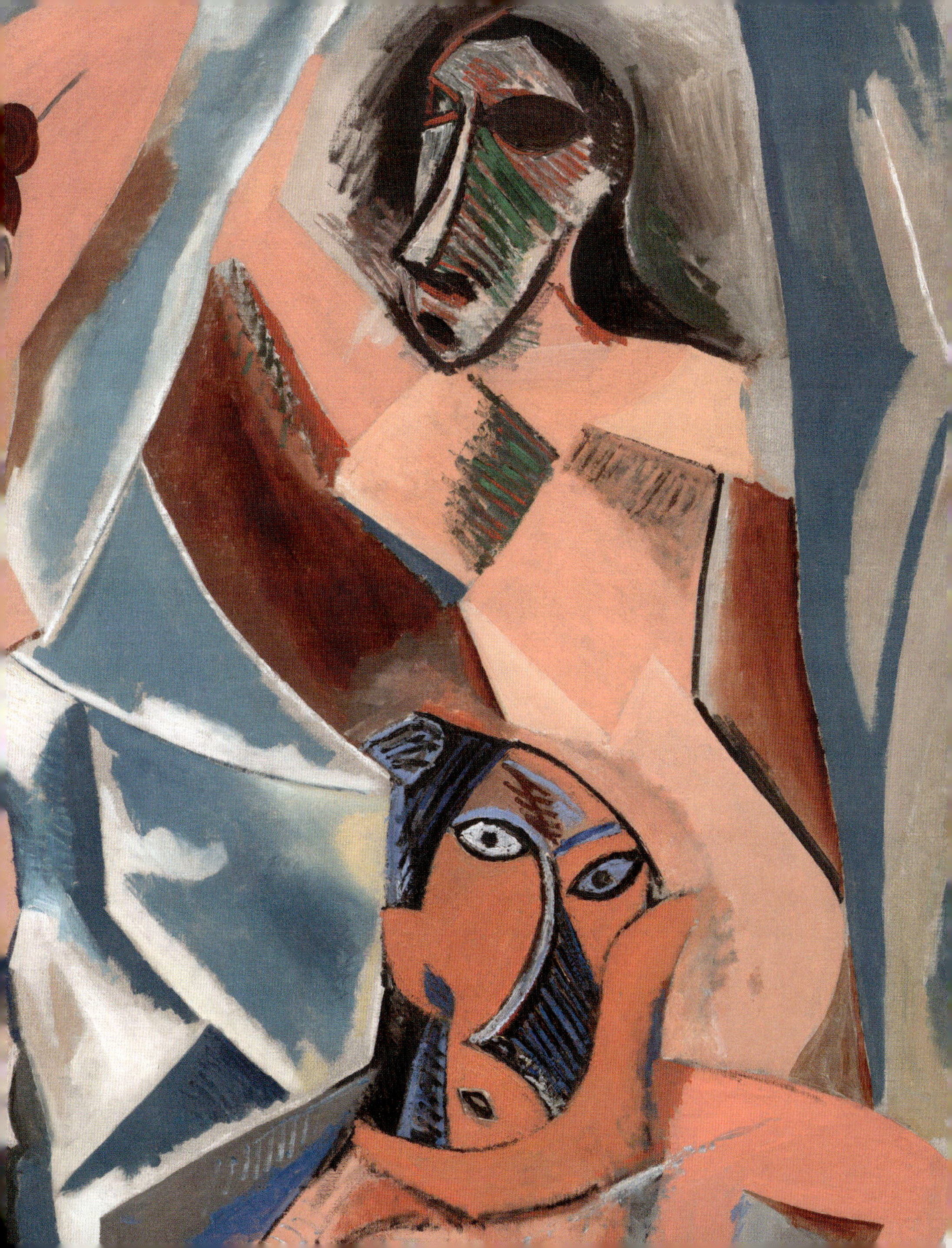

When Pablo Picasso showed *Les Demoiselles d'Avignon* to the world, many people hated it. But as so often happens in art history, his radical statement turned out to be ground-breaking. Picasso's carefully structured mish-mash of shapes and colors was the first step toward an art movement that exploits our *pareidolia* like no other: cubism. It inspired artists to move further and further away from realism, breaking the world down into abstract shapes and reassembling them in ways that trick our brain into recognizing what it sees, while at the same time challenging how we perceive the world. It's designed to make you feel uncomfortable.

Speaking of discomfort, these five ladies don't look particularly at ease. There are no smiles—just unnerving gazes and twisted poses. Maybe it's because they're prostitutes from Avignon Street in Barcelona's red-light district. Maybe they feel like objects of male desire. Or maybe, just maybe, these women aren't uncomfortable at all. Maybe they feel powerful, confronting us with their strength and daring us to stare back, turning the tables and making us feel uncomfortable instead.

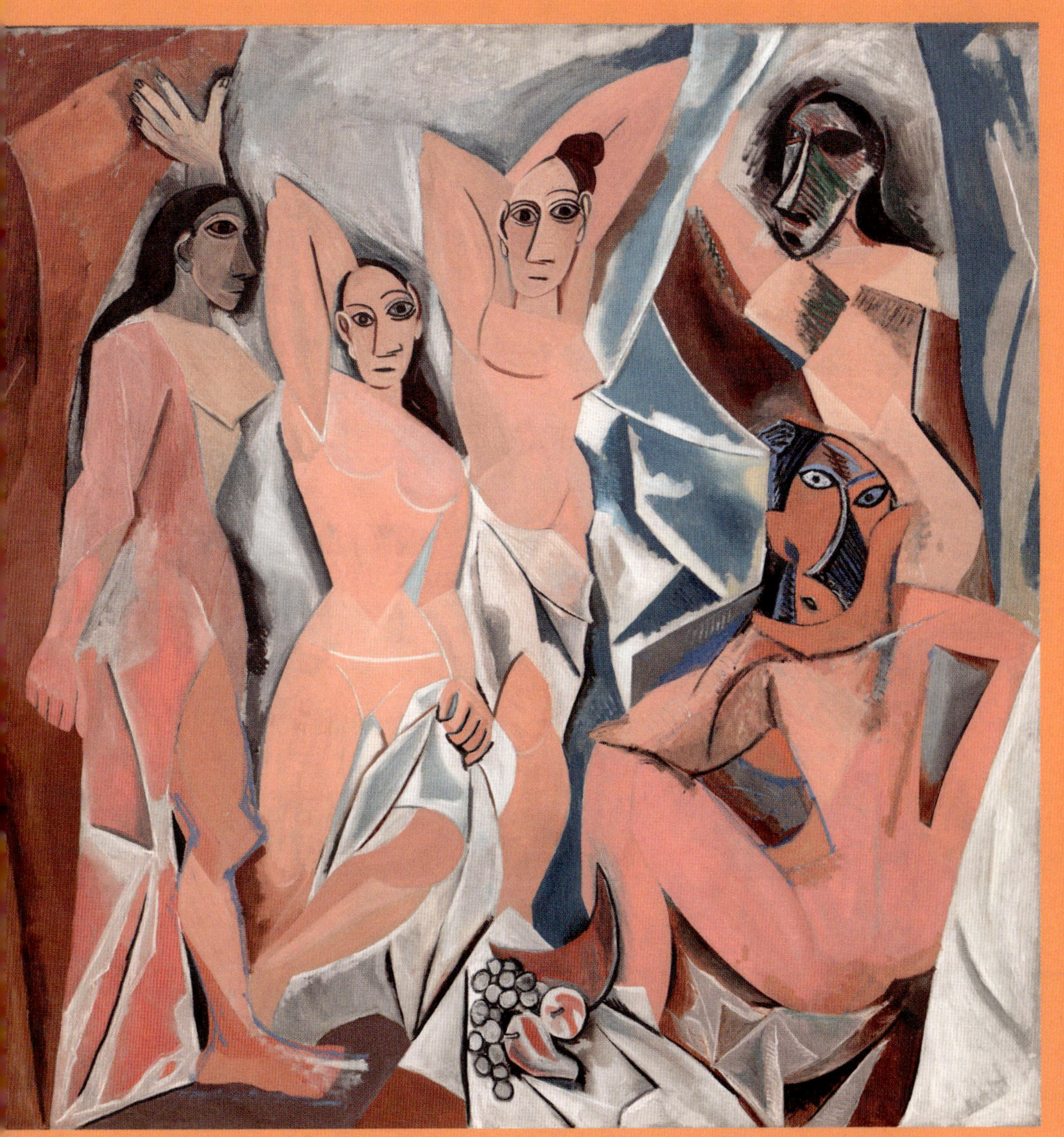

Pablo Picasso, *Les Demoiselles d'Avignon*, 1907.

angelic awkwardness

This is what a cookie sees when I discover it has raisins. But of course, in reality, this isn't my face and cookies don't have eyes. This facial expression belongs to an angel that is either disgusted, angry, constipated or all of the above. At least, that's what you would think. But in fact, she is *none* of the above.

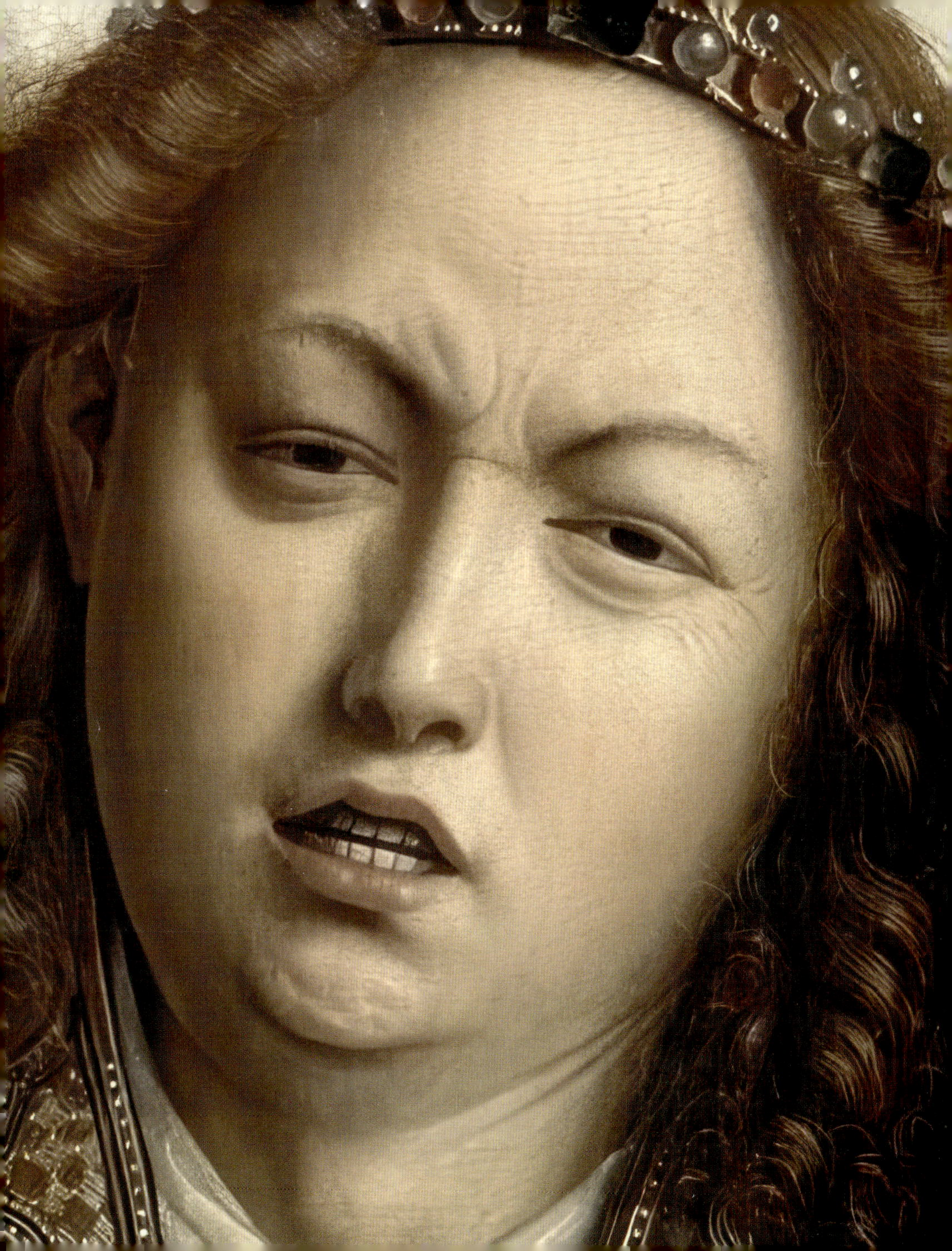

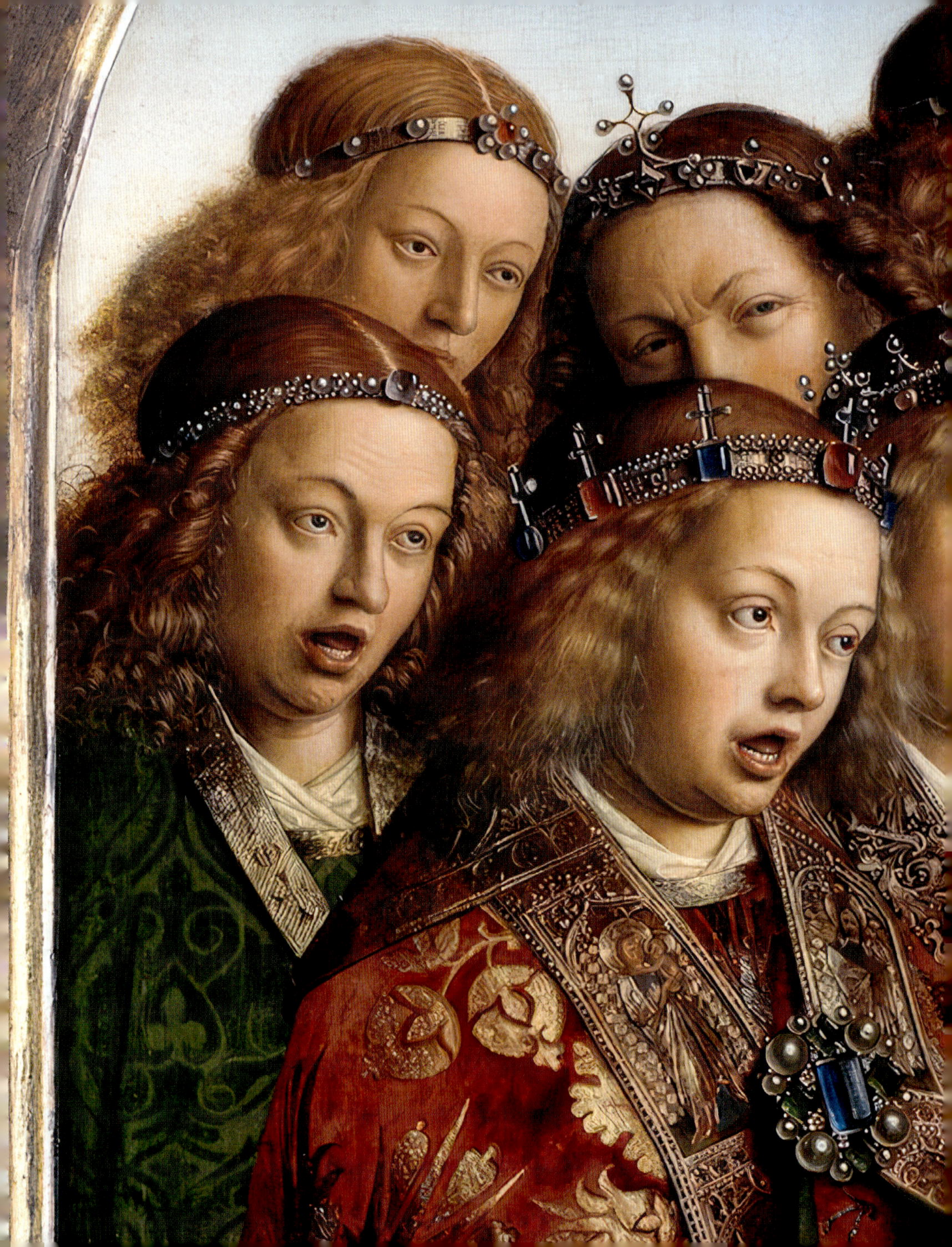

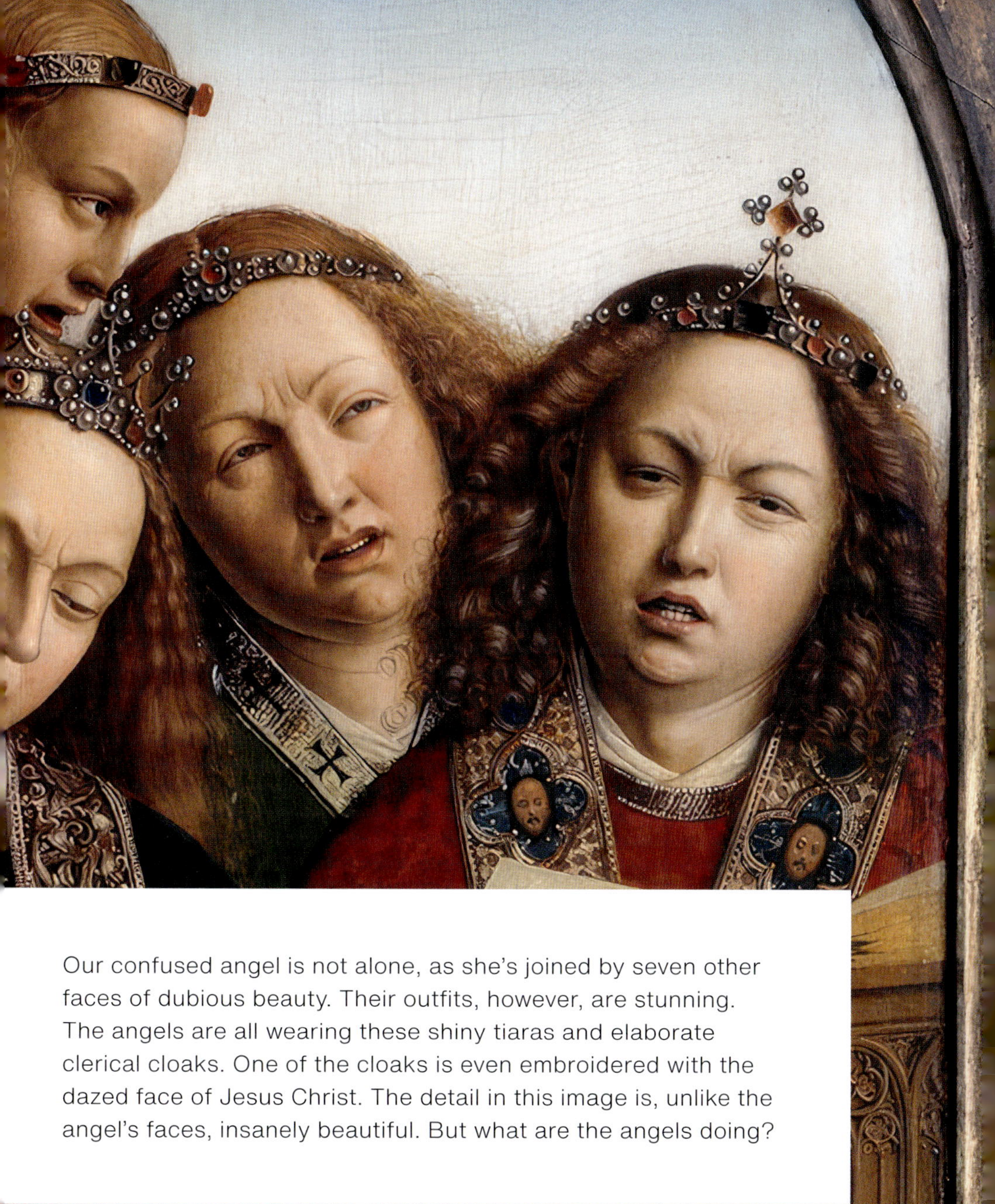

Our confused angel is not alone, as she's joined by seven other faces of dubious beauty. Their outfits, however, are stunning. The angels are all wearing these shiny tiaras and elaborate clerical cloaks. One of the cloaks is even embroidered with the dazed face of Jesus Christ. The detail in this image is, unlike the angel's faces, insanely beautiful. But what are the angels doing?

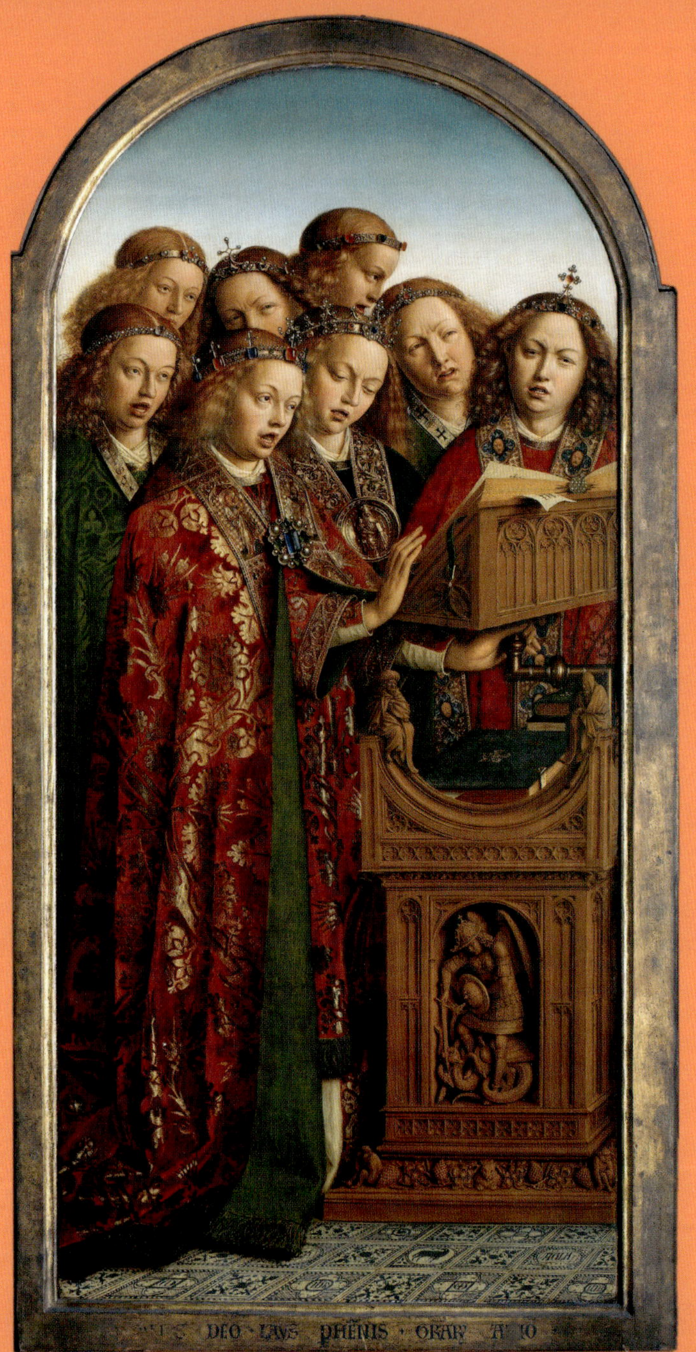

Jan van Eyck, *The Singing Angels* from *The Ghent Altarpiece*, 1432.

Jan van Eyck, the upper panels of *The Ghent Altarpiece*, 1432.

They're singing. You're looking at *The Singing Angels*, painted by the Flemish Renaissance master Jan van Eyck as part of his 12-panel behemoth of a painting called *The Ghent Altarpiece*. You might notice that these particular angels don't have wings. However, angel specialists have identified them as being legit angels because their panel sits on the right-hand side of God on his golden throne. On the far left-hand side of God's panel, you'll notice another band of musical angels. Together, these two swiveling panels reflect the fact that—according to medieval theories—the gates of heaven open up to the tones of divine music. So, likewise, when you open the side-panels of the altarpiece, the musical angels appear. All to say: Jan thought this through.

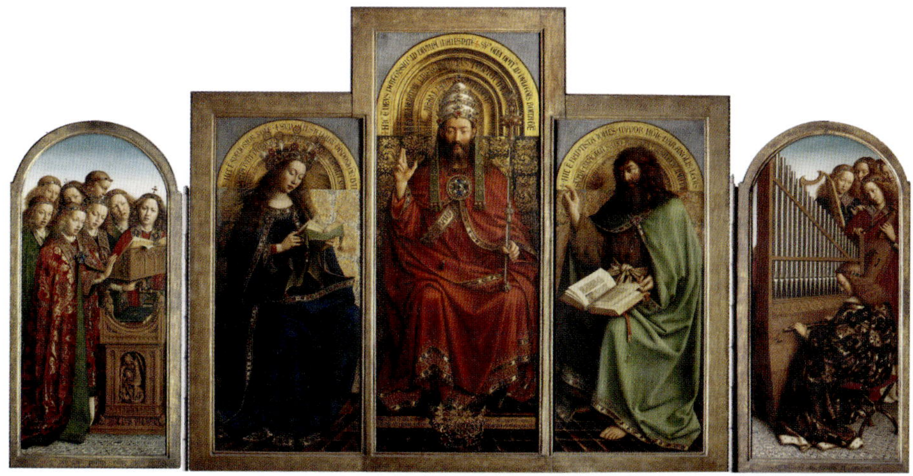

The odd expressions of these angels do make you wonder: Is this what a singing face looks like? Well, yes. Art historians and musicologists have studied the faces and concluded that the angels are probably singing in *polyphony*—meaning each of them is tackling a different tone or melodic line, which taken together probably sounds awesome.

And it gets better, because considering the position of their mouths, specialists have even been able to identify who is singing soprano, alto, tenor and bass. Just to point out: Jan van Eyck was so good, he didn't just paint some random silly faces. He painted some incredibly *realistic* silly faces.

well, i'll be damned

This magnificently oversized nose isn't just a facial feature; it's a statement. This majestic peak with a beautiful shiny tip and two nostrils is spacious enough to shelter a small family. Needless to say, I love this man's sniffer. But as splendid as it is, this is not the nose of a happy man. In fact, it belongs to a deeply distressed soul.

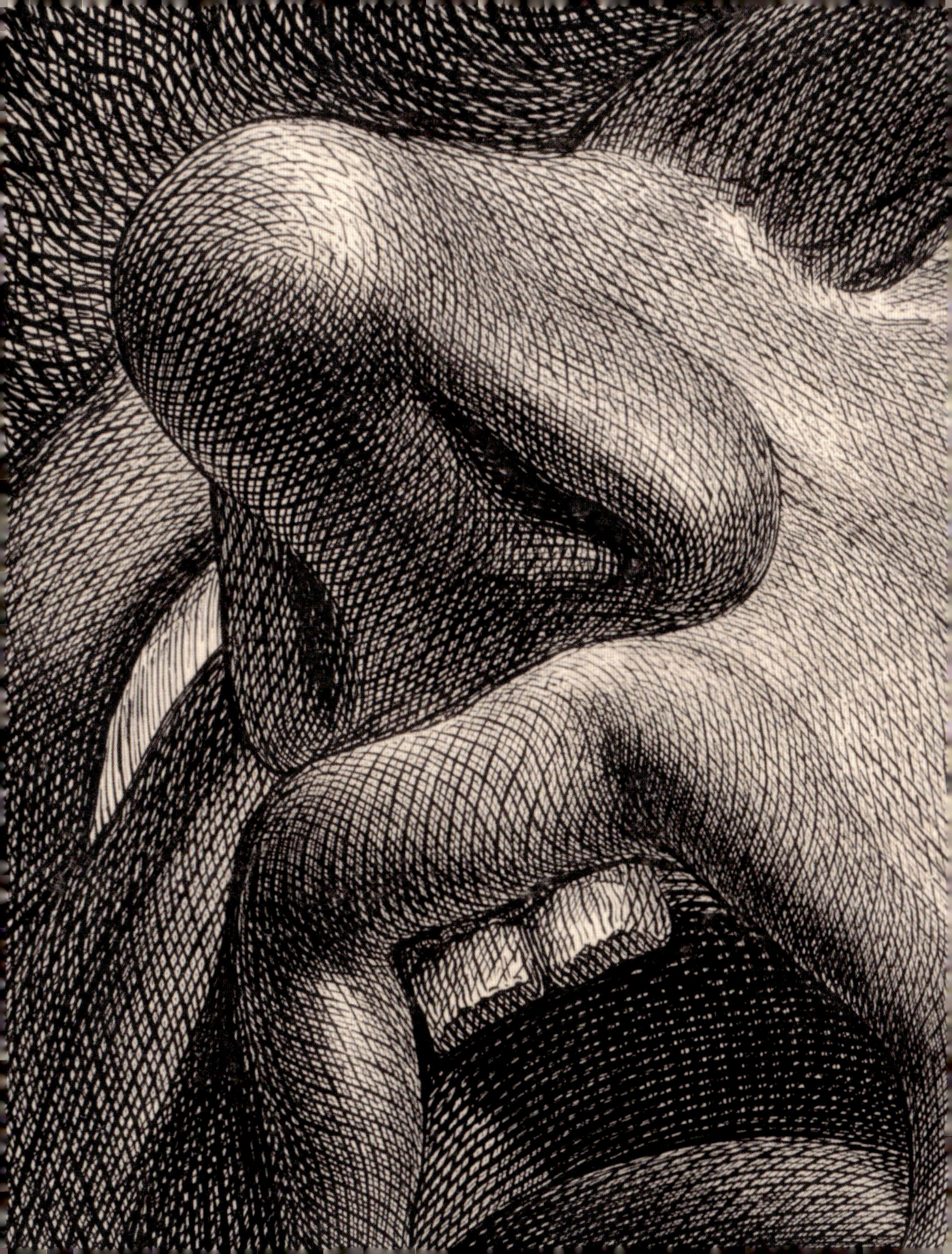

Check out those big soft lips framing a gaping mouth with two adorable teeth on full display. This poor soul is screaming in agony, as if he just stepped on a lost Lego® piece. But no, this man isn't suffering from the intolerable pains of a plastic brick; he's suffering from the intolerable pains of hell. Which, come to think of it, might be one and the same.

This engraving was crafted by the English poet William Blake. Besides being the author of lofty poems, Blake was also an incredible engraver. The one you're looking at showcases his skill spectacularly. If you lean in and look closely, you'll notice that the image is made up of thousands of criss-crossing lines. The variation in their density creates a beautiful interplay of shadows and highlights, forming this silent, screaming face.

William Blake, *Head of a Damned Soul in Dante's Inferno*, c. 1789.

The scream belongs to a damned soul from Dante Alighieri's epic *La Divina Commedia (The Divine Comedy)*. Behind him, the blazing fires of hell rage. Even his hair looks like it's going up in flames. Blake probably created the image as an illustration for *Essays on Physiognomy*, a book about human expressions. But his engraving never made it into the book, because just like the man's nose, it was colossal. Too huge to fit on the pages.

I like to think that when Blake heard this unfortunate news, his own facial expression was very similar to that of the damned soul in his engraving.

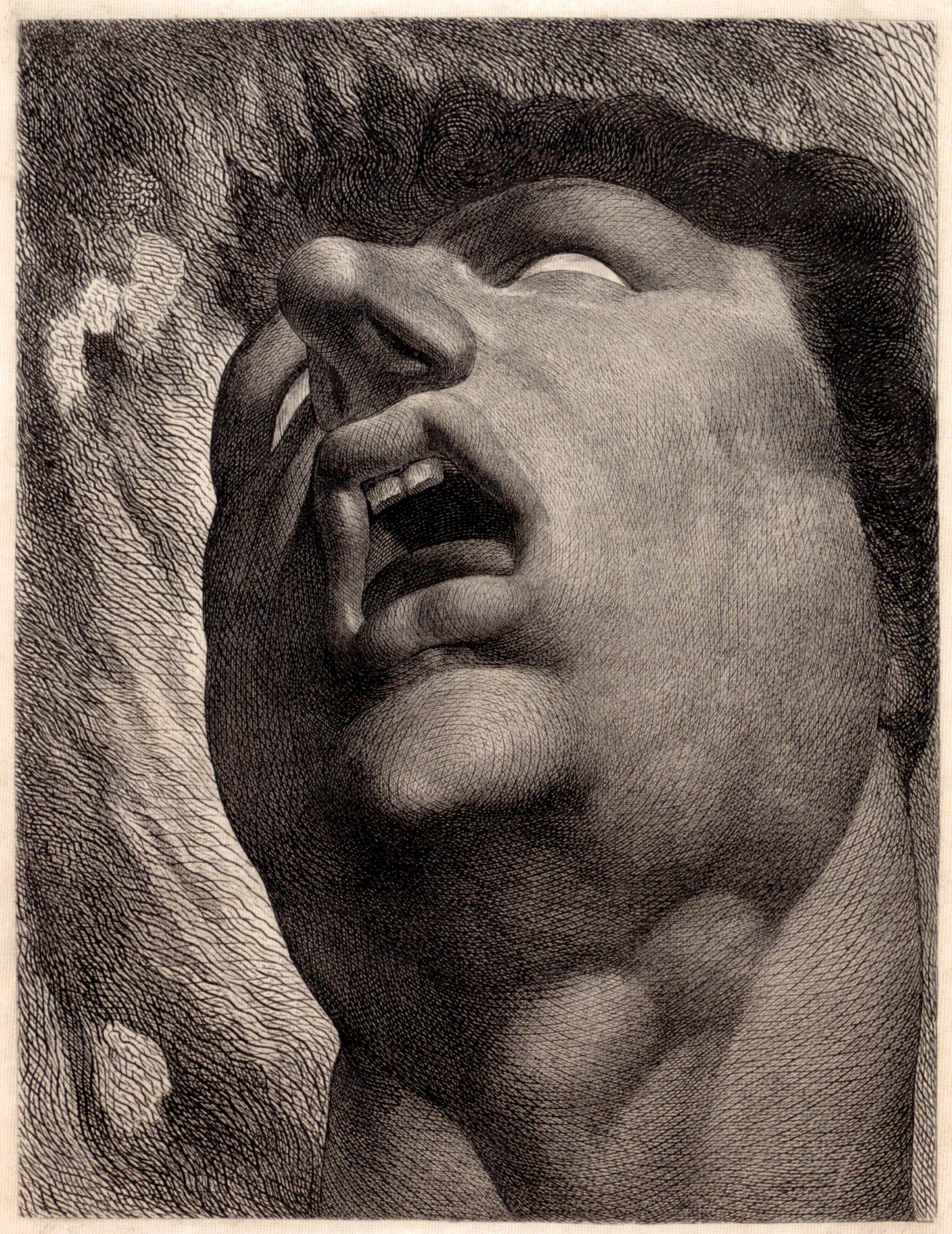

roses are red, my guests are dead

The look on this man's puffy face glows with a mix of fascination and amusement. There's a mischievous little grin, wide eyes and two rosy cheeks, probably the result of drinking too many fancy cups of expensive wine. This guy is having a blast, because he's a guest at an emperor's extravagant party.

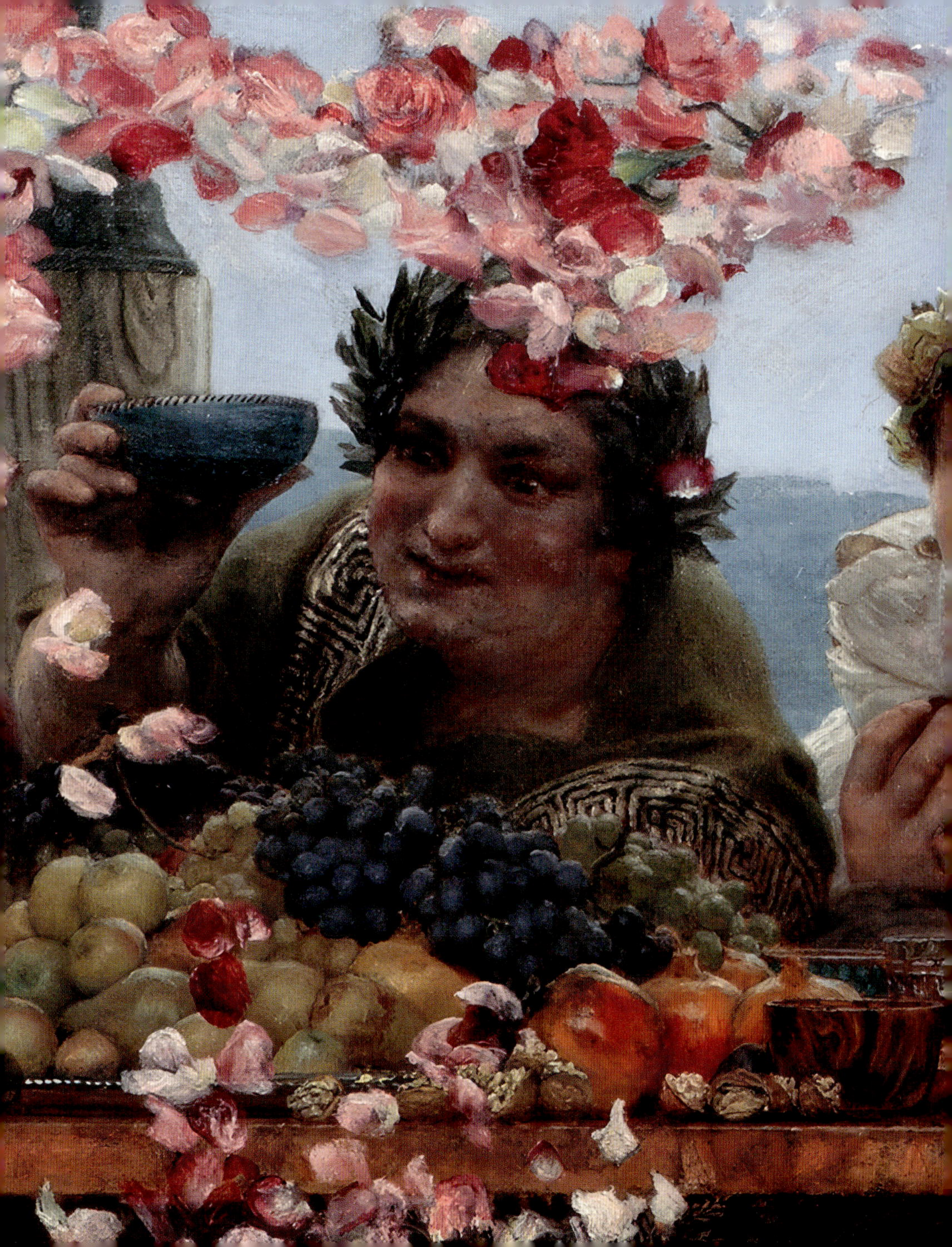

Behold: the Roman Emperor Heliogabalus—the guy with the golden robe and smug face on the left—and his lounging squad of wine drinking, fruit eating party people. Behind them lie the rolling hills of Rome and a beautiful, clear, blue sky. In the foreground, a bunch of rose petals dance in the wind. What a wonderful, colorful day.

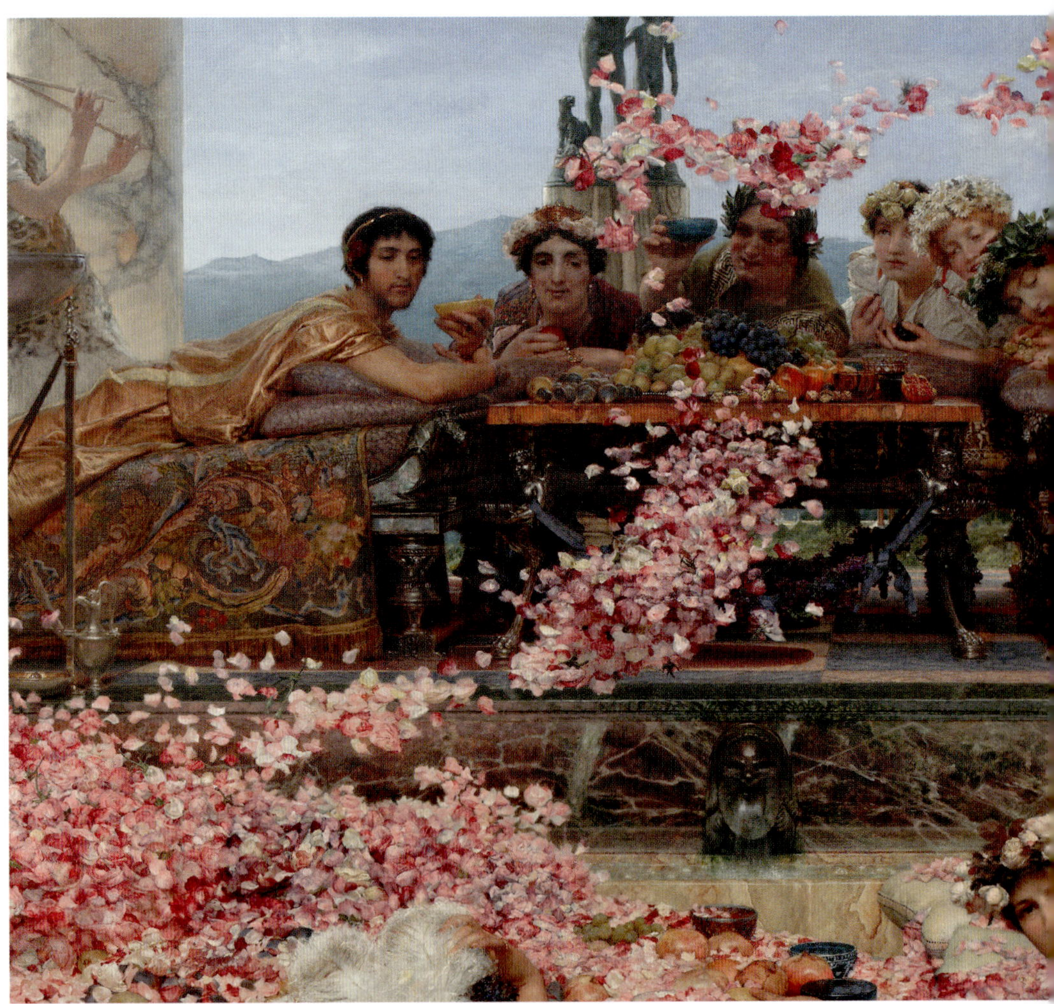

But in reality, it isn't . . . really. Yes, these people are enjoying themselves, but they're also displaying an incredible amount of misplaced nonchalance, because the event unfolding before their eyes is very disturbing. Though, I have to add, kind of romantic, as well.

Sir Lawrence Alma-Tadema, *The Roses of Heliogabalus*, 1888.

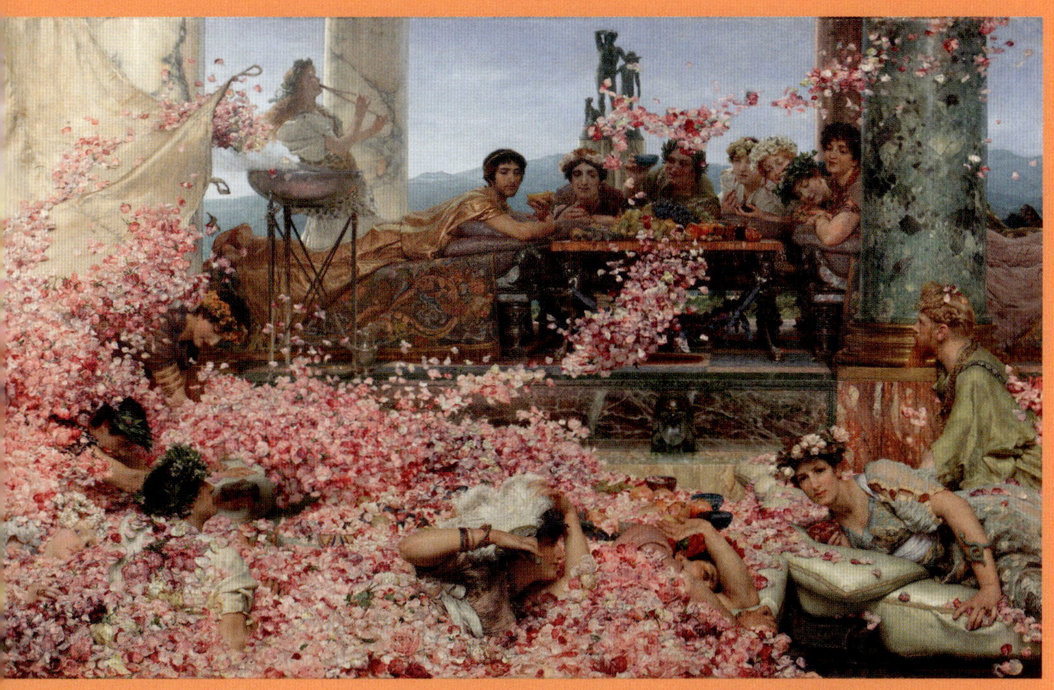

It's quite the spectacle. Look at that vast sea of pink, containing thousands of delicate rose petals, engulfing the partygoers in front of the emperor and his posse. Turns out our jolly emperor was quite the prankster. According to the *Historia Augusta*, a collection of biographies of Roman emperors, Heliogabalus invited these guests to his palace to indulge in a drinking party and an accompanying orgy. But unbeknownst to the party people, the false ceiling above their heads was rigged for a twisted prank.

After several hours of drunken fun, the hidden cloth gave way, releasing a deadly downpour of rose petals. At first, it must have been lovely—being drunk on love and wine and having these soft, rosy petals swirling on your woozy head. Very lovely indeed, until the party people realized that the rosy rain just kept pouring down. Petal puddles grew into suffocating petal mountains.

Desperately, the guests gasped for air, getting smothered under the weight, choking on the petals.

And at the center of it all, Heliogabalus and his crew just keep on gazing and drinking, raising their cups and having the time of their lives. Our jolly emperor's cruel joke was complete, and his guests had been condemned to death by flowers, smothered in a sea of petals. Pranked.

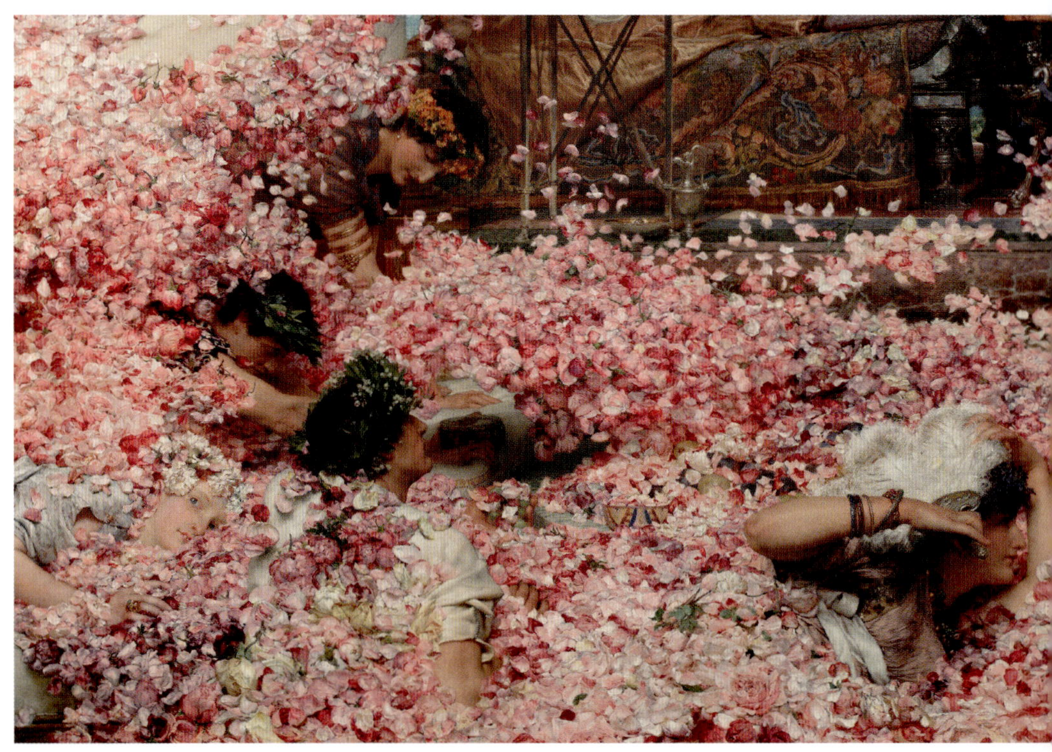

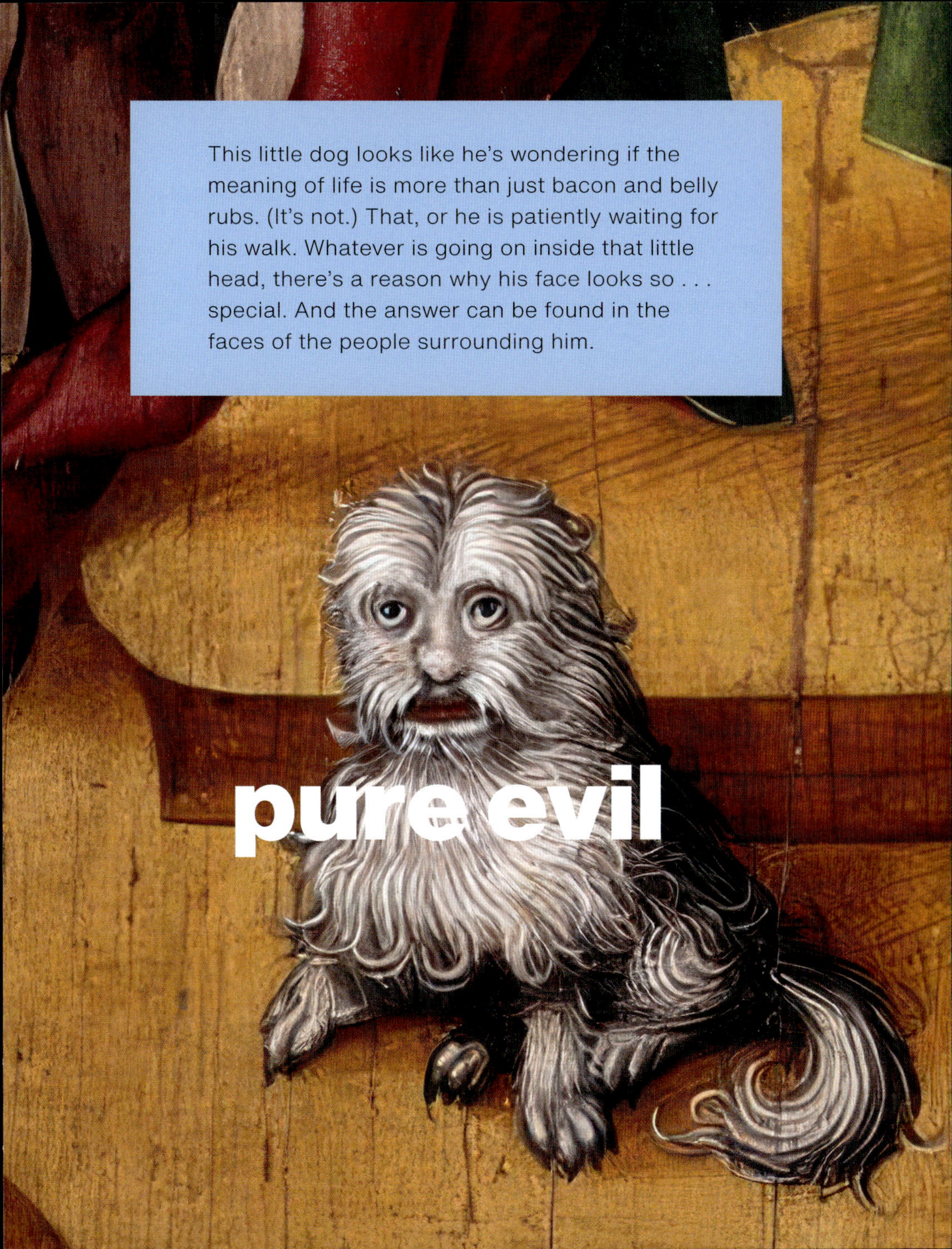

This little dog looks like he's wondering if the meaning of life is more than just bacon and belly rubs. (It's not.) That, or he is patiently waiting for his walk. Whatever is going on inside that little head, there's a reason why his face looks so . . . special. And the answer can be found in the faces of the people surrounding him.

pure evil

It seems our curly friend is calmly sitting through a violent Bible scene. Good boy. Behind him, Jesus is being challenged by Herod Antipas to perform a miracle. But Jesus remains silent, and Herod sends our poor savior to Pilate. If you don't know what happens next, don't worry—you'll find out later in this book.

Anyway, the painting is just one part of a greater altarpiece depicting the different stages of Christ's final days and suffering. Little is known about this late 15th-century work or the artist behind it. What we do know is that the little dog seated at Herod's feet looks incredibly funny, which is a bit alarming, especially considering the fact that this cute little fluffy animal probably symbolizes the people who tormented Christ. Because in late medieval Passion literature, it was common to refer to those people as being "mad dogs."

This might explain why the dog's oddball face looks remarkably similar to the weird faces of the people in the crowd. Jesus's tormentors obviously weren't very popular back in medieval times, so giving them ugly faces was an obvious choice. So there you have it: This little dog isn't pondering the meaning of life or quietly sitting through a violent Bible scene—he is busy symbolizing pure evil. Bad doggy.

Maître à l'œillet et au brin de lavande de Baden et atelier, *Retable de la passion*, c. 1500.

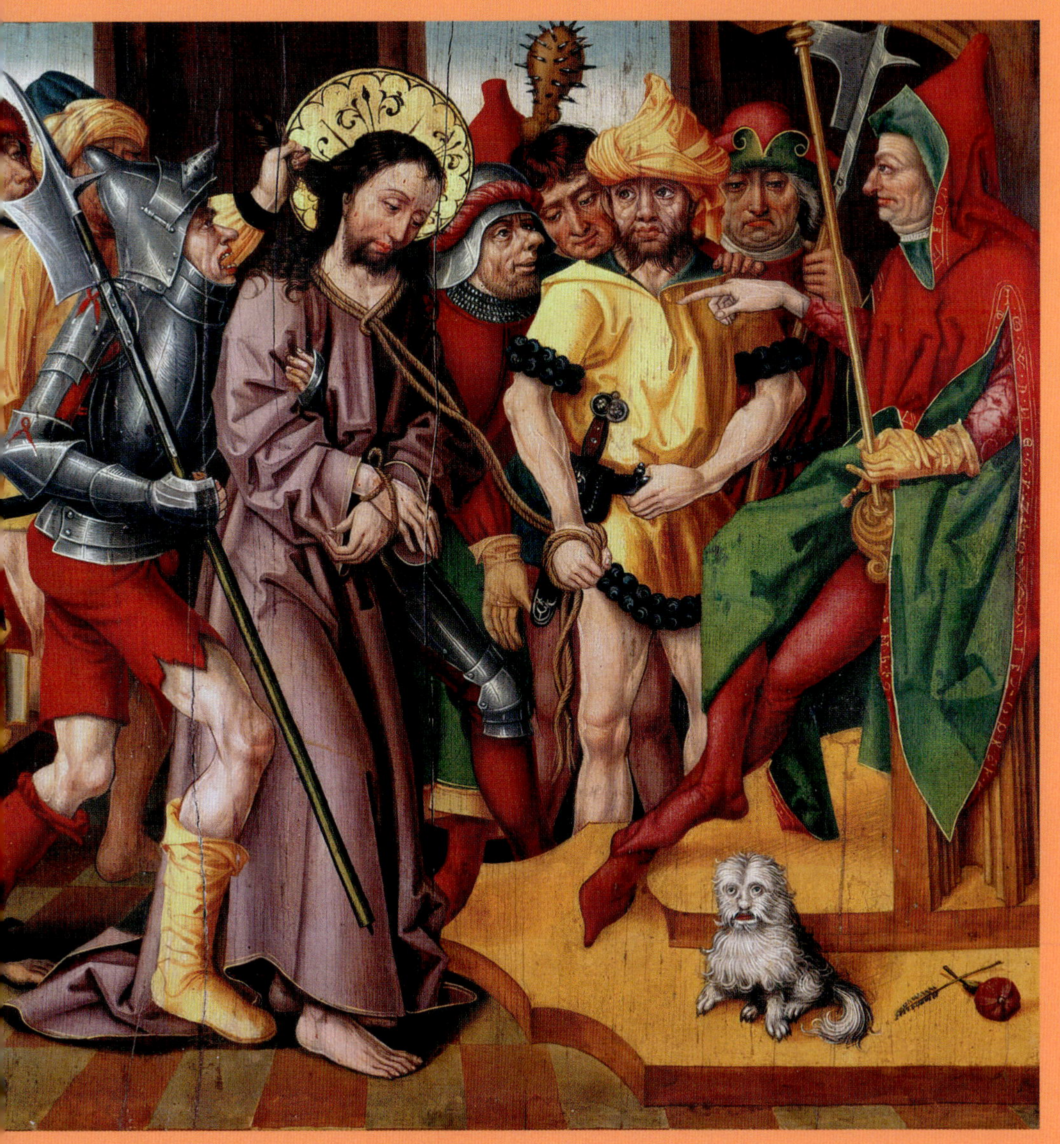

Saturn's late-night snack

Feeling ravenous for junk food after a night out? Totally normal. Alcohol activates your brain's hypothalamus, triggering your appetite. Nothing to be ashamed of, but this man's wild eyes do suggest he's slightly embarrassed—mortified even. It's like he's been caught mid-bite while having a nocturnal snack of what seems to be a big chunk of dried sausage. Which, of course, it isn't.

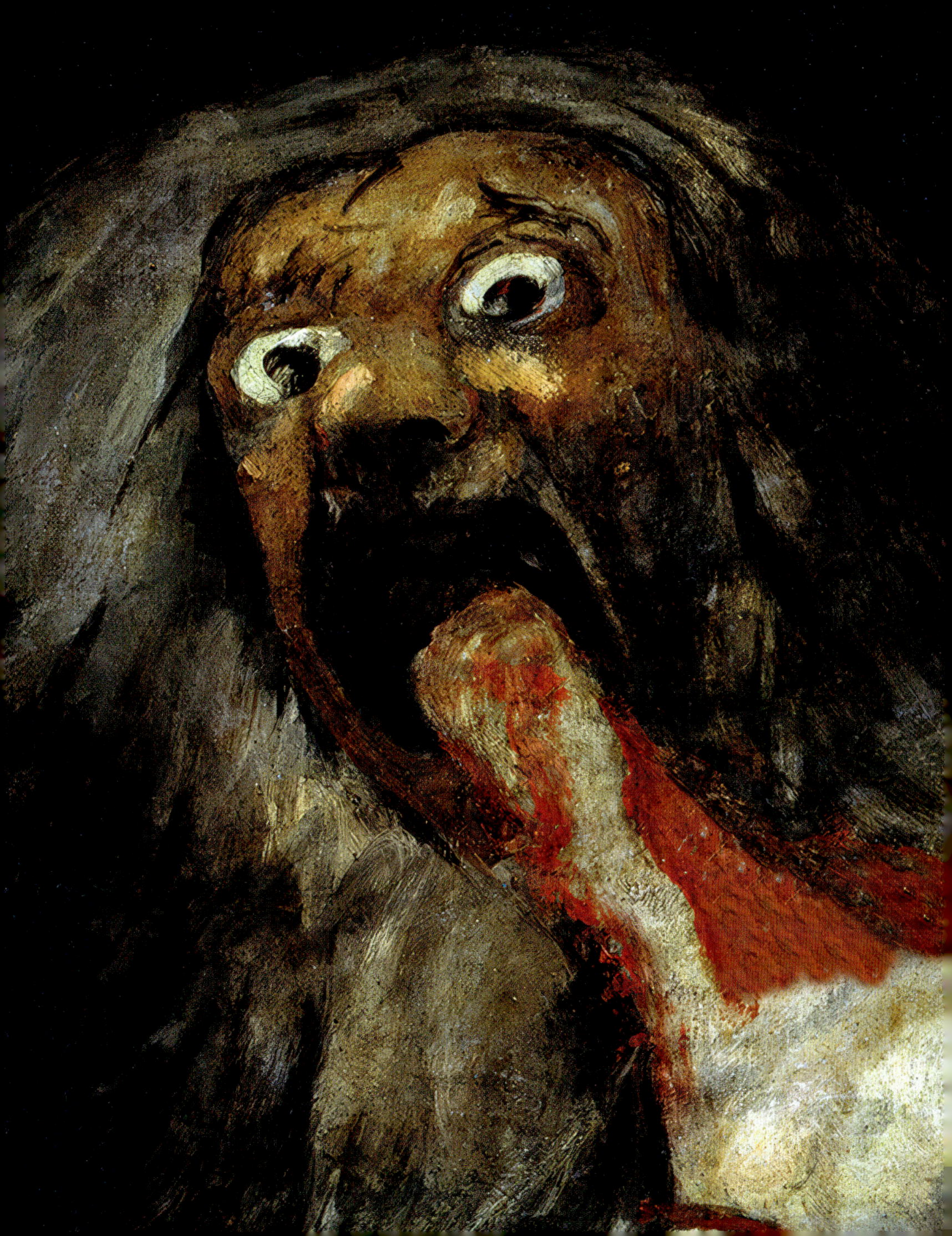

"Eat what you love" is a great culinary motto, but this wild-eyed monster has taken it several steps too far. Because the *saucisson*? It's actually his own son. And we've caught him in the act of devouring him. The painting is vicious. Just look at those clawing hands. They're gripping the spine with blood-stained fingers, white knuckles digging into the flesh, as if this creature is in the middle of ripping the carcass in two. The poor son's head, right arm, and left hand have already been consumed by the big black hole in his father's face. You can almost hear him chewing, munching and crunching.

Saturn Devouring His Son by the Spanish master Francisco Goya is a monster of a painting. It might be one of the scariest things that has ever been put on canvas. It shows the Roman god Saturn eating one of his sons, because a prophecy by the goddess Gaia revealed that one day Saturn would be overthrown by one of his children.

Francisco Goya, *Saturn Devouring His Son*, c. 1820–1823.

But Goya's Saturn isn't a mighty deity; it's an ugly, old, naked monster. No big muscles. No long beard. No beauty. Just wild hair, long bulky limbs and a deranged face. It's remarkable how Goya painted Saturn like a ferocious monster emerging from the darkness, while at the same time also showing his fear and shame at being caught. Because Saturn's bulging eyes don't just point out his insanity, but also his panic. He's acting in a state of frenzy because he's afraid of being ousted by his own blood.

It's the same crazed expression as someone caught raiding the fridge in the dead of night, devouring the last bit of sausage, surrounded by darkness and only lit by the little light in the fridge. Which, unlike devouring your own son, is nothing to be ashamed of.

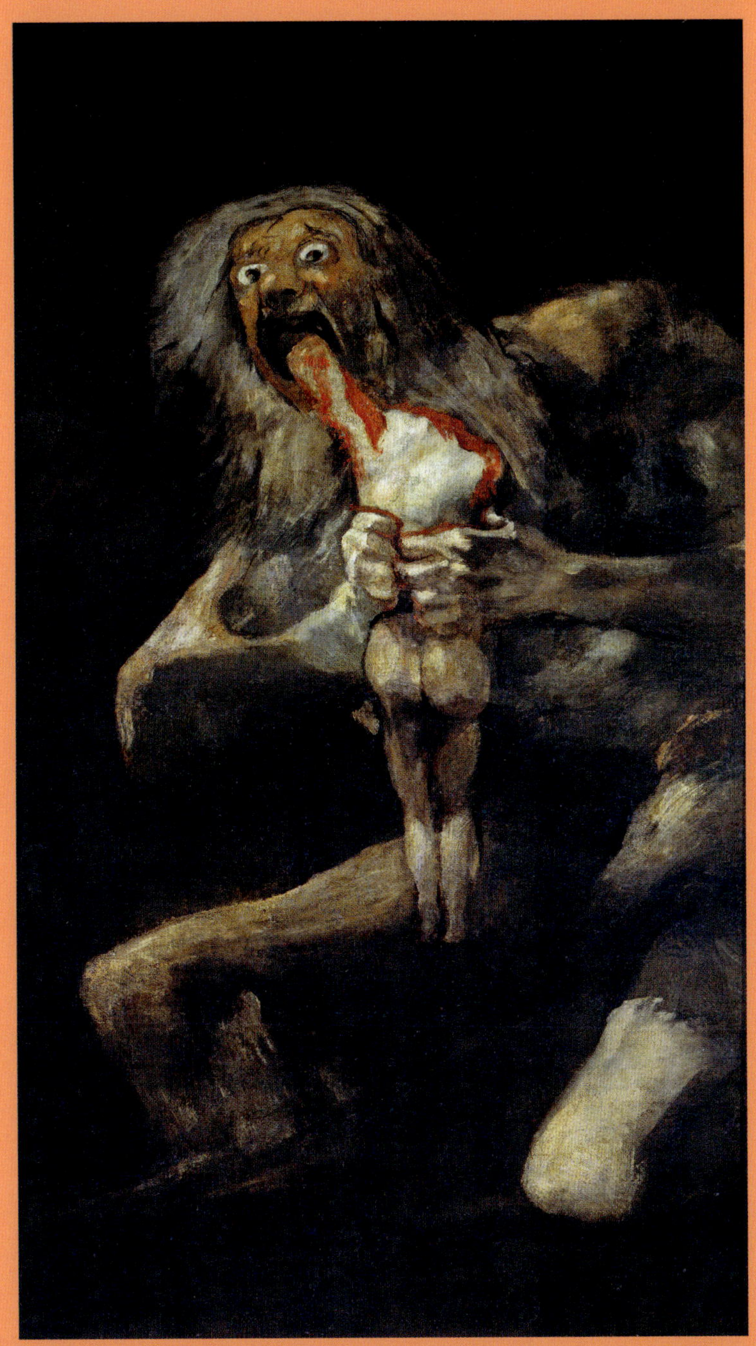

where is the groom?

This 16th-century stupid face radiates a blend of surprise and mild alarm. The man's eyes are wide open and his gaze is slightly asymmetrical, as if he is in the middle of a sudden realization. "Oh my gosh, did I forget to lock the barn doors?"

Or perhaps this isn't a panicked look, but a pleading one. Maybe this man is just very hungry. He is desperately clutching an empty bowl and eyeing us with a look that demands a refill of whatever it is he's spooning. Impatient and slightly rude, if you ask me. Let's zoom out and see what's going on exactly.

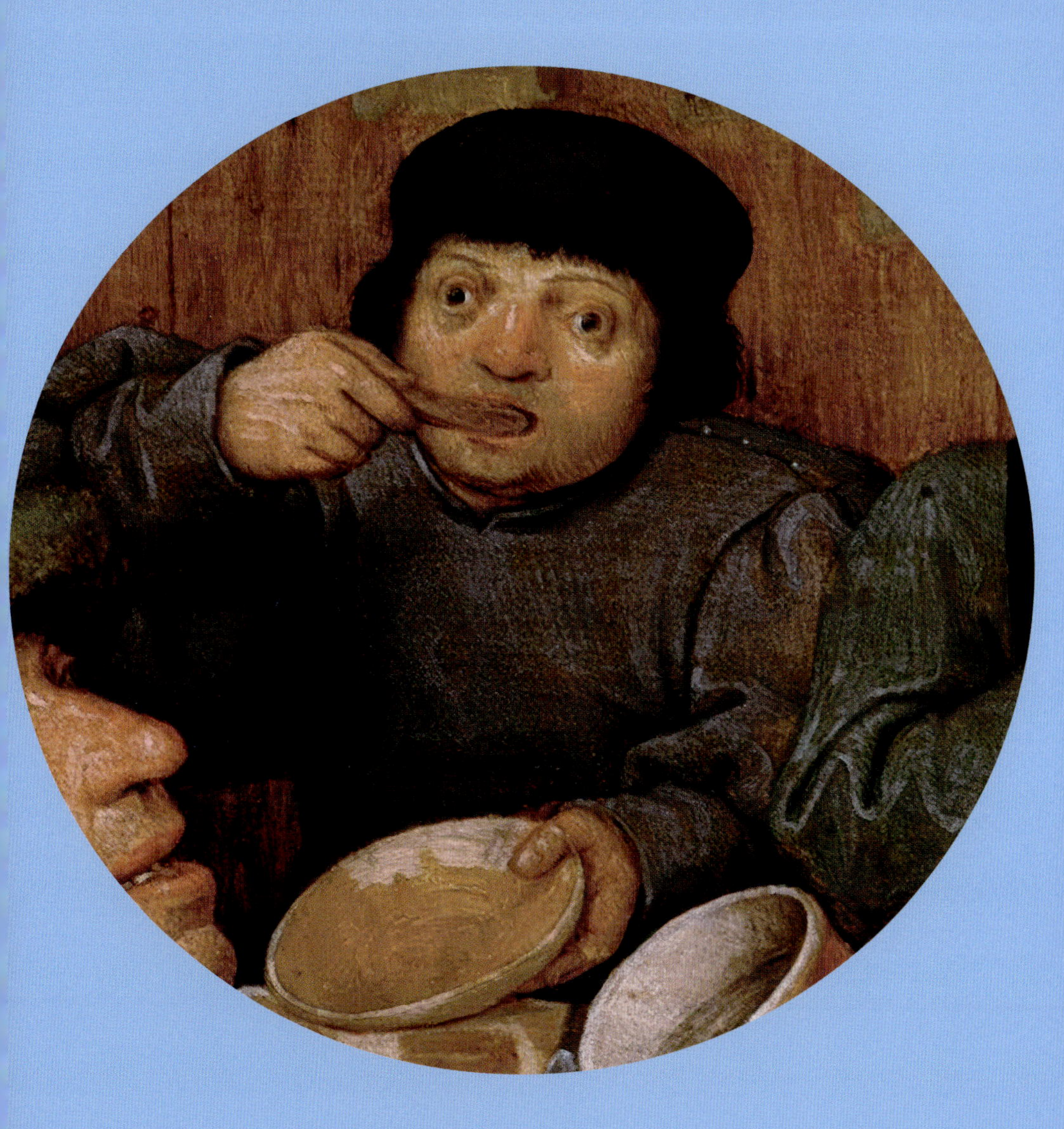

The Peasant Wedding by Pieter Bruegel the Elder shows a farmers' feast in full swing. People are drinking and eagerly passing out bowls of soup or some sort of thick porridge. Our hungry friend is in luck as a steaming refill is on its way.

And just three spots to the right of our cross-eyed farmer sits a glowing young woman. She's all smiles, and for good reason, because this is her wedding party. She's wearing a festive crown, her hands folded in her lap, with her proud parents beside her. Good times all around. But where's her husband? Spotting the bride is a no-brainer, but we can't see an obvious groom. Maybe it's the man with the green cap in the middle, wearing a dark coat and holding a jug. Or perhaps it's the man with the red cap, serving up plates of food for his guests. Or maybe there is no groom at all. If so, the painting would be a nod to an old Dutch proverb: "It's a poor man who cannot even be present at his own wedding."

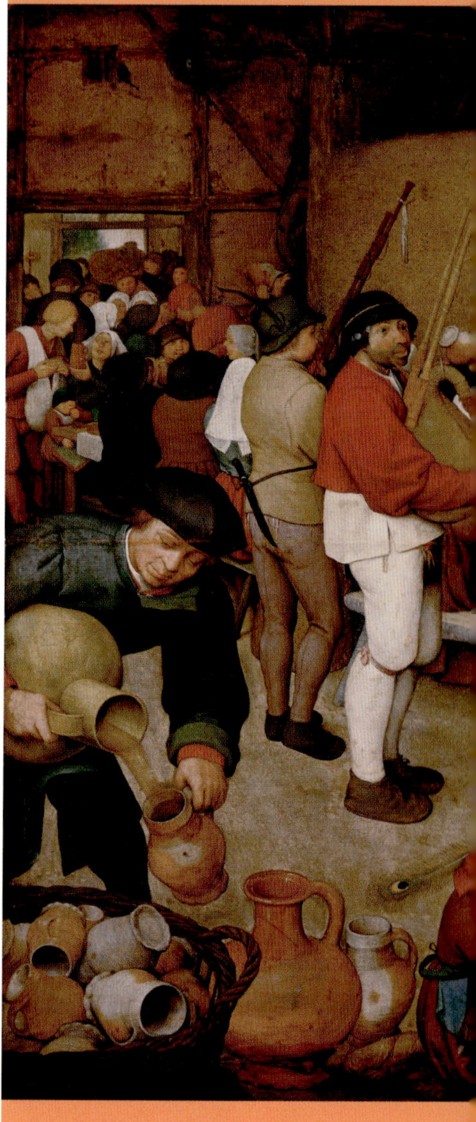

Pieter Bruegel the Elder, *The Peasant Wedding*, 1568.

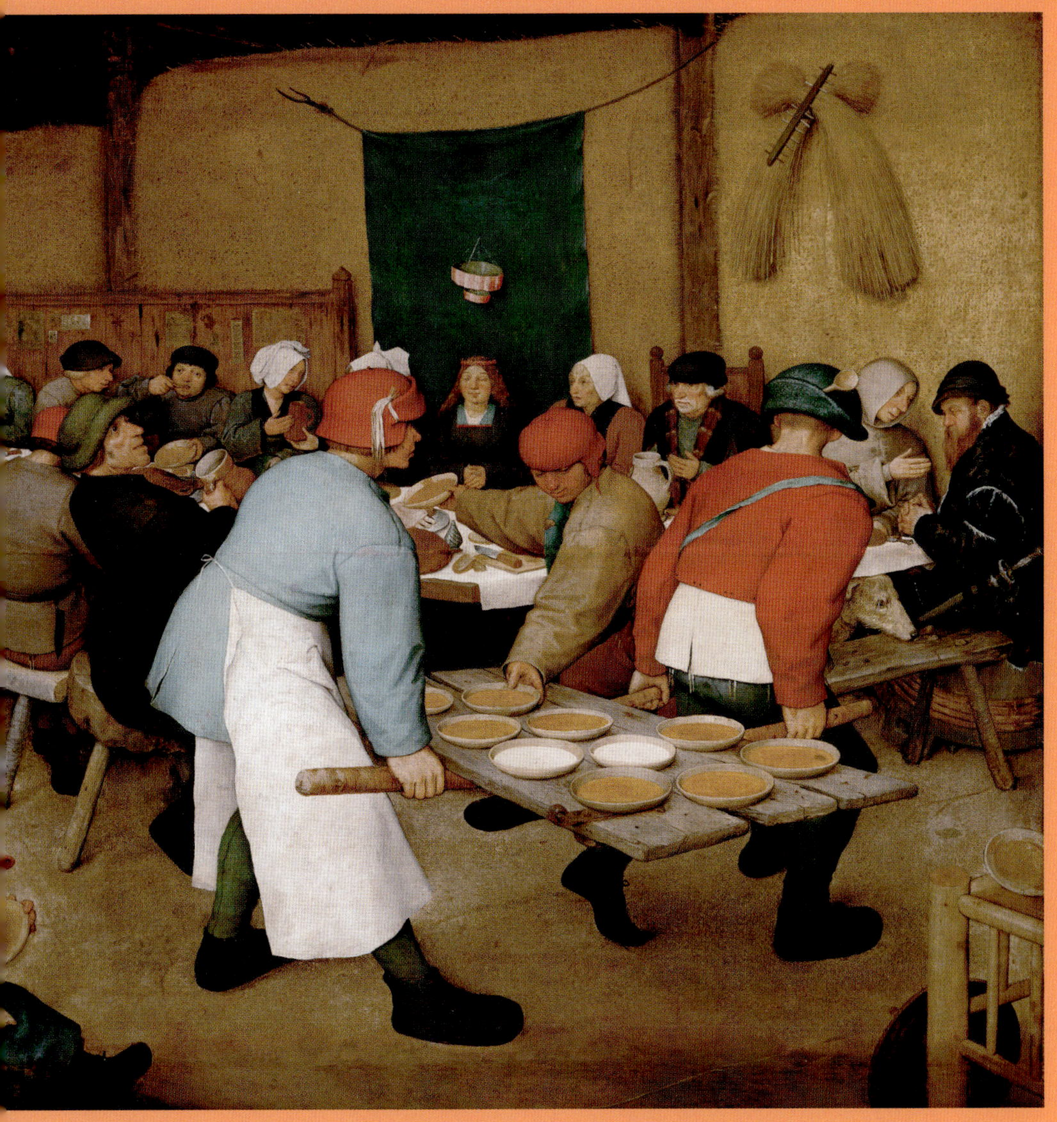

But there's yet another possibility. Maybe, just maybe, our hungry, cross-eyed farmer is, in fact, the groom. If this is the case, the couple seated to his right could be his parents, visibly cringing at their son's gluttony and lack of decorum.

excuse me?

I'm no ophthalmologist, but at first glance, it seems to me that this lovely lady has a serious case of *strabismus*. Look deep into her eyes and you'll instantly see what *strabismus* means. But, as they say, first impressions can be deceiving, because this beautiful pair of misaligned eyes isn't due to a vision disorder. No, it's the result of an incredible talent for multitasking. Let's have a properly aligned look at this colorful fresco.

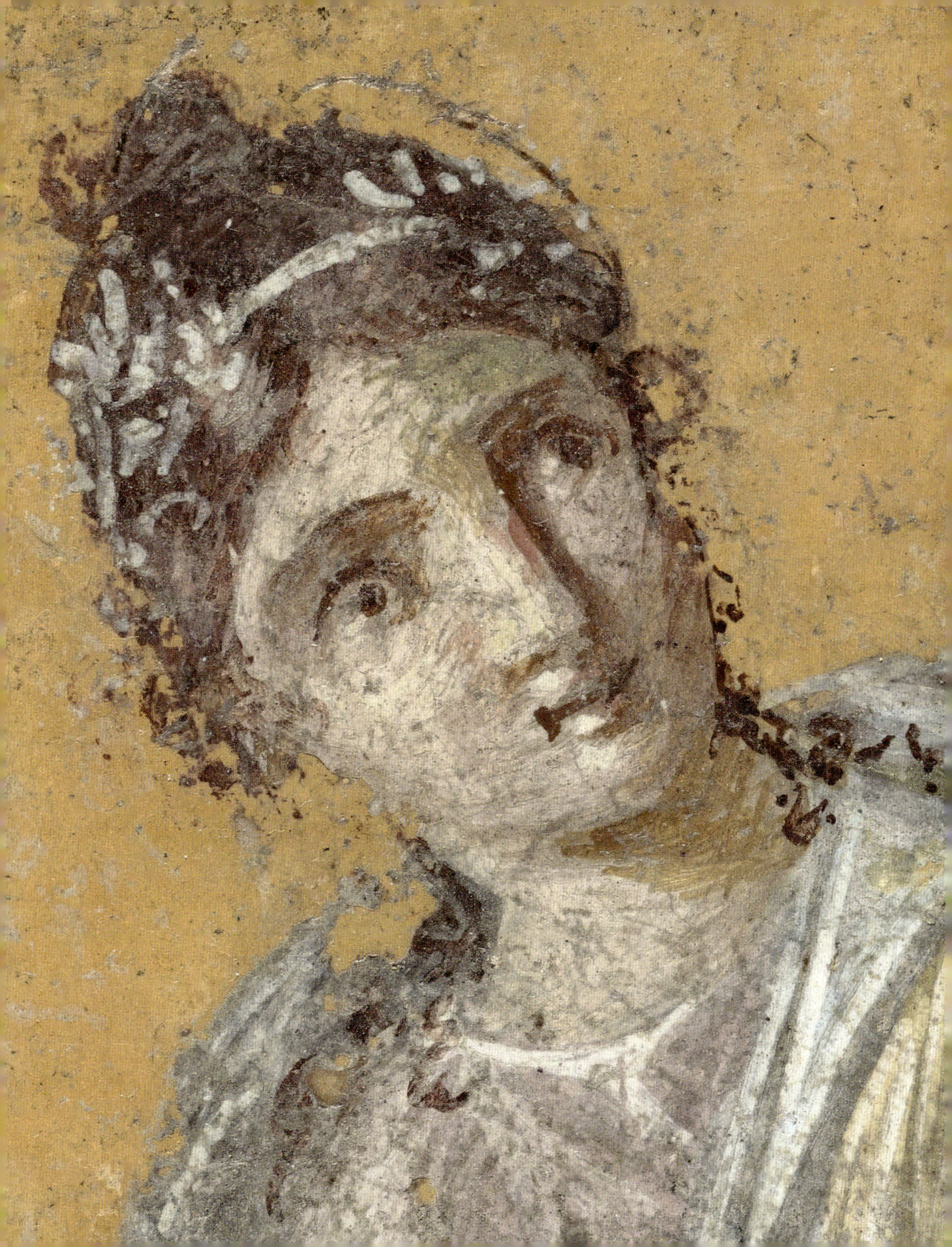

This fresco once adorned the walls of a fancy villa in Pompeii. And you probably know what that means. In 79 AD, Mount Vesuvius woke up and buried this little beauty under a thick layer of dust and lava. It stayed there undisturbed for ages until, in 1755, a bunch of treasure hunters found what they were looking for: a Roman villa filled with valuable artifacts. Which they robbed. They removed the frescoes from the walls, took them to France, and when they were done, they reburied the villa.

Fast-forward to the early 20th century, when a group of sane archaeologists undertook another excavation and (re)discovered the huge complex with luxurious baths, public gardens and spectacular art. It all belonged to Julia Felix, a Pompeiian business woman and public figure with loads of money and great taste. And among the many artworks in her villa, there was also a series of colorful frescoes depicting the Greek muses, the inspirational goddesses of the arts and science.

Which brings us to our cross-eyed lady. She is Urania, the muse of astronomy and astrology. And according to mythology, she always keeps her eyes pointed upwards to the heavens. Or, in this case, one eye on the heavens and the other on her globe. However, no matter how broad her eyesight might have been, there is one thing she probably didn't see coming: that darned avalanche of dust and lava.

Unknown artist, *The Muse Urania*, c. 79 AD.

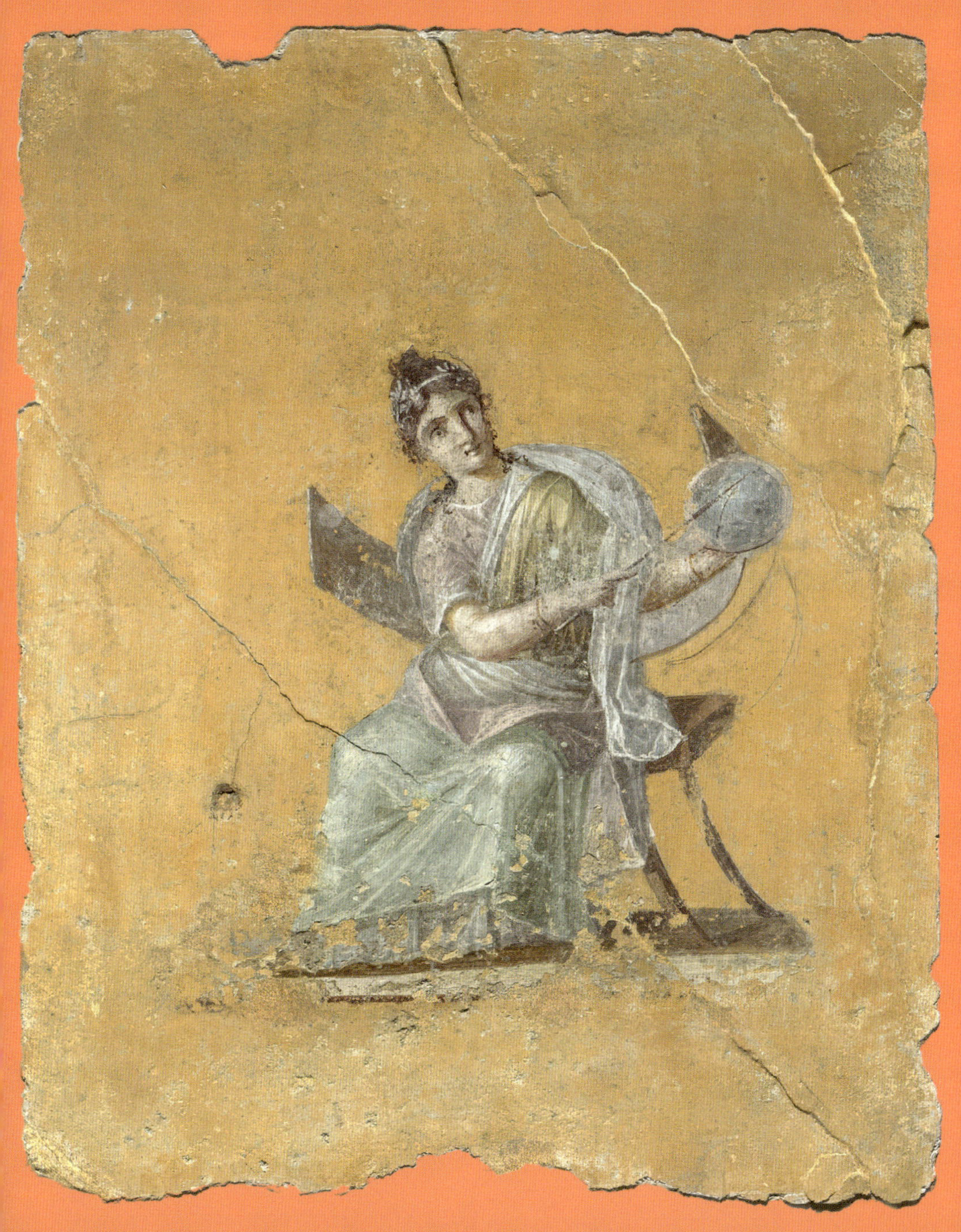

Some artists only need a couple of brushstrokes to bring a pair of eyes to life. Vincent van Gogh was one of them. With three curved lines and two dabs of paint, he captured two blue, staring irises. This man's gaze is empty, and for good reason.

Van Gogh painted this gnarly face in 1889 during his stay at the Saint-Paul Asylum in Saint-Rémy-de-Provence. Battling severe mental health struggles, he suffered from periods of illness in which he just couldn't paint. He was exhausted. But between those attacks, painting became a vital source of comfort and relief, and he worked at a furious pace.

During his one-year stay at the asylum, Van Gogh created an astounding 172 paintings—that we know of. He was incredibly productive. This quick oil sketch is one of only two portraits he made of fellow patients. The face has a large, crooked nose, sunken cheeks and a quite remarkable scalp. Let's have a look.

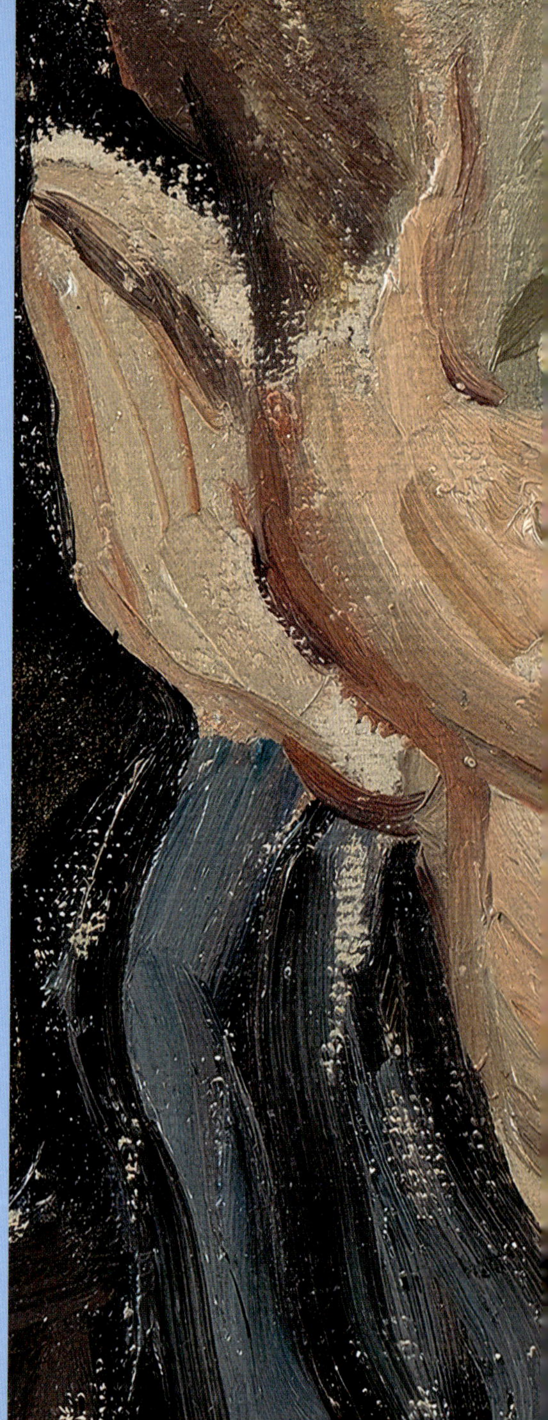

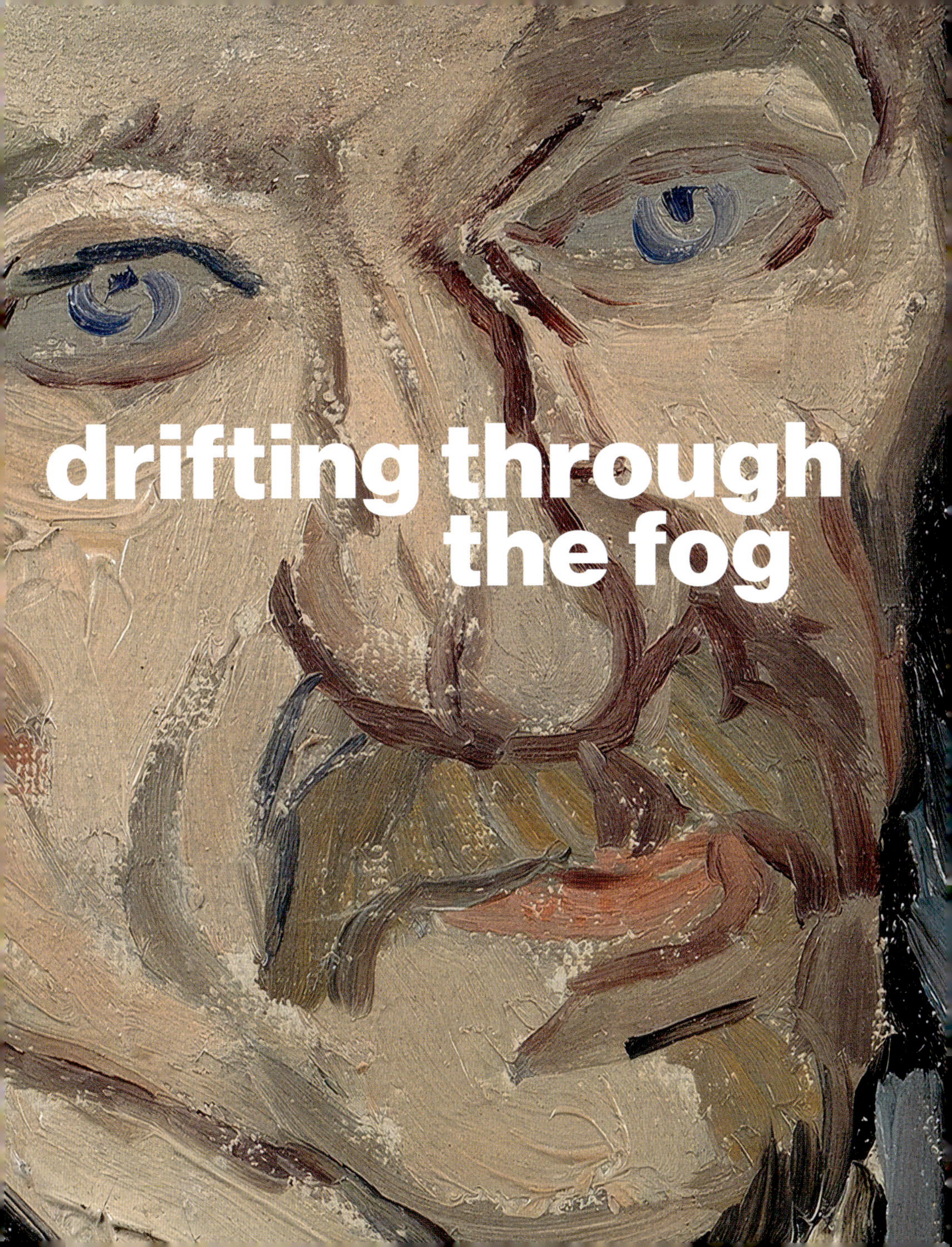
drifting through
the fog

Before we get to the scalp, let's carefully check out the rest of the painting, because, as you can tell, Van Gogh was a fast painter. His rapid and textured brushstrokes give this portrait a raw and unsettling atmosphere. Every line is urgent, as if he were racing to capture something that was slipping through his fingers. But the foggy scalp? That wasn't part of his original plan.

You might interpret the smudges and hazy outline of this man's head as a visual metaphor for his mental illness. It's very tempting, but the truth is a bit more mundane. The portrait got damaged not long after it was painted. We still don't know what exactly happened—maybe it was mishandled or perhaps it suffered water damage. But either way, I think it's a happy accident. Because the imperfections are actually quite fitting, as the smudges add even more unrest to this portrait. They say the eyes are the windows to the soul, but the soul behind these blue irises is lost and confused, as if it's drifting through a fog.

Vincent van Gogh, *Portrait of a Man*, 1889.

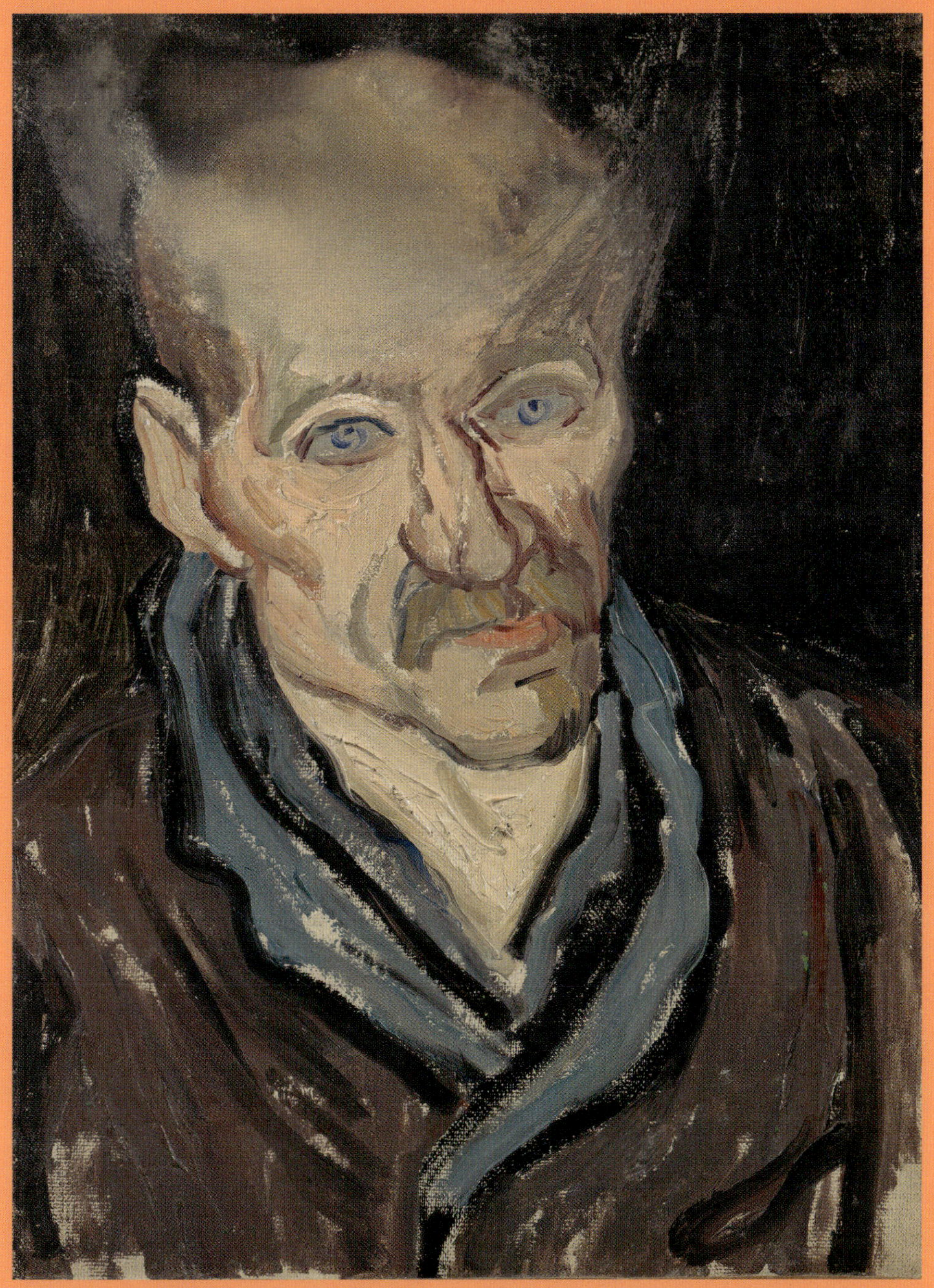

Here's another beautiful eye by Vincent van Gogh, this time painted with more detail. The beautiful blue-green iris stands out. It has a heart-shaped black pupil, staring into the distance, and a tiny fleck of white and brown to add a little reflection. But the eyelid is drooping. Is this person sad? Is he suffering from some sort of melancholy? Let's see.

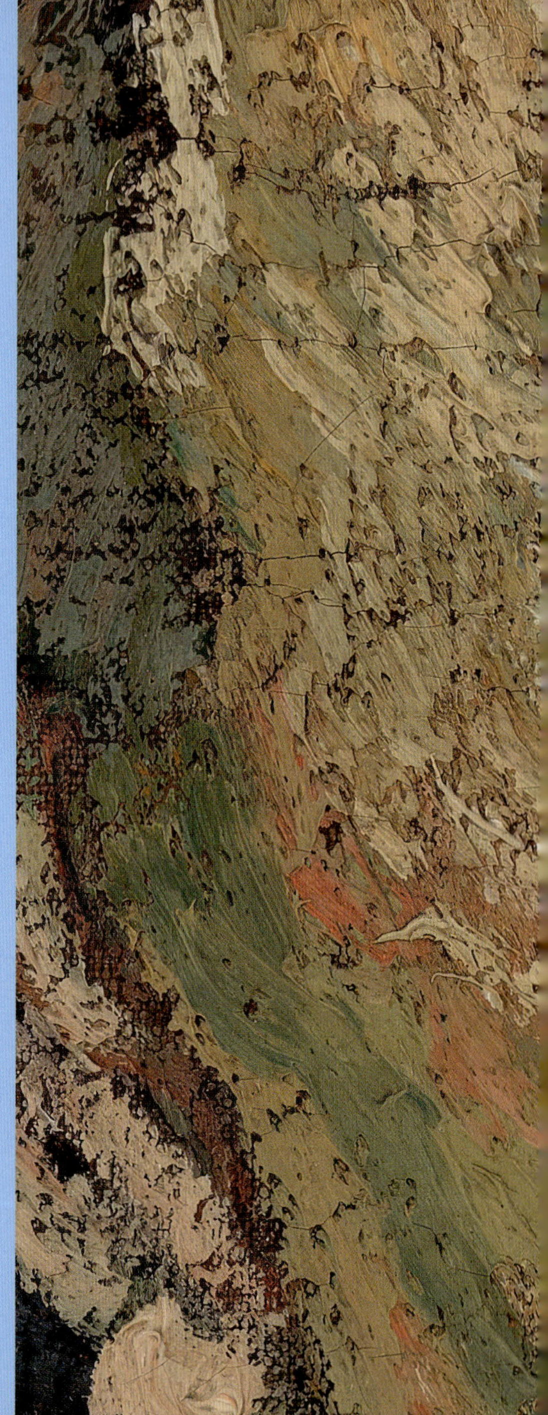

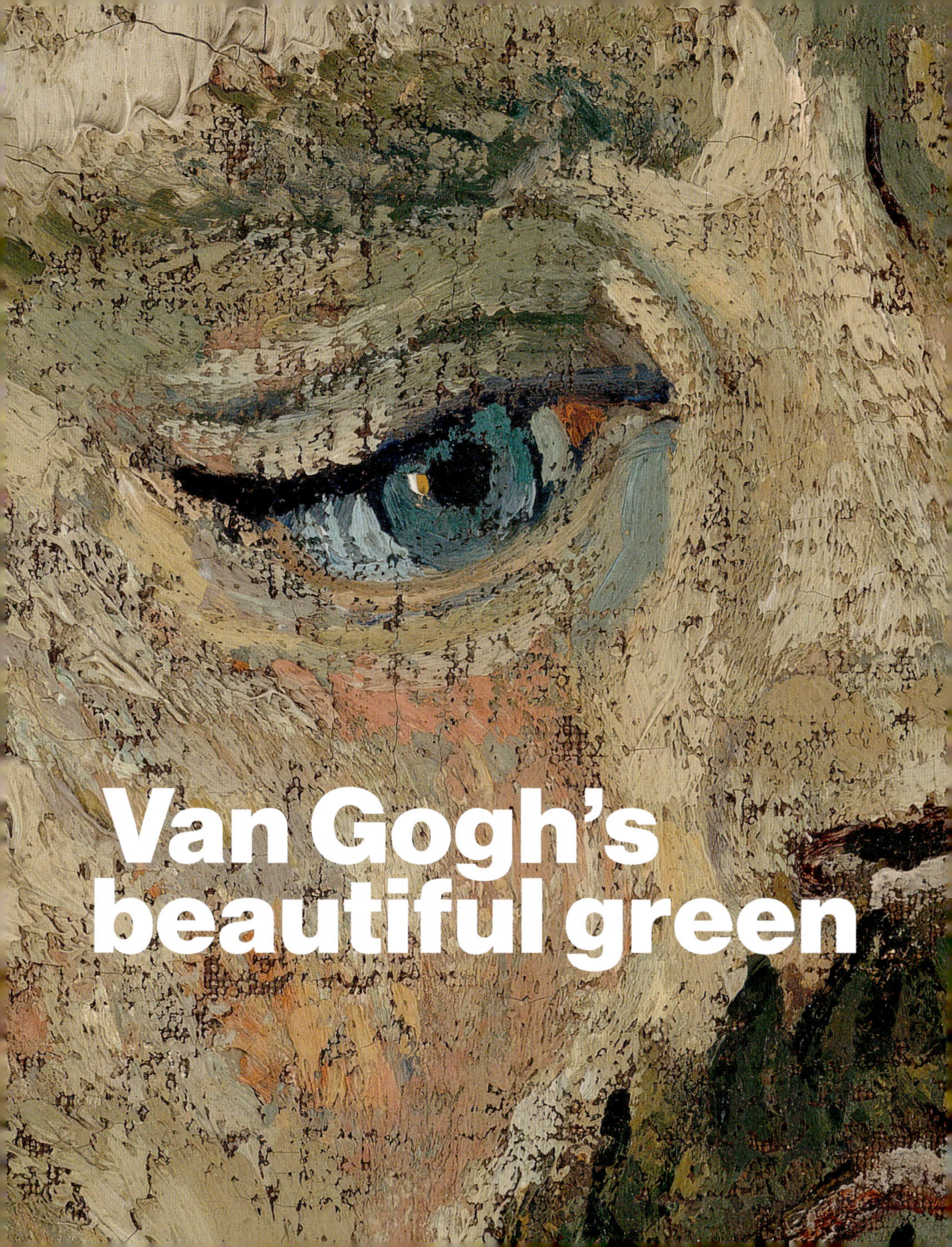

Van Gogh's beautiful green

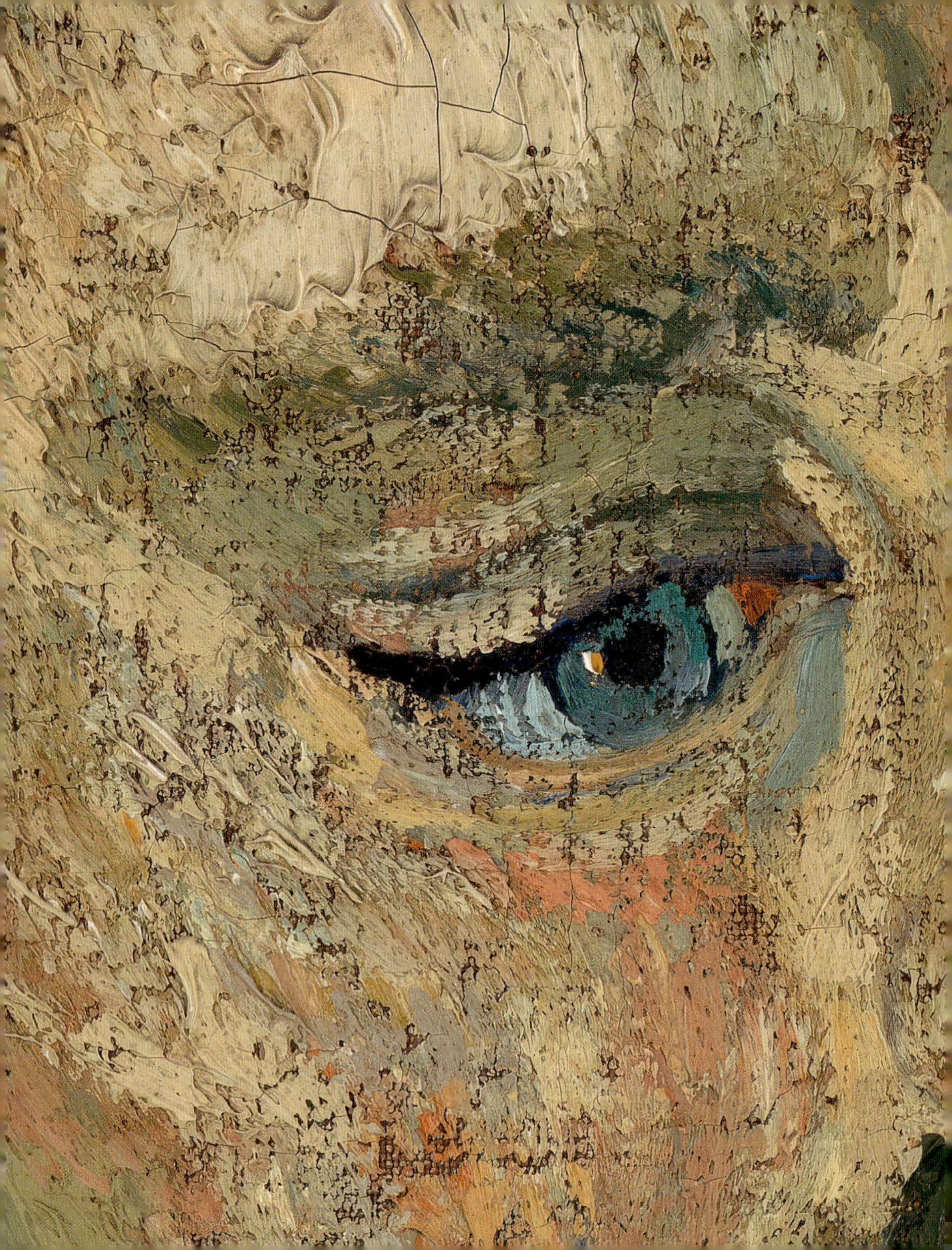

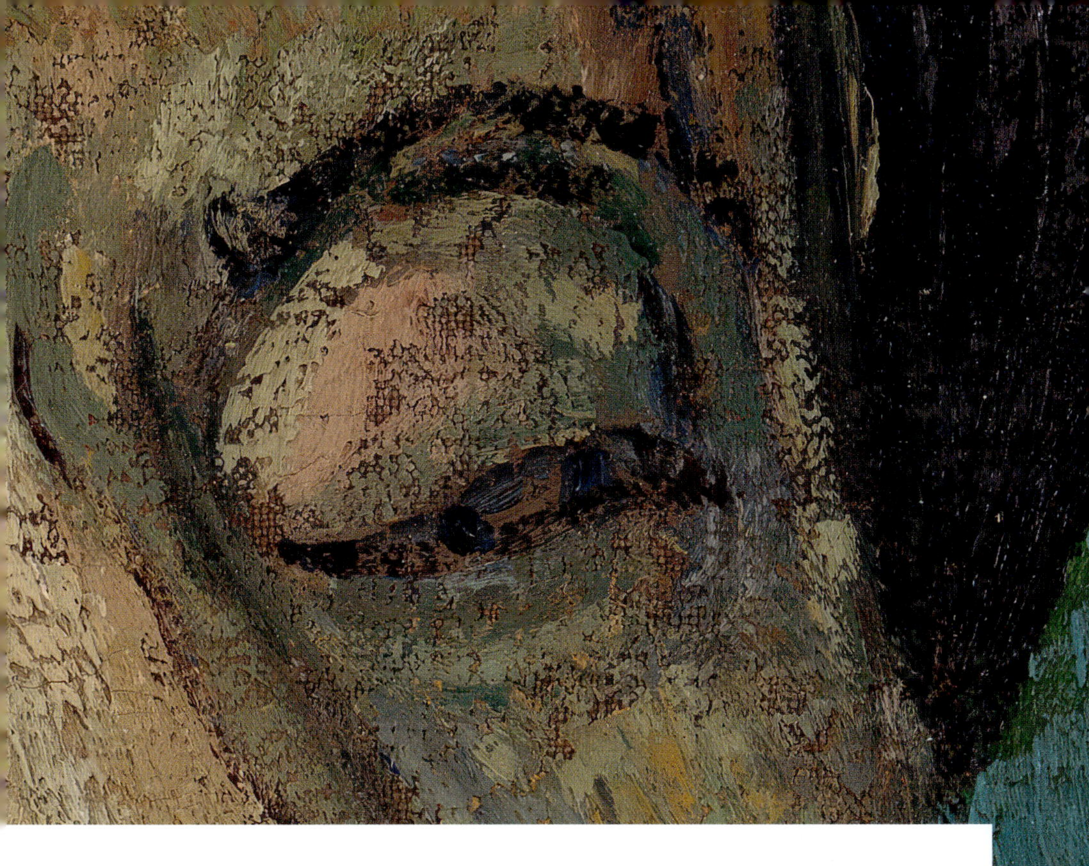

The second eye is closed, the eyelid relaxed with a brow that seems to be incomplete. This is definitely not a playful wink. There's more going on, because these eyes belong to another patient from the Saint-Paul Asylum. It's possible that the man was blind in one eye. Or he might have had an eye disease. Or maybe his eyeball was missing altogether. We can't be sure, but it must have intrigued Van Gogh. After all, he was missing an ear after he cut it off during a mental breakdown. Maybe he felt a connection?

Portrait of a One-Eyed Man is just one of many paintings that show Van Gogh's mastery as a colorist. Just look at the background. Van Gogh often painted backgrounds that reflected the sitter's energy or personality. In this case, he created a pulsating backdrop in the same green hue as the patient's eye, only broken by some swirls of smoke. The bright orange glow at the tip of the cigarette reveals that the man is in the middle of taking a puff.

Following one of his crises, Van Gogh became frightened of his fellow asylum patients, yet still he painted them. In a letter to his mother, Van Gogh wrote about creating these portraits: "It is strange that when one is with them for some time and is used to them, one no longer thinks about their being mad." Being with his fellow patients, gazing at them, painting them, might have tempered his fears. In fact, to me, this painting doesn't show fear. To the contrary, it radiates sympathy.

Vincent van Gogh, *Portrait of a One-Eyed Man*, 1889.

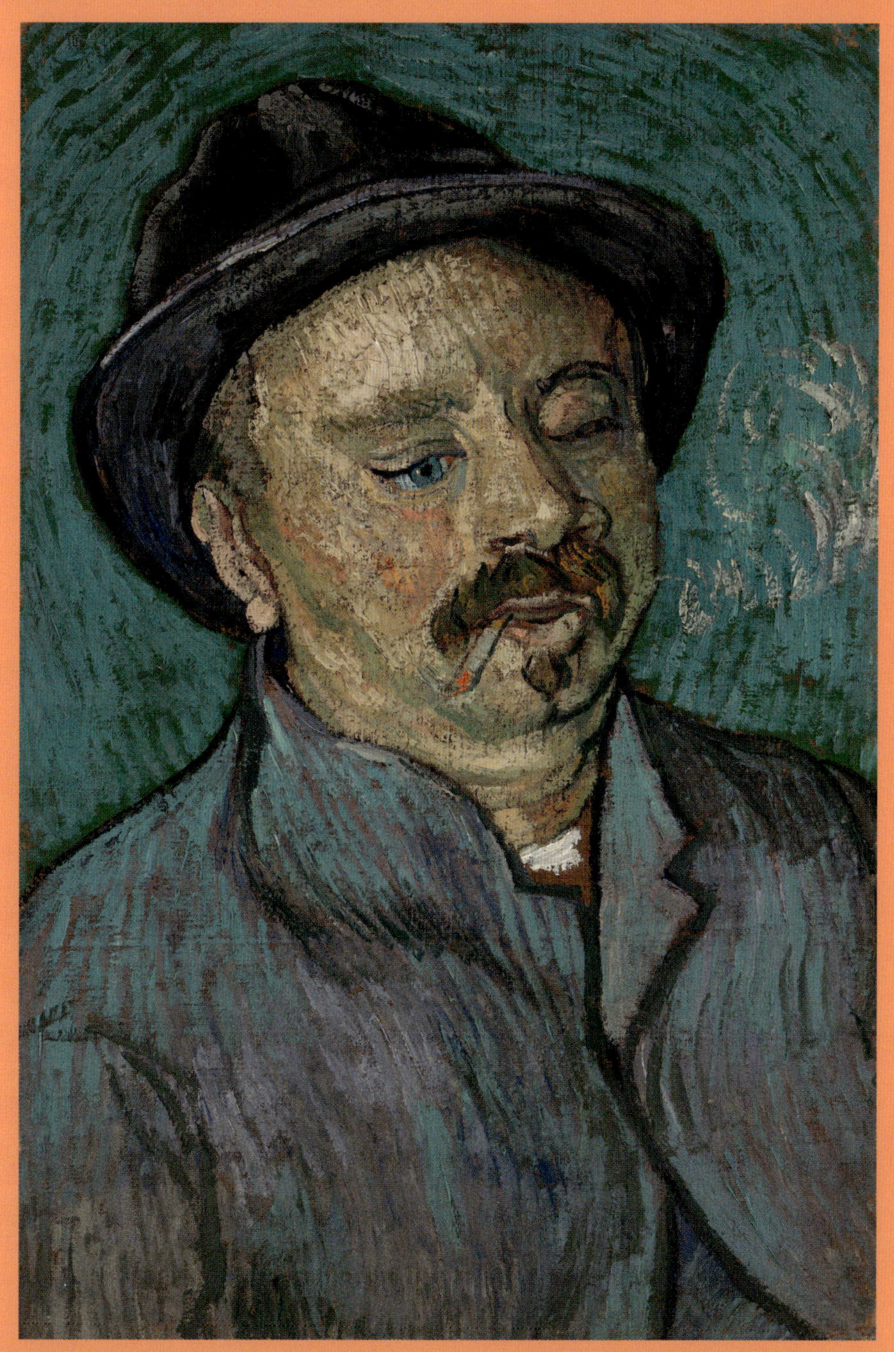

a fair deal

Here's yet another broken eye. Though calling it an "eye" might be generous, as it looks more like a swollen tomato. The skin around it is twisted, the colors are deeply concerning and the nose has collapsed. And yet, somehow, it's still unmistakably human. This swollen tomato belongs to Francis Bacon, the British painter who once described himself as being "drunk since the age of 15." Which might explain why he created so many unsettling portraits of distorted faces. Could be, but there's more to it.

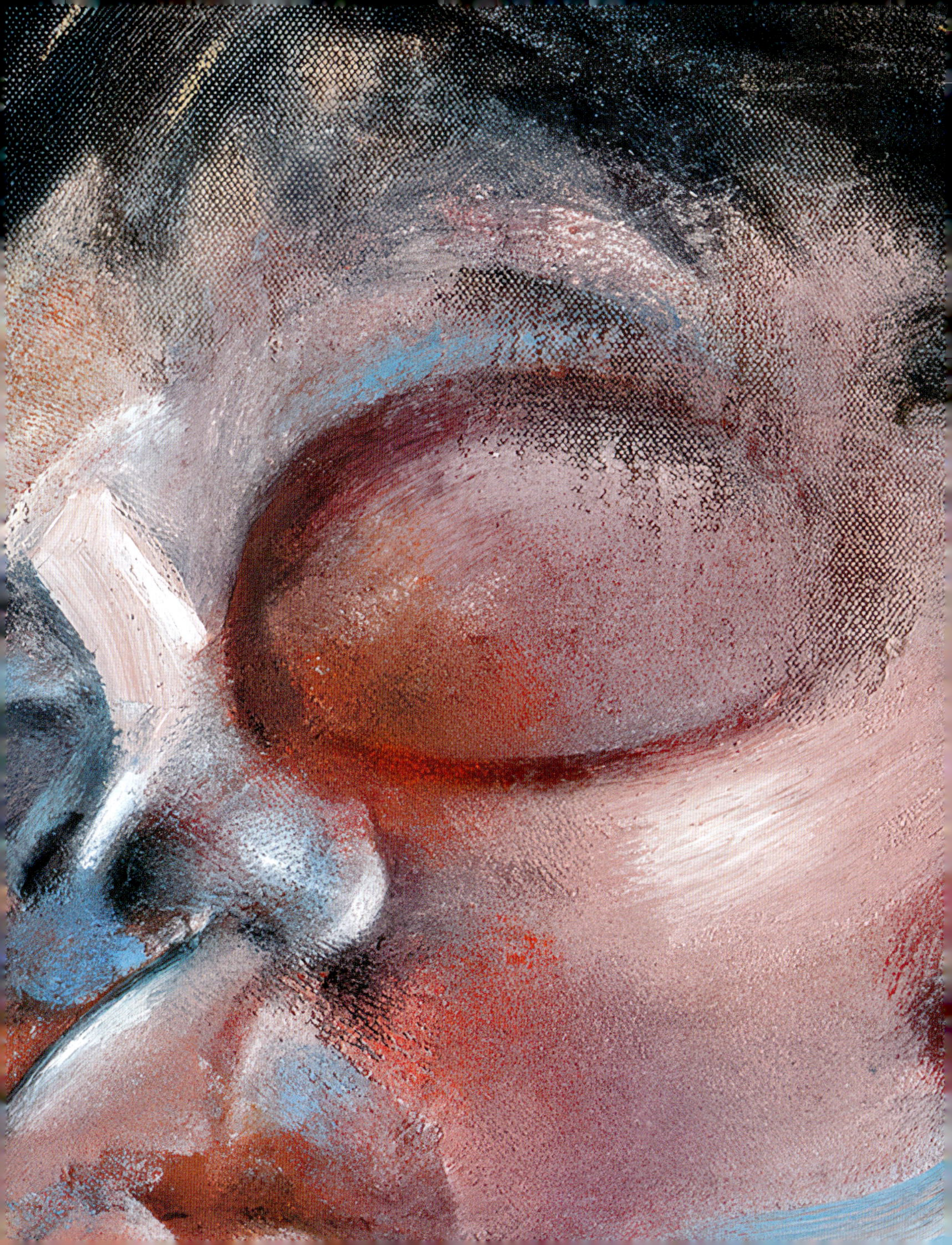

The greenish background, the lapel jacket and that closed eyelid—this self-portrait is pretty reminiscent of Van Gogh's portrait of his fellow asylum patient (page 130). In fact, when Bacon painted this, he was also in a very troubled state of mind.

His former lover, George Dyer, had passed away the year before, and Bacon spent the following decade obsessively painting searing self-portraits like the one you're looking at. He said, "I've done a lot of self-portraits, really because people have been dying around me like flies, and I've had nobody else to paint but myself." These twisted, frightening faces became mirrors of his loneliness and grief.

Francis Bacon, *Self-Portrait with Injured Eye*, 1972.

This particular portrait tells the story of a drunken brawl Bacon had in his studio with one of his lovers. It's filled with the violent energy of a fight: his jaw twisted from a punch, his left eyelid swollen and red, his broken nose bent sideways. The fight is so violent that Bacon's eye gets punched from its socket. The drunken artist calls his doctor, who urges him to go to the hospital, but Bacon refuses—he fears the gossip and bad press. So the doctor comes over and in the filth and chaos of Bacon's studio, the poor man sews Bacon's eye back in place. To thank him, Bacon gives the doctor one of his paintings, which, I think, was a very fair transaction.

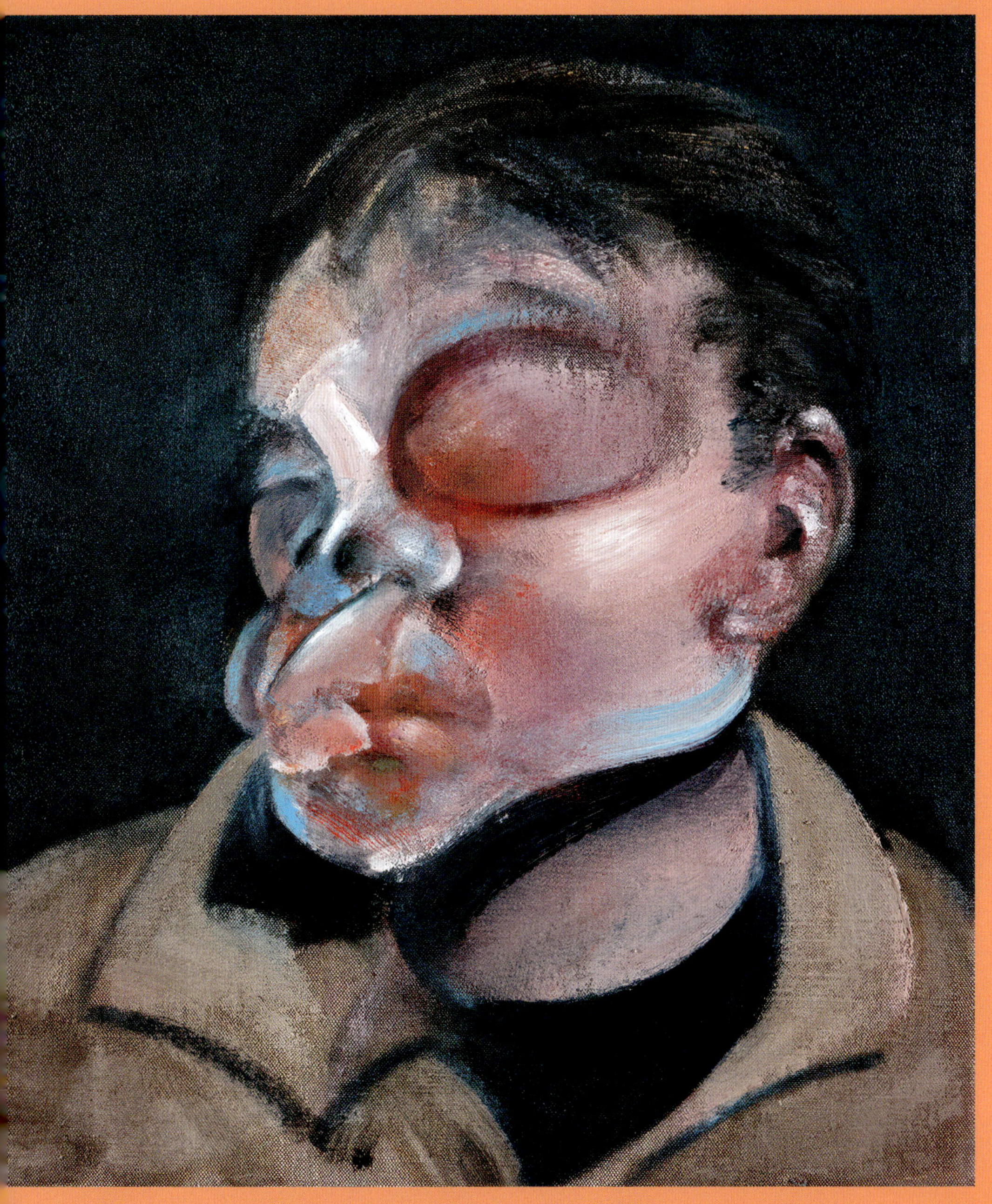

boys will be boys

Of all the mythological creatures, satyrs might be the weirdest. Which is quite the feat, considering the Greeks seasoned their stories with centaurs (part human, part horse), minotaurs (part human, part bull), chimera (part lion, part goat, part snake) and a busload of other strange cocktails.

But the satyr sticks out, and not just because of its bizarre looks. Don't get me wrong, humans with goat's horns, ears and legs score high on the oddball ranking, but it's the way they *act* that separates them from the rest. Because satyrs are little assholes that love to party. They are rowdy. They drink. They harass women. And they often sport exaggerated erections. In this case, we're looking at a very young satyr that seems to be either drunk or horny. Quite controversial if you ask me, but age is never an issue in mythology.

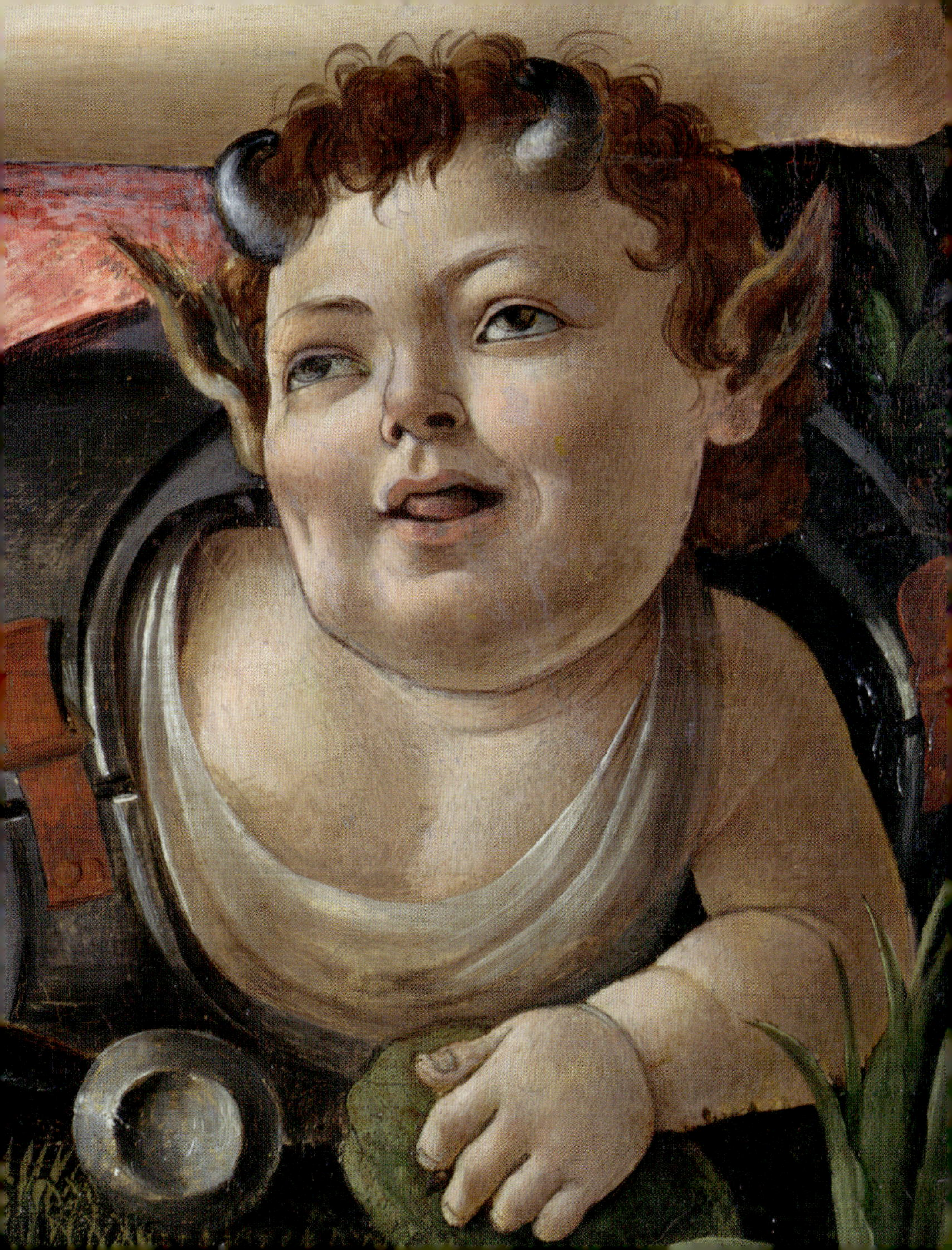

Zooming out, we discover the reason behind this creature's stupid face. He is not intoxicated by wine or women, but probably by the green piece of fruit under his left arm. Because according to one theory, this satyr is holding a thorn apple, a plant that causes delirium and drowsiness. Let's hope he's too drunk to wield the sword he is caressing.

Anyway, what's up with the naked guy casually leaning on our friend's curly fur? It's Mars, the Roman god of war. Yes, *Roman*—which might surprise you, since satyrs are Greek creatures. But in the Renaissance, artists didn't mind mixing up mythologies. Anyway, our Roman friend is so fast asleep that not even a blaring shell can wake him up. We should also consider the fact that Mars isn't just leaning on the drunk satyr's head, but also on the chest-piece of his armor. Why would a god of war so carelessly remove his armor and weapons?

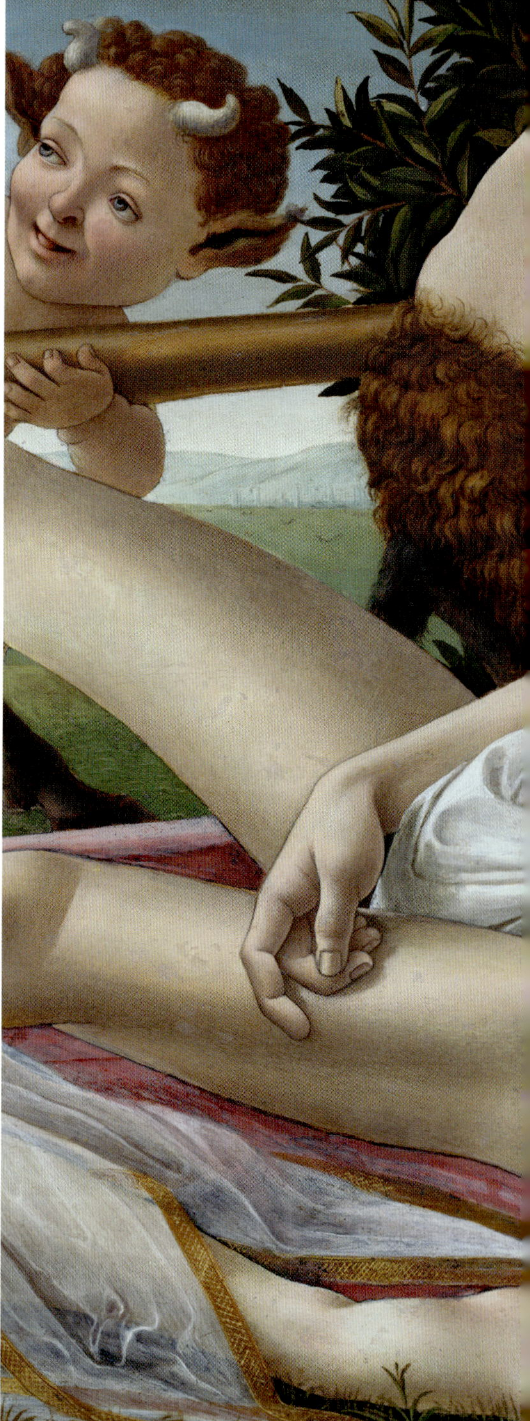

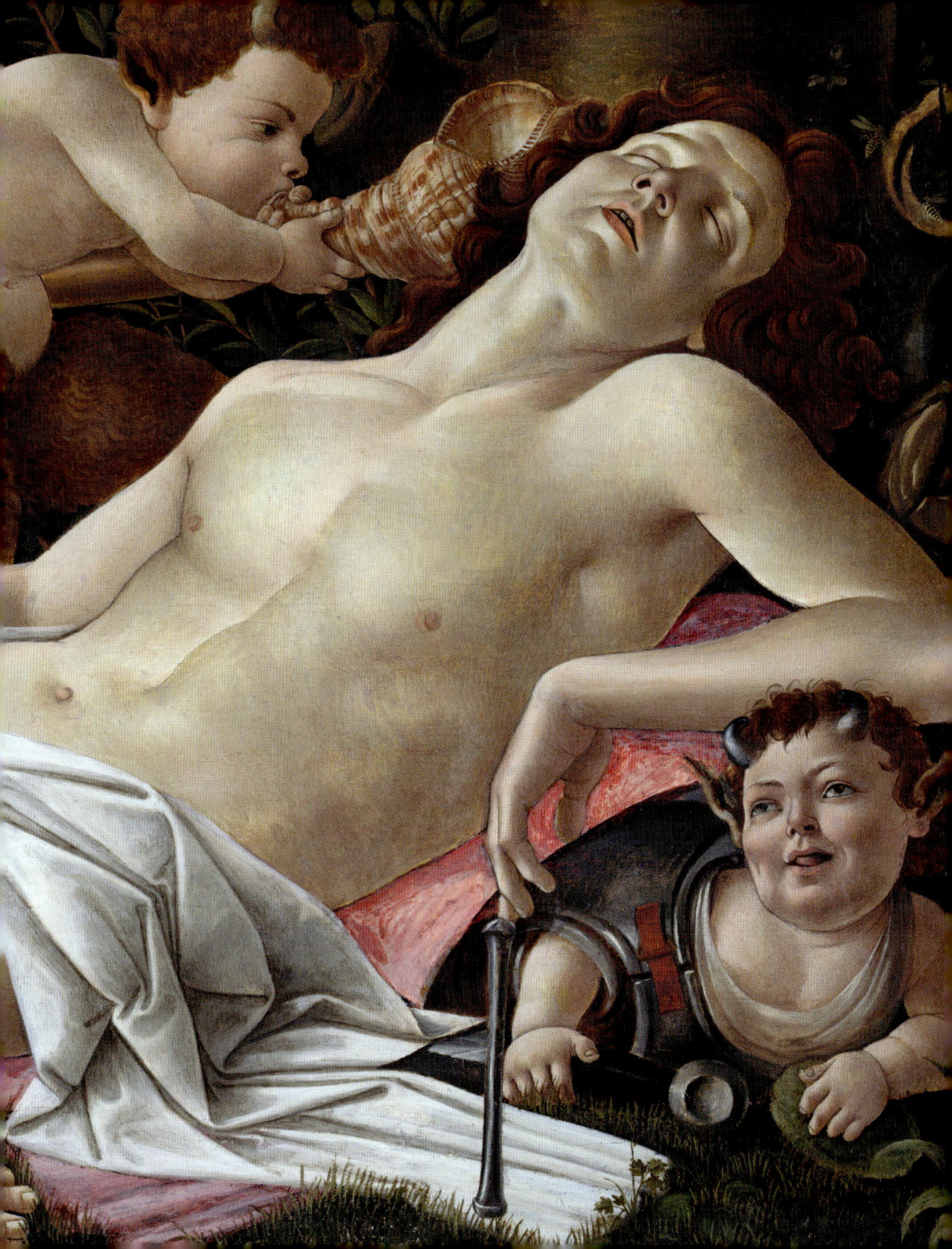

Sandro Botticelli, *Venus and Mars*, 1485.

Because he fell victim to the charms of Venus, the Roman goddess of love, beauty, sex and victory. The result? A deep, post-coital slumber. One conclusion we could draw from this scene is that love conquers war—literally—as Mars's weapons and armor have been playfully seized by four mischievous satyrs. After all, Venus isn't just about romance. She's the goddess of *victory*.

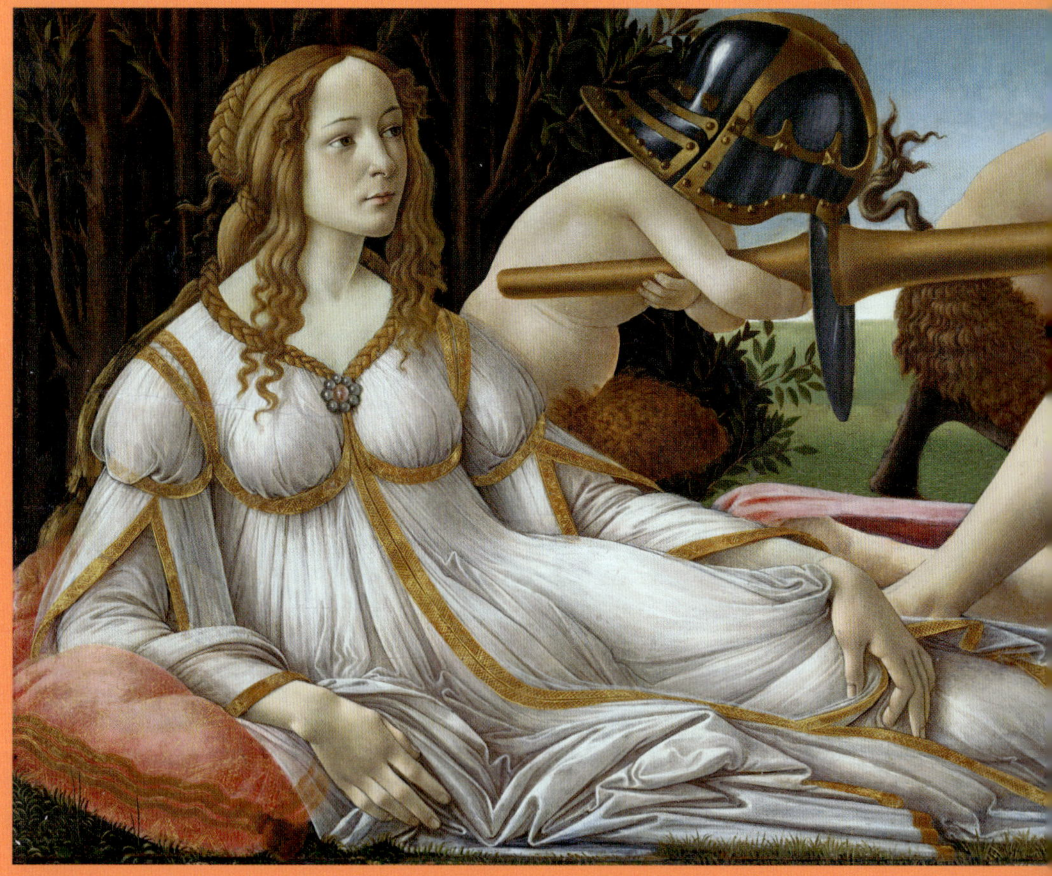

But of course, there's more. Because this Renaissance masterpiece was probably made to celebrate a marriage. It was to be hung in the couple's bedroom not just as a piece of sensuous decoration, but also to help them in their quest for male heirs. Because at the time, people believed that women gazing upon beautiful male bodies were more likely to give birth to boys. But maybe it also serves as a warning. Because the four boys in this painting aren't the kind of boys you want hanging around in your bedroom.

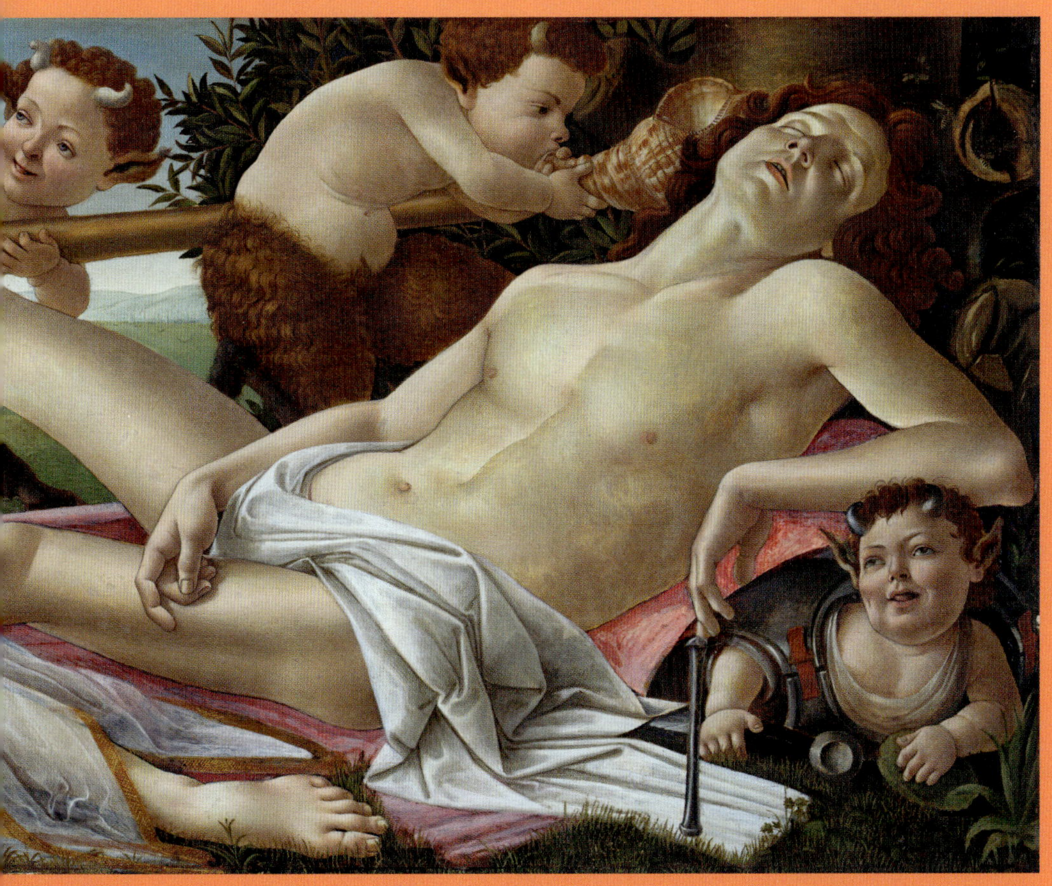

cats will be cats

There are countless reasons why we humans adore cats. They're cute, soft and warm. They give us attention, soothe our anxiety and help relieve our loneliness. But they also have the wonderful potential to be incredibly stupid, which is why cat videos remain an immensely popular staple of Internet culture. We just love to watch them missing their jumps, sliding off countertops and chasing laser pointers.

This particular feline face looks like it has just seen a laser pointer for the first time in its life, mesmerized by the little wiggling dot and fully prepared to smack straight into the wall. Pure comedy gold. It could explain the oddball expression, if it weren't for the fact that laser pointers didn't exist in 1650.

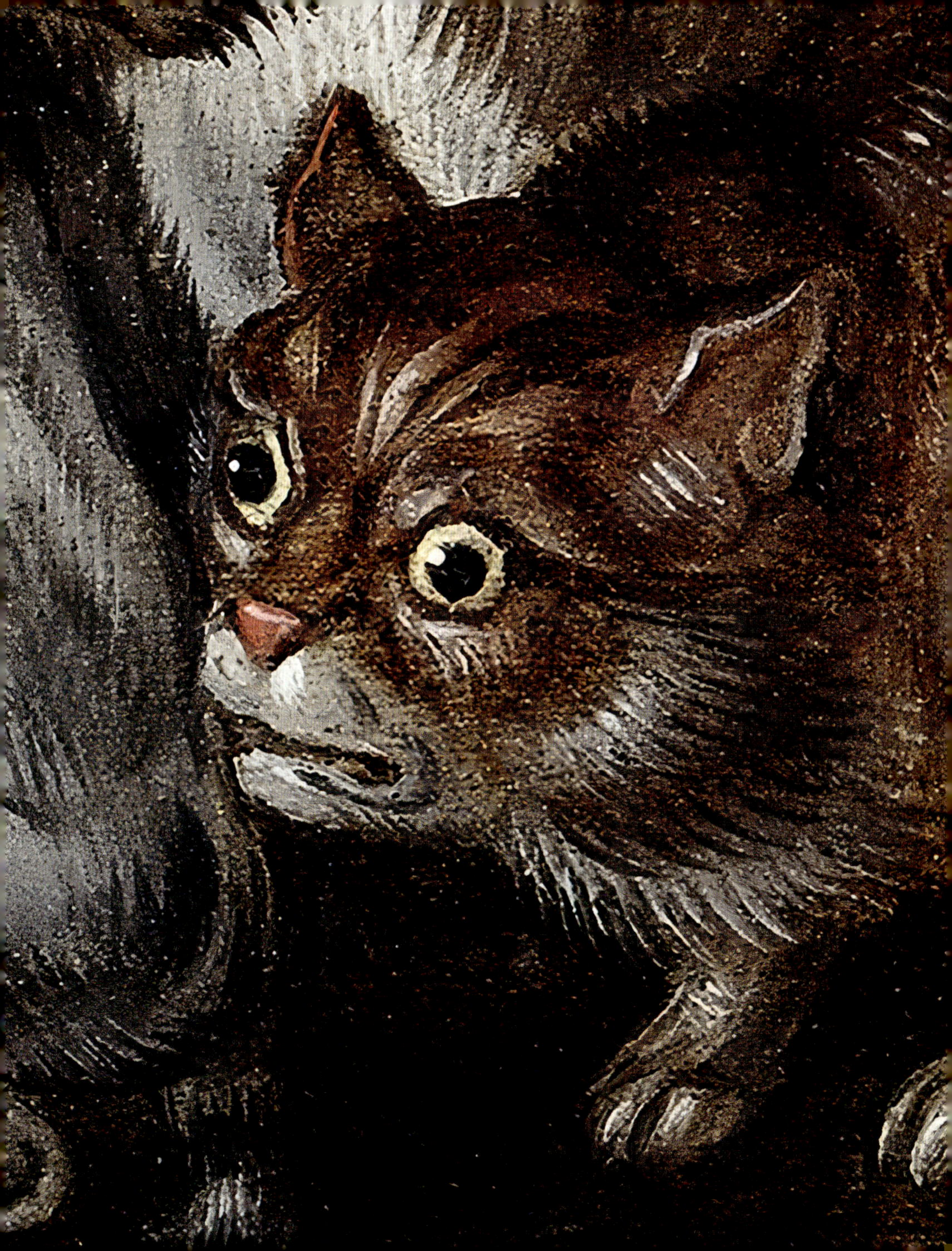

Our confused cat is surrounded by a crew of equally puzzled friends. One of them wears a pair of glasses. Another plays the trombone with eyes begging for help. And the rest stare at a book of sheet music with slack jaws and furrowed brows. But if you look closely, they're not studying the sheets to play a symphony. No, they're baffled because, to them, the notes look like mice. The left page is what we see; the right page is what the cats are seeing.

The artist, Jan van Kessel, is trying to teach us something with this odd little scene. He painted a bunch of cats that are acting like humans, but he's probably trying to point out the impossibility of this situation—that no matter what tricks you try to teach them, cats will always remain cats.

Because animals don't follow sheet music—they only follow their instincts. Which in this case are screaming, "What are these tiny windows on my nose? Why am I holding a shiny slidey honk machine? And why the hell are these mice flat and impossible to eat?" To us, these cats look hilariously silly, but they're just being themselves. And all the while, they're taking advantage of our warmth and care. So who's the stupid one here?

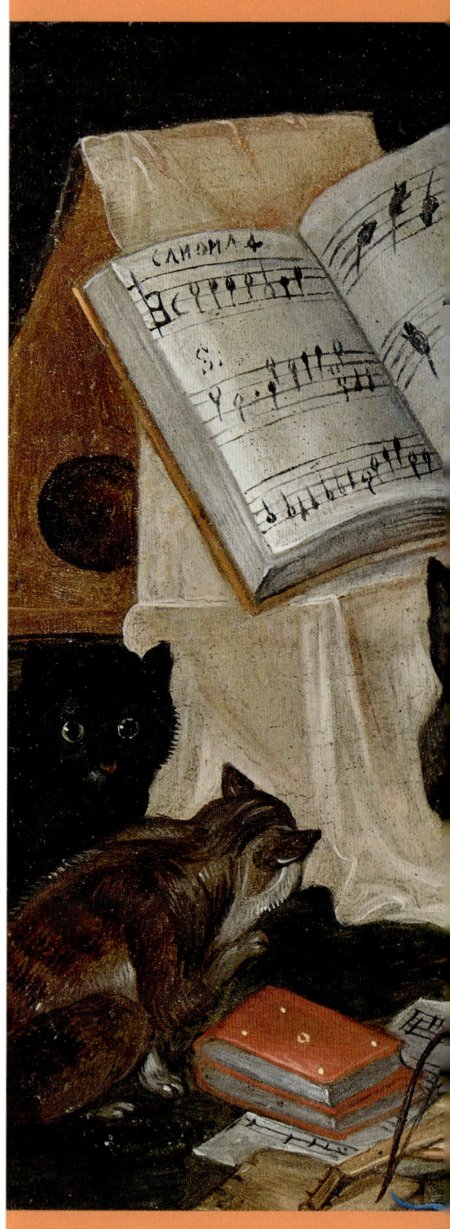

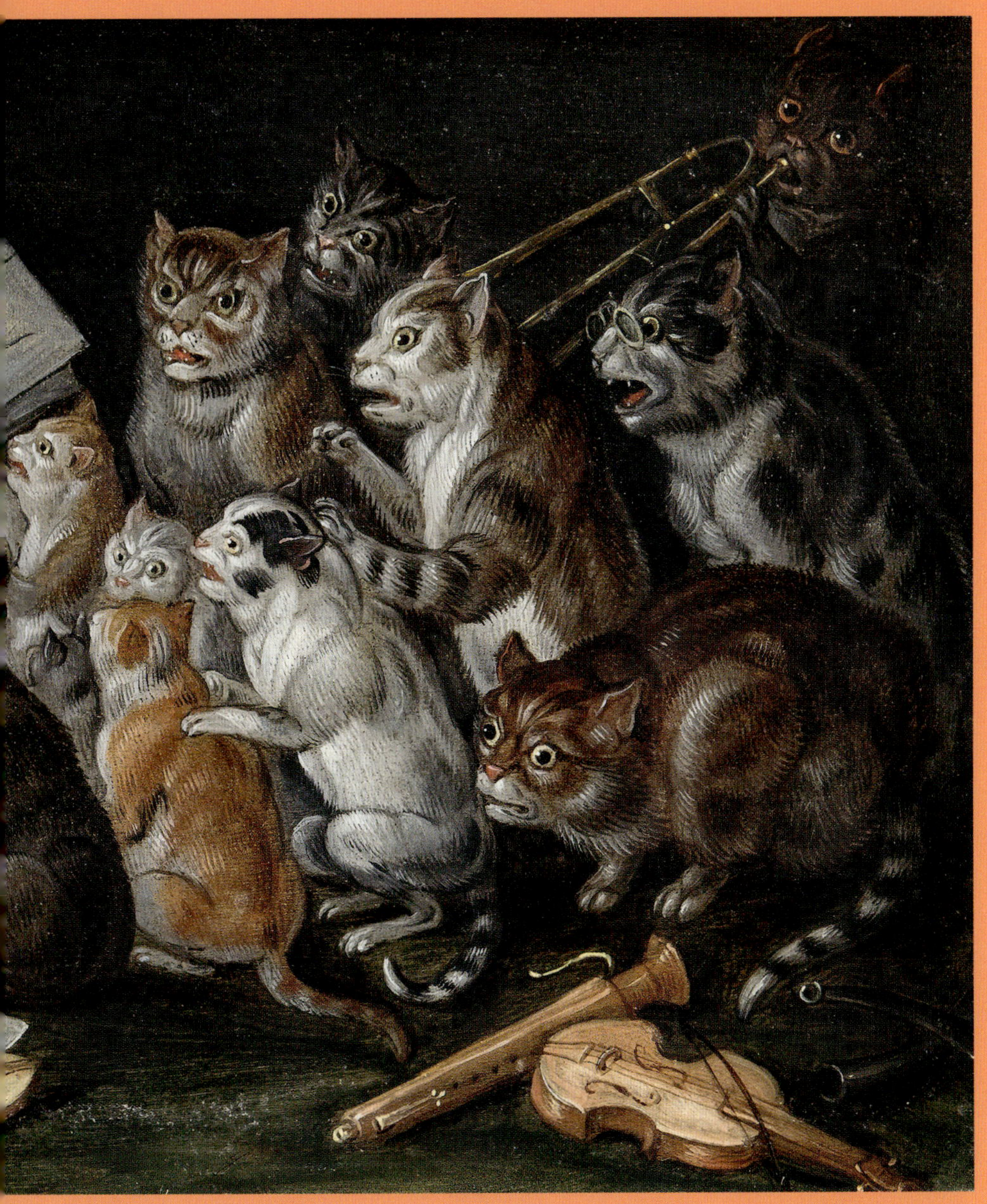

Jan van Kessel, *The Concert of Cats*, 1650.

the fastest painter ever

Now here's a stupid face of intense concentration. What's this man doing that requires such an amount of focus? Is he painting? Examining a restaurant menu? Decoding the manual of his brand new IKEA® wardrobe? Regardless, judging by that furrowed brow and the little tip of his tongue peeking out of his mouth, he's clearly in deep, deep thought. Let's see what's going on in that grotesque little noggin.

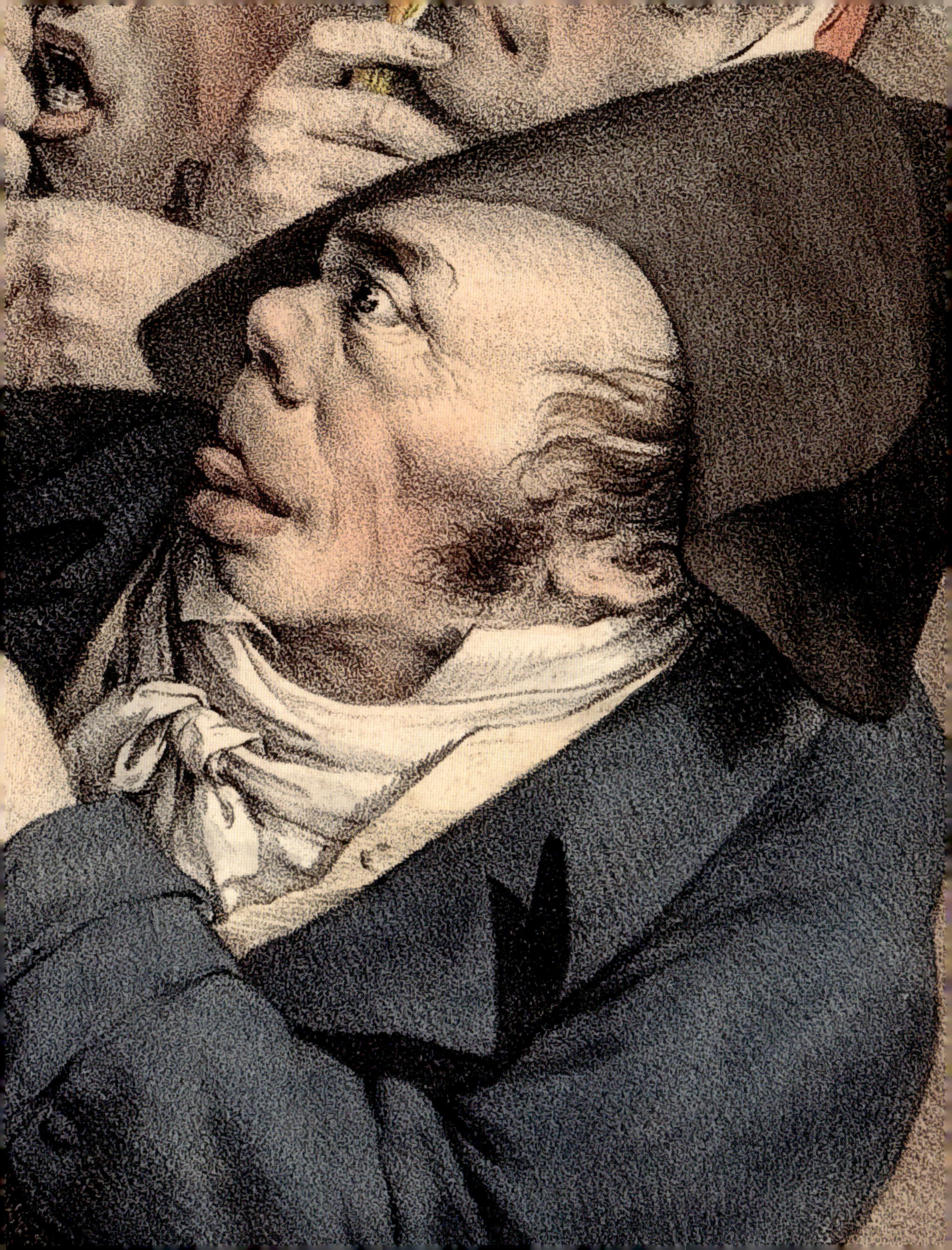

Our friend isn't alone, as he's joined by four other men with glorious noses and receding hairlines. They've got their fingers pointing, glasses perched and magnifiers raised, working hard to decode whatever they are studying.

You're looking at a hand-colored lithograph by one of the fastest painters of his time. Louis-Léopold Boilly boasted he could finish a portrait in less than two hours' time. Over his lifetime, he churned out more than 5,000 portraits. Needless to say, this man loved painting faces. And not just any faces—*weird* faces too. The five gentlemen you are looking at are part of Boilly's *Recueil de Grimaces* or *Collection of Grimaces*, a portfolio of 96 lithographs dedicated to all kinds of stupid expressions. The title of this particular artwork is *The Art Connoisseurs*, so it's not hard to guess what these gazers have their eyes locked on.

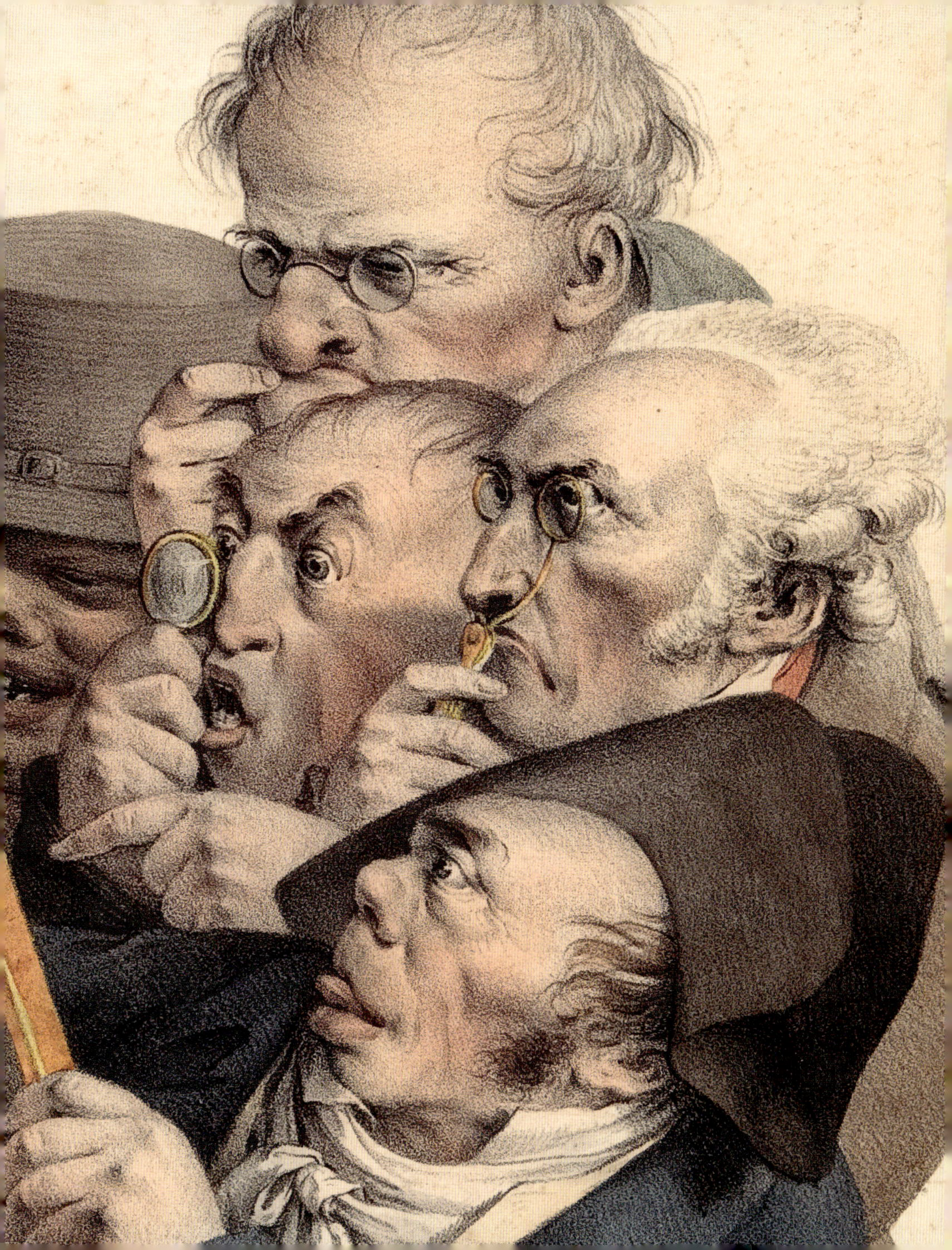

The one single woman, pushed aside by five serious art critics, is a pretty accurate reflection of women's place in art history. Boilly loved poking fun at social types like lawyers, politicians and so-called art connoisseurs, undermining their self-importance by turning them into grotesque caricatures with ugly noses and twisted grimaces. But the woman in this drawing was spared from such mockery, remaining hidden behind the artwork. Perhaps it's Boilly's way of saying that these men might think they're the experts, but it's the women they push aside who possess the keenest eye.

Louis-Léopold Boilly, *The Art Connoisseurs*, 1823–1828.

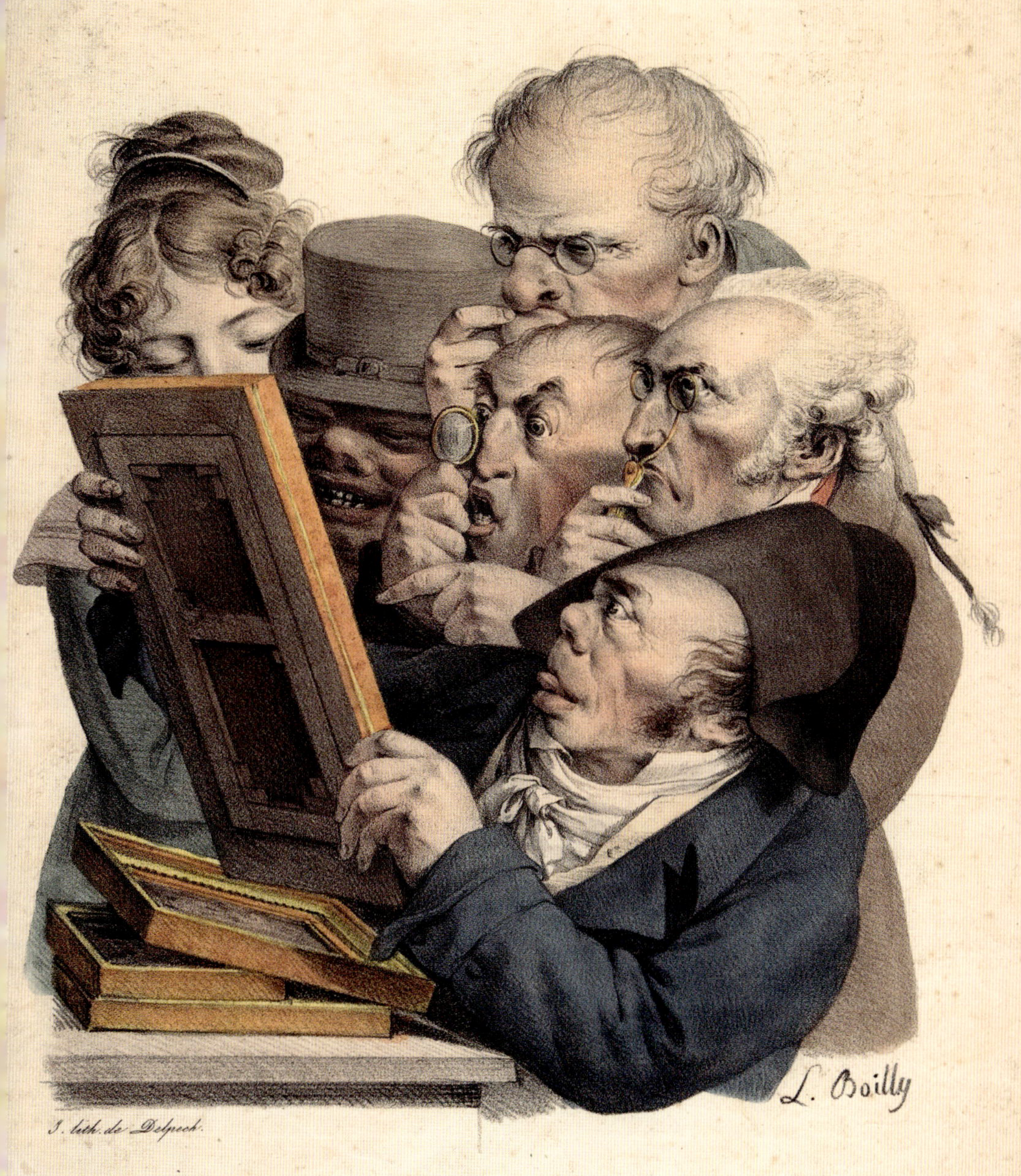

Les amateurs de tableaux

a tiger in despair

This tiger looks like he is in the middle of a surprise colon exam, which, if true, would make this a fascinating painting. But I'm afraid that's not what's happening here. No, the source of this animal's anguish isn't located behind him. It's directly above him. But before we turn the page, let's look at the tiger's face. Because this animal seems to be in distress. His ears are pinned back, his pupils are dilated and his whiskers are all over the place. Now, let's zoom out.

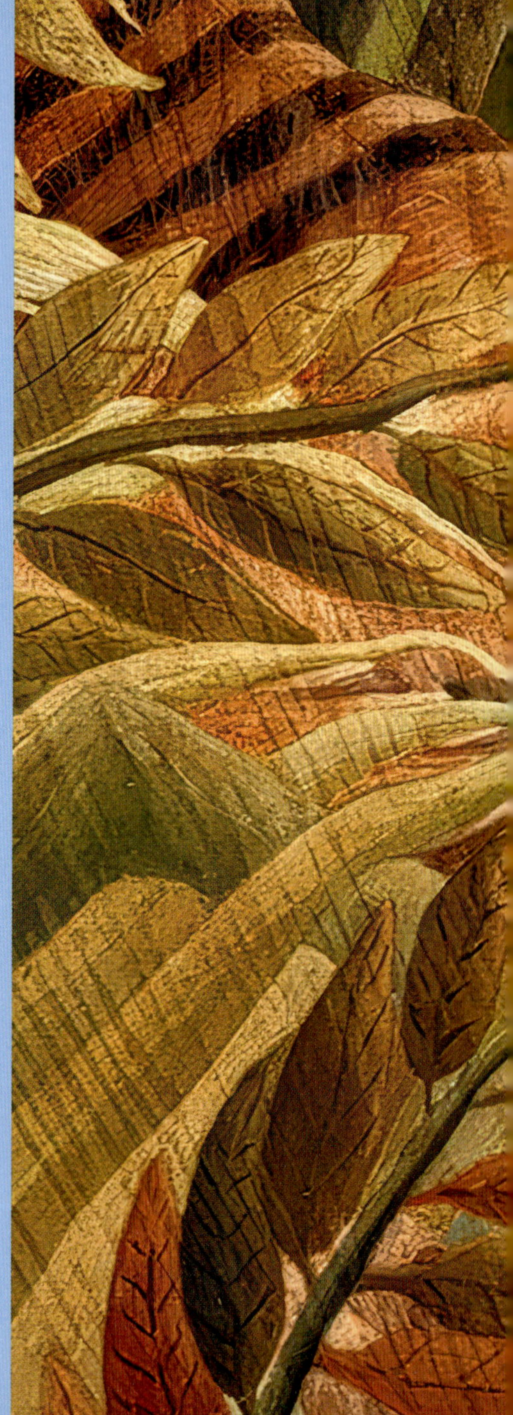

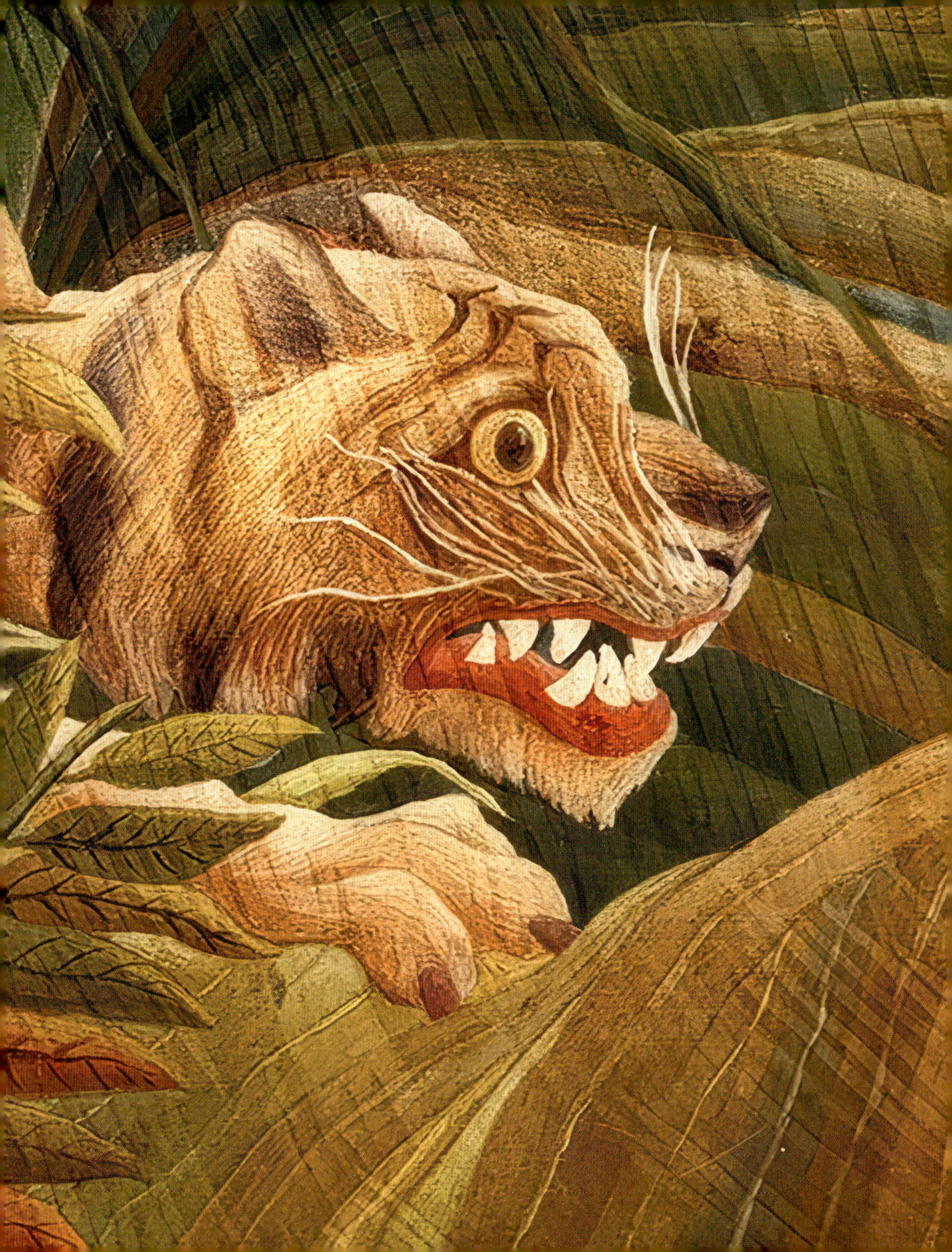

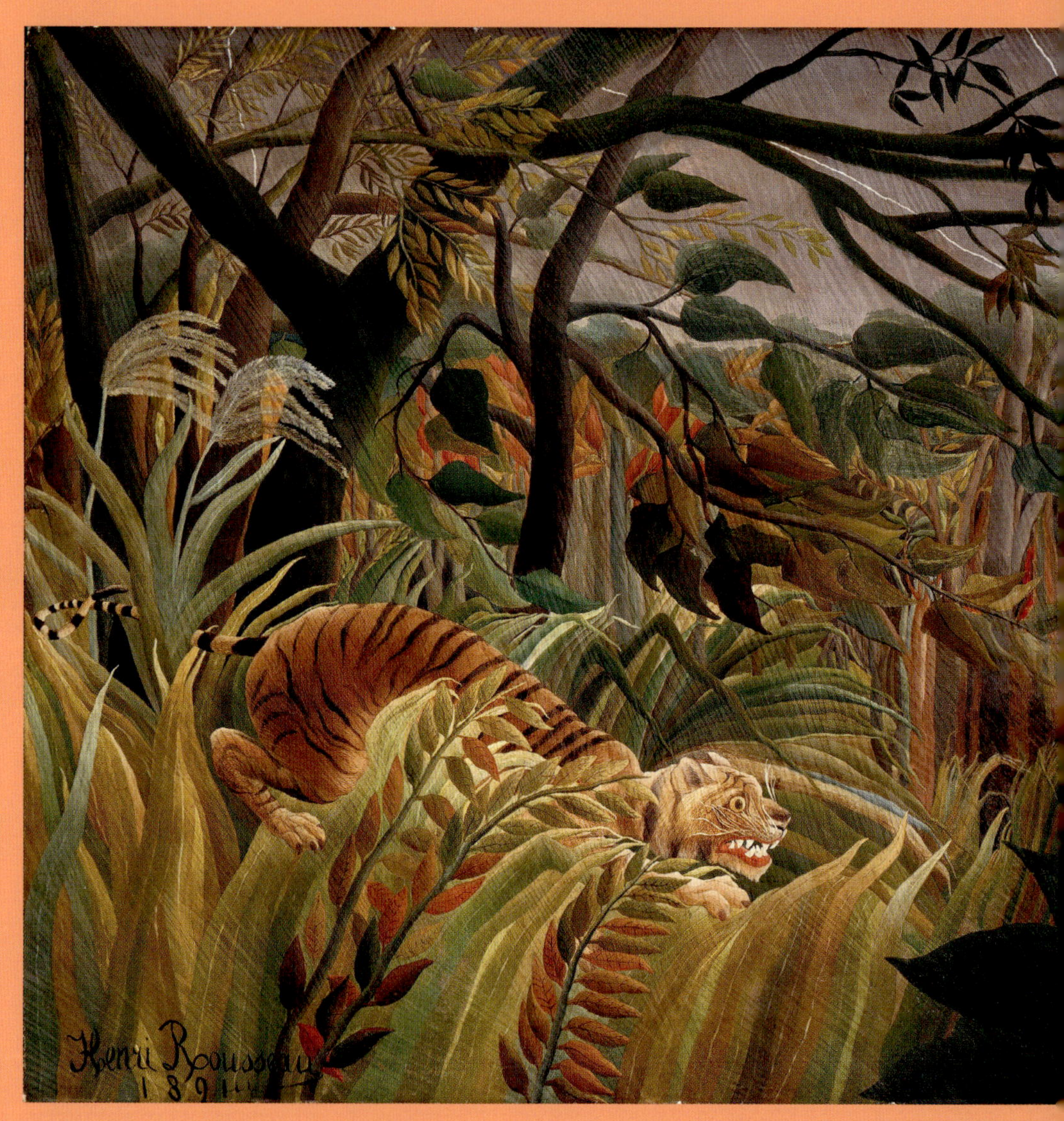

Henri Rousseau, *Tiger in a Tropical Storm* or *Surprised!*, 1891.

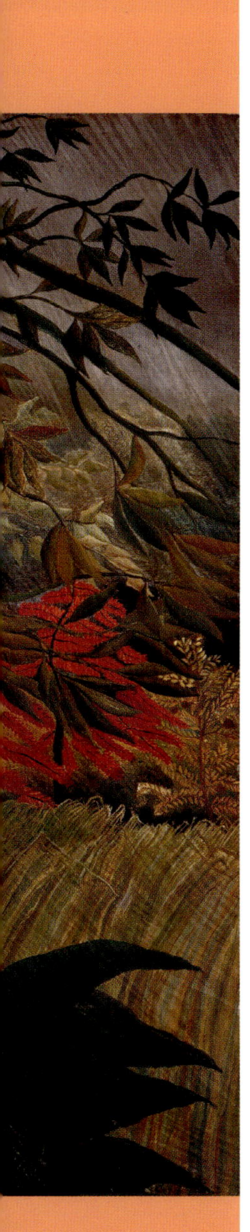

This banger of a painting is called *Tiger in a Tropical Storm,* and it was created by Henri Rousseau, an entirely self-taught artist whose day job was collecting money in Paris—Rousseau was a toll booth operator who just happened to love painting. He only began creating art seriously in his early forties, and by age 49, he retired from his job to devote himself full-time to painting. And as it often goes in art history, Rousseau got mocked by critics during his lifetime, only to get recognized as a genius after his death.

The artist originally titled this painting *Surprised!* So our striped friend isn't just scared, he's startled, probably by the flash of lightning ripping through the stormy sky or the deafening roaring thunder that follows. This tiger stands awkwardly in the middle of a fierce tropical storm with raging streaks of rain, dancing branches and multiple layers of lush, green jungle.

What we don't see is the tiger's prey, which the painter left just beyond the edge of the canvas. Still, the animal looks ready to pounce. Head low, haunches high and a back paw that seems to be twitching with anticipation. Granted, the posture is a bit awkward—as if he accidentally walked onto the Broadway set of *Cats*—but he's definitely ready for a catch. Will the tiger's snack escape, leaving him with nothing but a mouthful of rainwater? Or will the prey be surprised by a tiger that even though it is exposed by a flash of lightning, will hold onto its careful composure and put those big pointy teeth where they belong: in a soft, wet and tender piece of tropical meat?

just another day at the holy office

This must be our Lord up in heaven. Big beard? Check. Golden halo? Check. Spitting fire? Check. Wait, what? Isn't spitting fire Satan's signature move? Well, not this time. Because today, it's God's turn to rain down some divine firepower, incinerating sinners with a casual calm that suggests it's just another day at the Holy Office. Let's take a closer look at who our dear Lord is casually turning into ash.

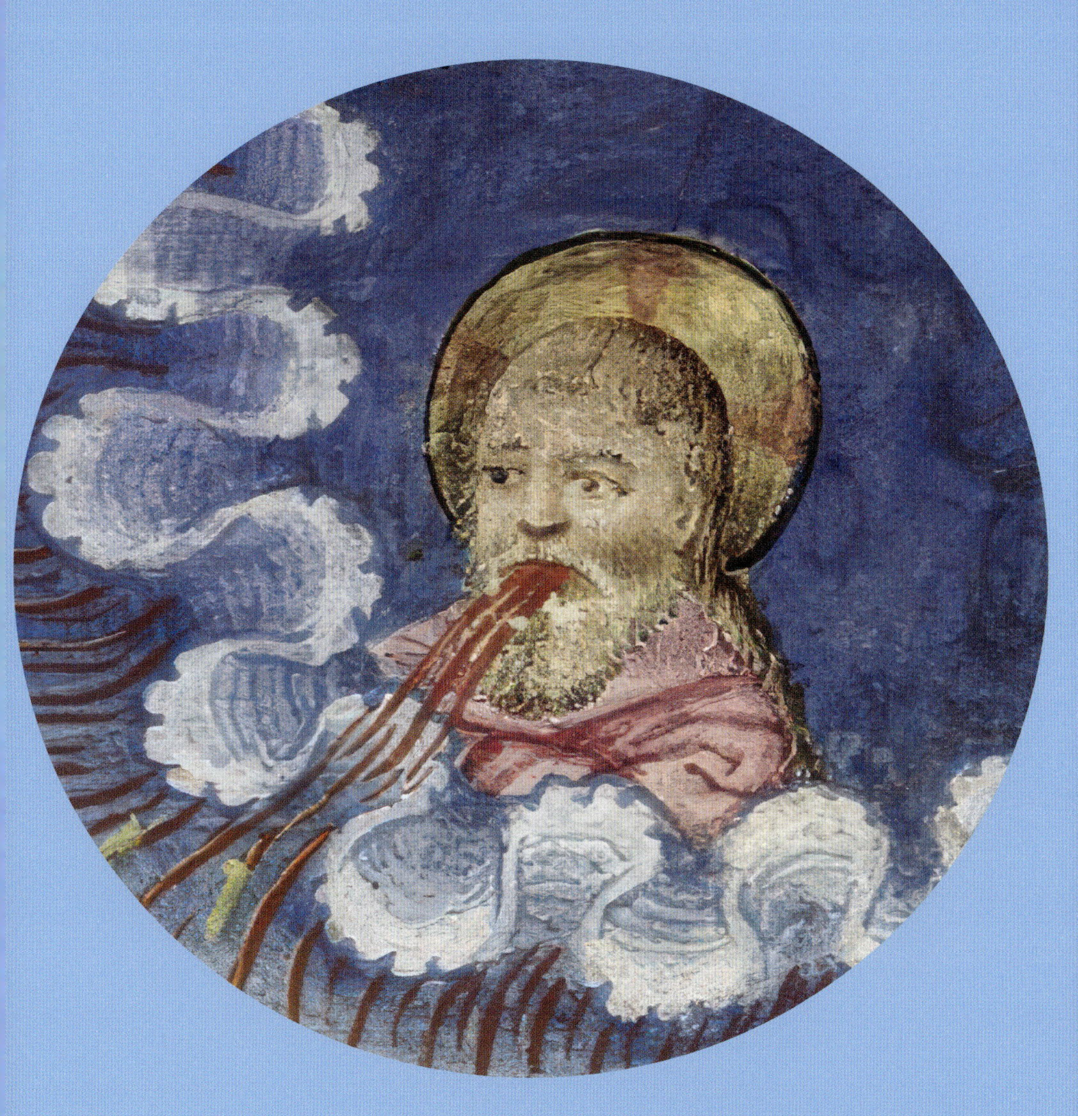

Well, well, well, if it isn't Mister Satan himself, complete with horns, spiky wings and a scorpion's tail. As usual, Satan is up to something. He's trying to ascend into the sky, carrying along a poor soul. He's clearly lost, since hell is supposed to be down below, nestled somewhere deep in the fiery depths of the earth. The sky is God's domain. Speaking of God, besides fire, he's also spitting out some weird green blobs. Are those . . . stomach juices?

No, the green blobs are pieces of sulfur or brimstone. In the Bible, fire and brimstone are the go-to ingredients for divine retribution. Consider them God's favorite tools for getting his point across. In this case, he's directing his wrath towards the Antichrist—the guy showing off his ballet moves. The Antichrist is a fake Jesus, orchestrated by Satan to deceive people into thinking he's the second coming.

One of the highlights of this risky performance is pretending to die and come back to life—you know, Jesus's signature move. So the melodramatic ballet dancing is in fact the Antichrist's way of feigning his own death. But his performance is so unconvincing that the Lord immediately sees through it. Just as Satan is theatrically lifting a "soul" up to the heavens, God saves the day with a breath of fire and brimstone, roasting Satan and his crowd of followers.

This bizarrely charming drawing is part of the *Book of the Vineyard (Livre de la Vigne)*, a medieval manuscript packed with Bible stories and the slightly insane illustrations that go with them. I highly recommend.

Unknown artist, Illustration from the *Livre de la Vigne* (fol. 36r), c. 1450–1470.

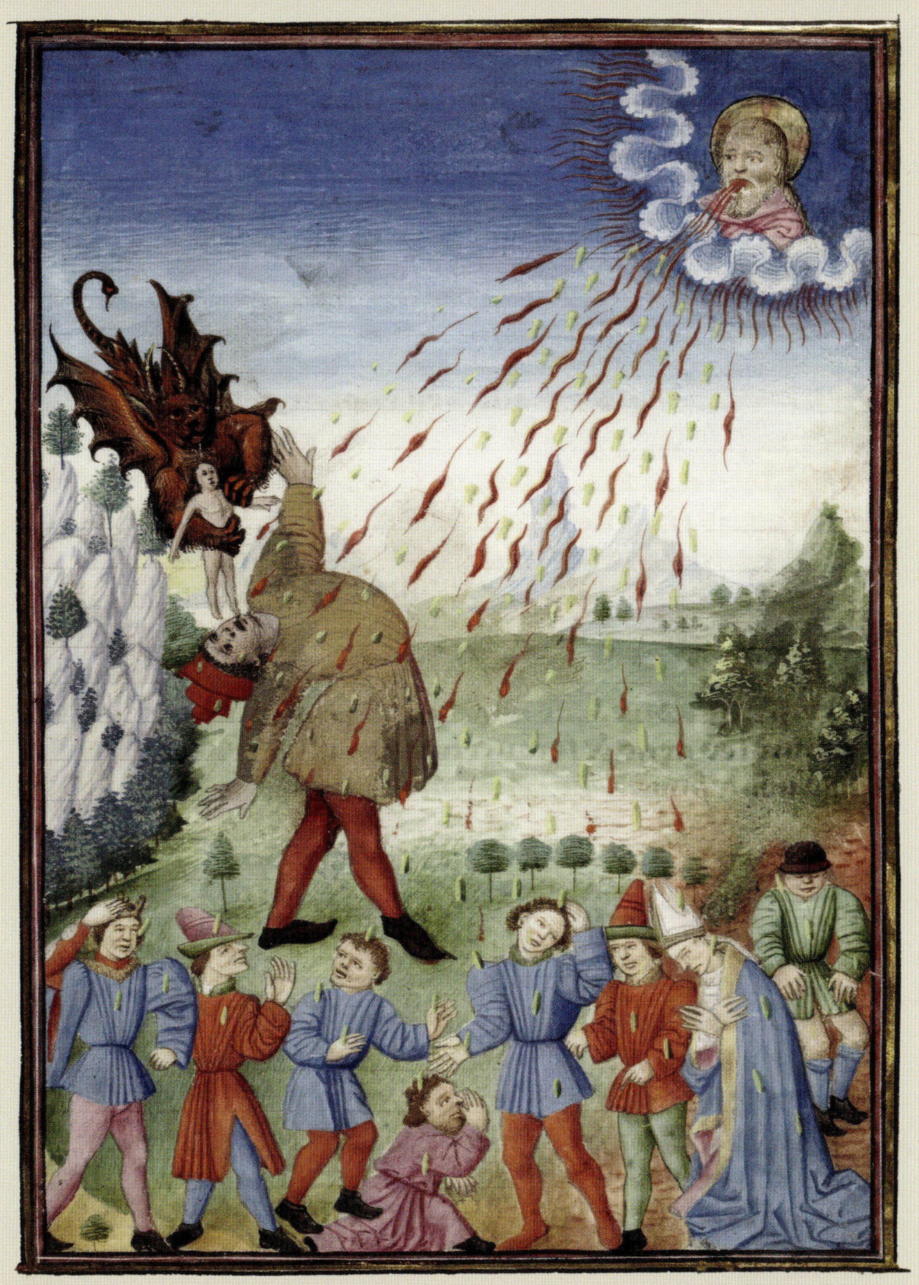

lip-locking and nipple-pinching

The Renaissance painter that came up with this bewildered face left no room for doubt: This person has issues. His face is contorted. He has wrinkles of pain around his eyes. He's clawing at his wavy black hair with long, bony fingers. And then there's that scream—which, besides seeming very loud, also reveals a complicated dental history. Let's see what all this desperation is about.

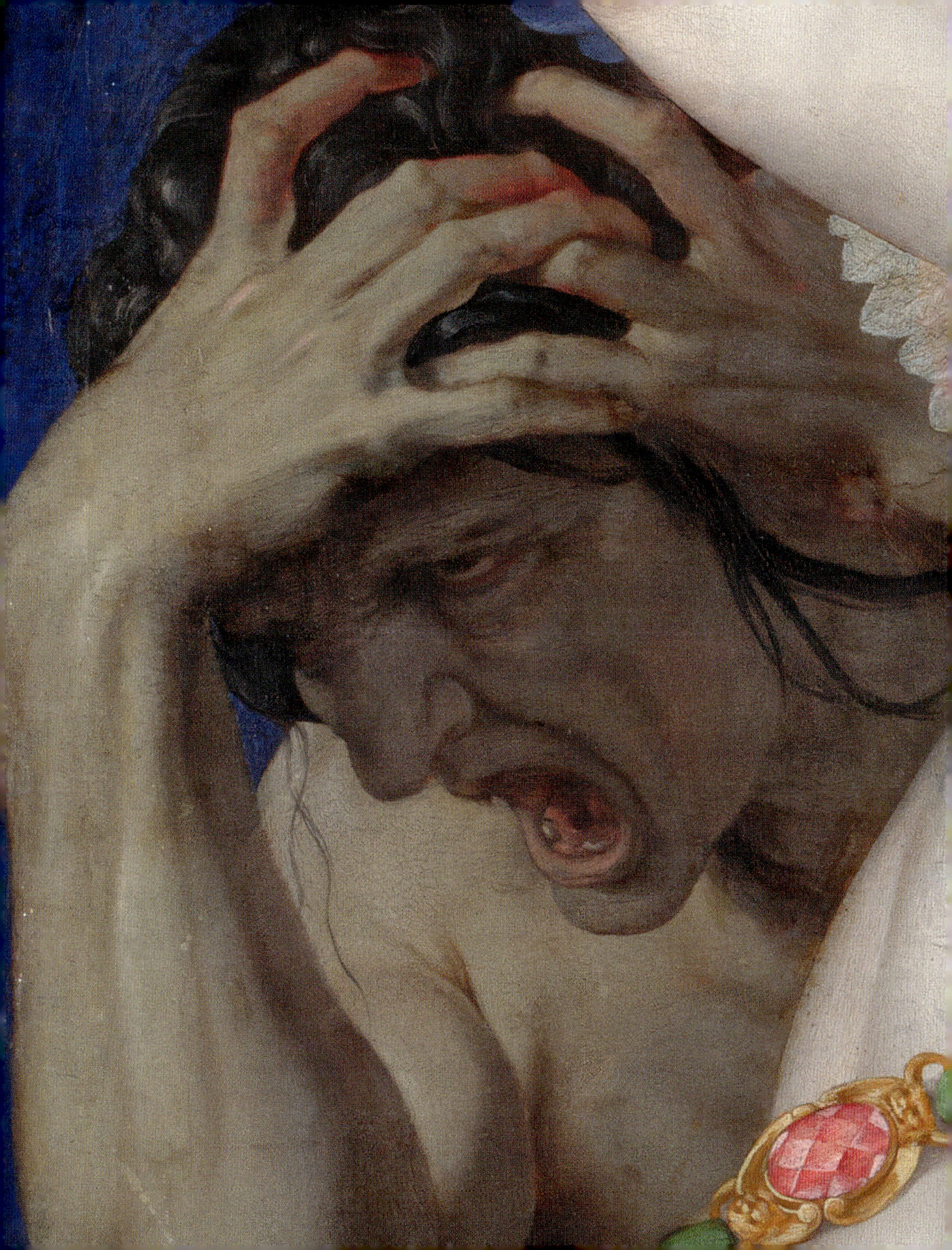

There's no dentist involved in this painting—the man's suffering is probably caused by the loving couple in front of him. Because love and pain go together like ice cream and headaches: If you go too hard, you might end up clawing your scalp. In that sense, our bewildered man might be suffering from a serious case of jealousy. He does look a bit greenish.

Meanwhile, the two lovers are lost in a rather enthusiastic embrace. There is nipple-squeezing, lip-locking and head-grabbing. The curly boy's colorful wings reveal that he's no ordinary kid—he's Cupid, the god of love. And his partner in this affectionate scene? Well, that's his mother, Venus. Mythology didn't shy away from complicated family dynamics.

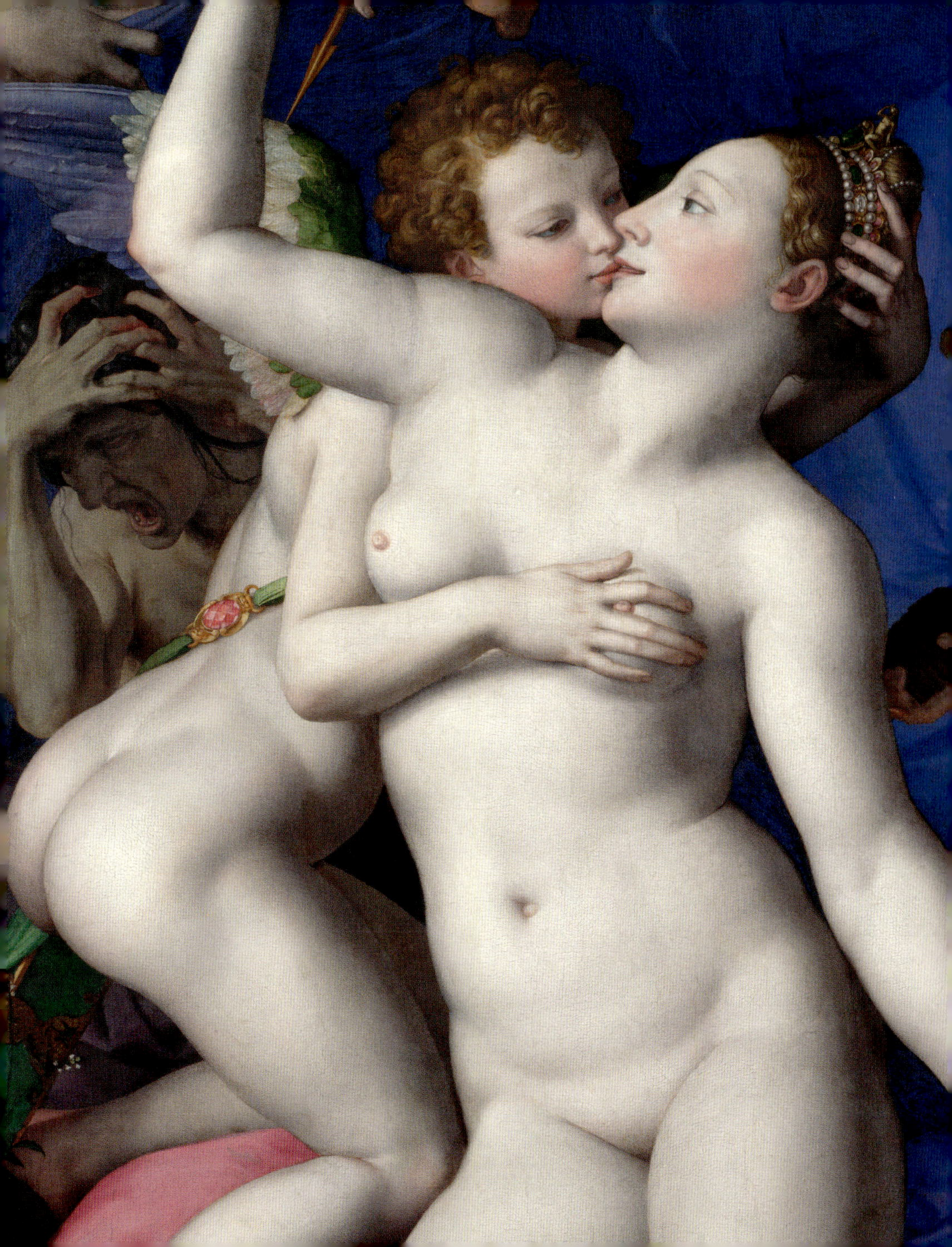

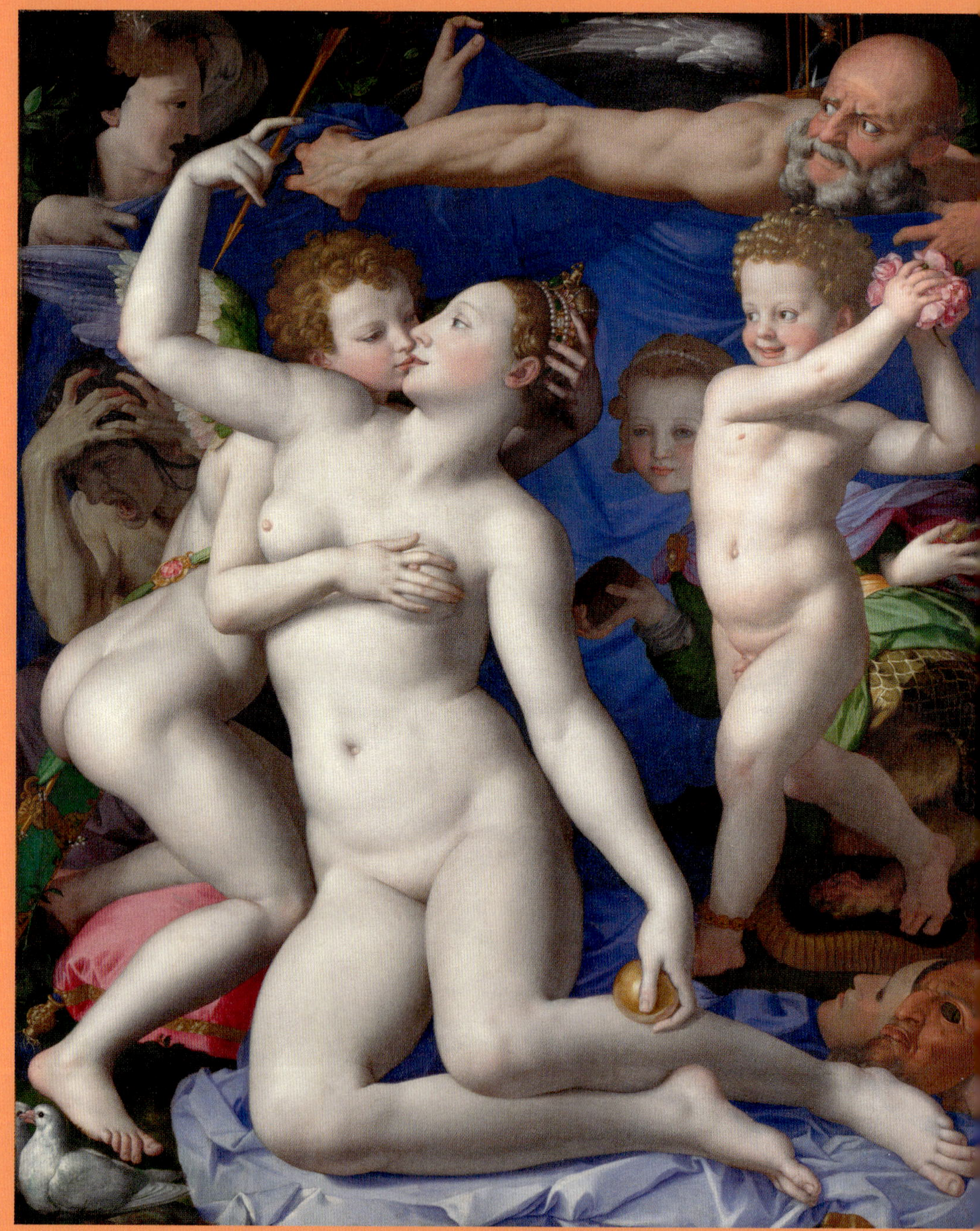

Zooming out, it's obvious that there's a lot to unpack, as we're suddenly dealing with a cast of seven strange creatures. Behind Cupid and Venus, a child stands ready to shower the incestuous couple with a handful of roses. He probably represents Folly, and his job in this painting is to highlight the lovers' poor judgment. He's all smiles and really seems to be enjoying his role.

But he has to be careful though, because behind him sits a girl who, despite her innocent face, is anything but. If you look closely, you'll notice that her hands are twisted and reversed, which is the least of our worries, because she also has a reptilian body with lion's feet and a long serpentine tail ending in a stinger. This girl is so weird that art historians can't agree on what she actually represents. Let's just say she's absolutely terrifying.

Bronzino, *An Allegory with Venus and Cupid*, c. 1545.

PS: Cupid's right foot is the famous foot featured in that other bizarre spectacle called *Monty Python's Flying Circus*.

In the top right corner, a bearded man with an hourglass on his back looks over this wild bunch of creatures. He might be Father Time, grasping a billowing blue sheet to either reveal or conceal the scene from another weirdo, sitting in the top left corner. This one has no eyes, only an empty mask for a face. He might represent Play or Oblivion, just like the two masks in the bottom right corner.

This painting is complicated, to say the least. But at its heart, the message is simple. Greek and Roman myths are filled with incestuous relationships like the one in this painting, and Bronzino has assembled an incredibly eccentric cast of creatures to emphatically say: Please don't.

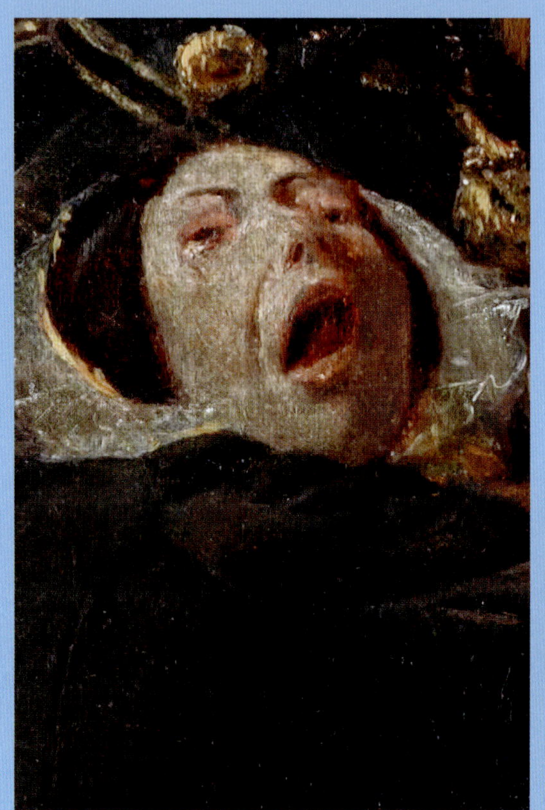

a party gone horribly wrong

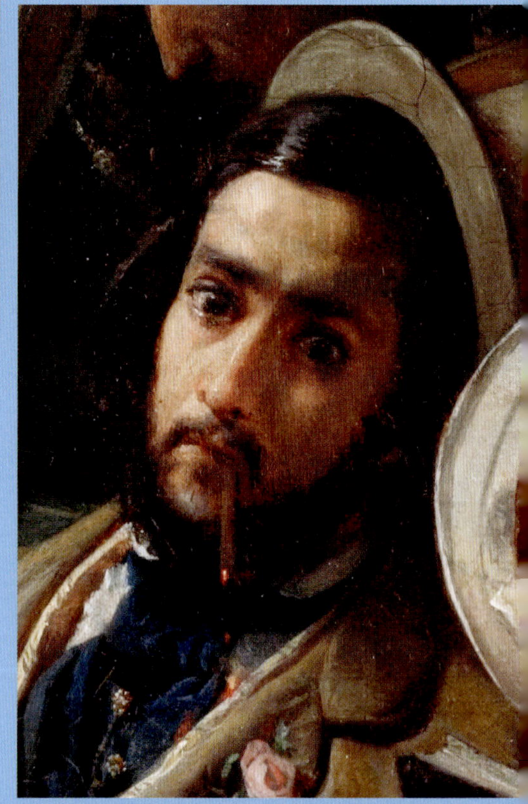

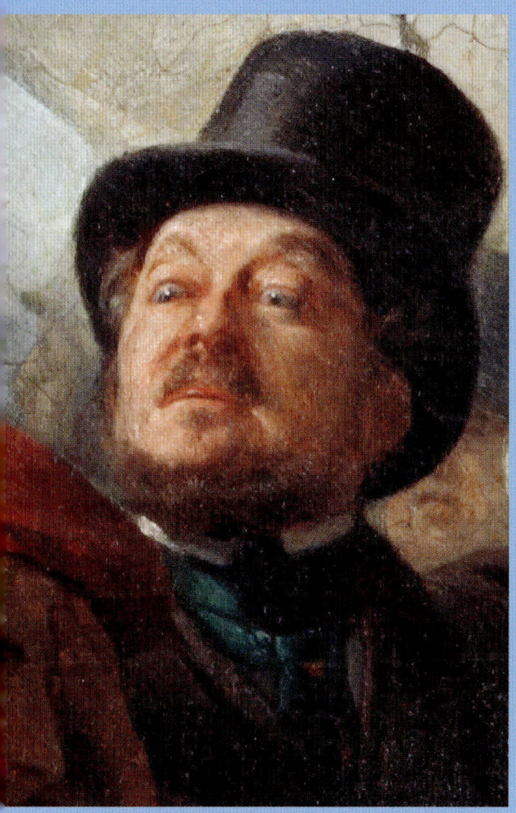

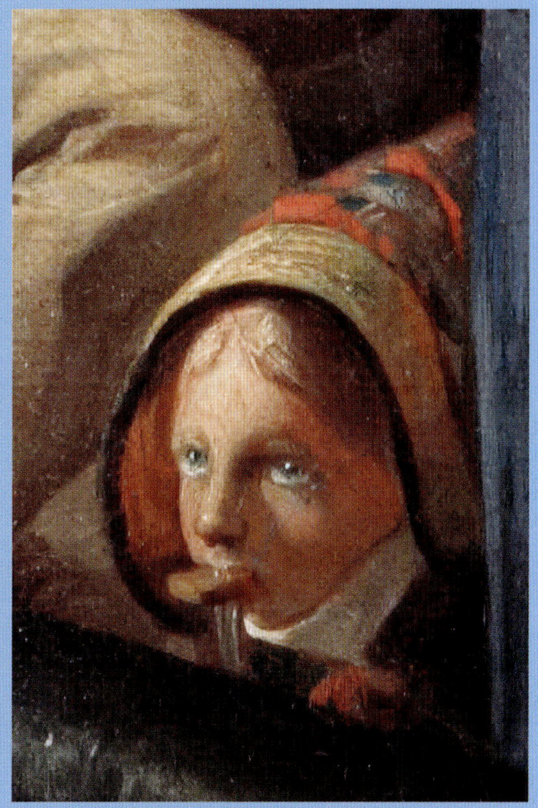

These four people are all trapped in the same horrible situation, which is captured in one incredible painting. The pale woman with the twisted mouth looks like she's just woken from her worst nightmare. Meanwhile, the gentleman next to her looks like he's about to start a fire, because those lips won't be clenching that cigar for much longer. Honestly, considering his glazed gaze, I'm not even sure if he's dead or alive. The guy with the fancy top hat, on the other hand, is very much alive, caught somewhere between surprise and horror. And finally, the kid with the sheepish eyes seems completely unfazed, casually nibbling a little snack while observing the chaos around her, which makes you wonder: What on earth is going on here?

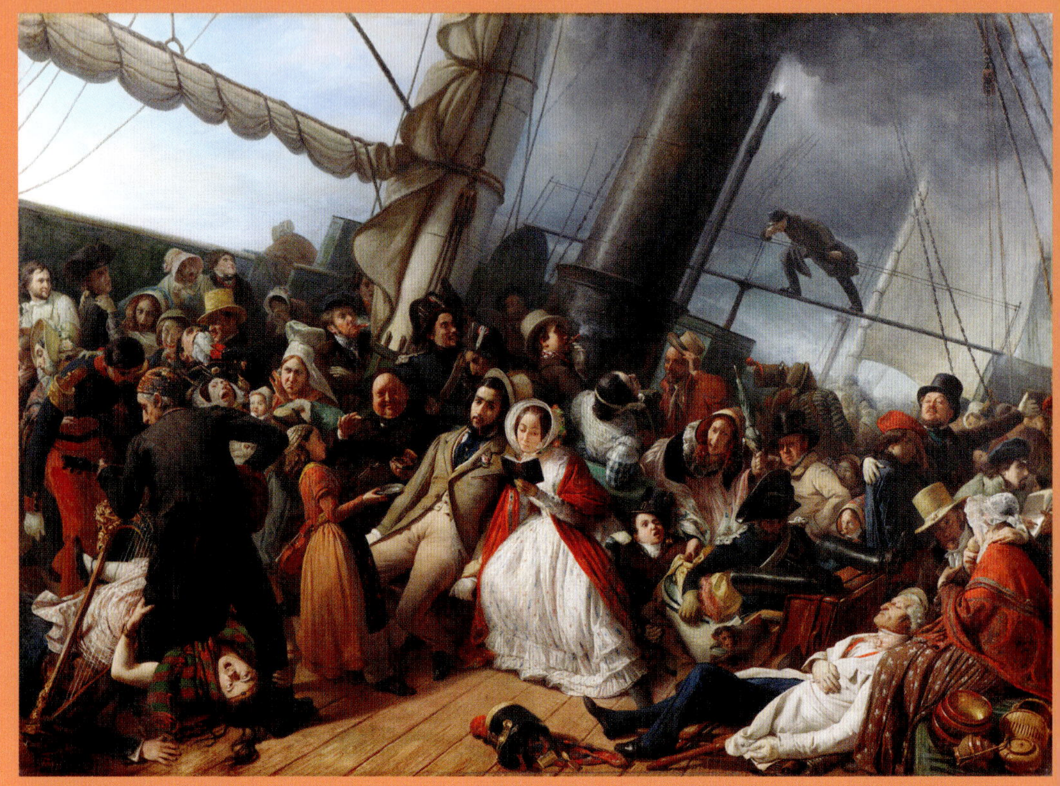

Now here's a true festival of stupid faces, and our cigar-clenching man seems to be the main act. The composition pulls our eyes straight to his distant gaze but also to the iron-stomached lady sitting next to him, probably his wife. She's holding his arm in support, all while being deeply engrossed in what must be an incredibly captivating book. If we could read her thoughts, they would probably say, "Jesus, darling, don't be such a whiner."

Seasickness at the Ball, on Board an English Corvette is a wonderful display of a 19th-century boat party gone horribly wrong. Just moments earlier, this beautiful crowd was probably having a great time, being all elegant and happily dancing to the tunes of a Romani band while

François-Auguste Biard, *Seasickness at the Ball, on Board an English Corvette*, c. 1860s.

crossing the Channel to England . . . until the weather turned, and hell broke loose. But as with any proper ship in distress, the band just keeps playing, or at least they try. The guitarist in the lower left corner is still plucking away, but the harpist has stumbled between his legs, gripping them for dear life. Meanwhile, the Romani girl standing next to them casually continues to ask for money.

Every person in this crowd is handling this highly uncomfortable situation in their own way. Some are screaming, others are eating and a few are just trying to keep their stomachs in check. The painter, François-Auguste Biard, had probably witnessed scenes like this firsthand. He was an experienced traveler who went on expeditions all around the world, and he loved to capture his adventures on canvas, never shying away from adding an extra pinch of drama. Or in this case, a thick layer of it. But hey, I'm not complaining. This painting is a gold mine of details. Just be careful though, because staring at it for too long might make you feel as sick as our friend with the cigar.

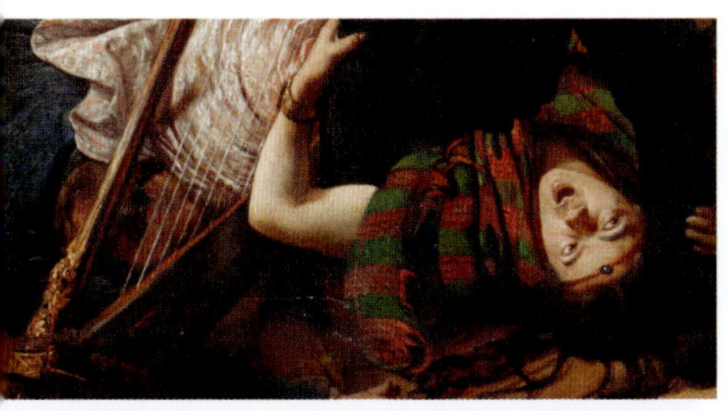

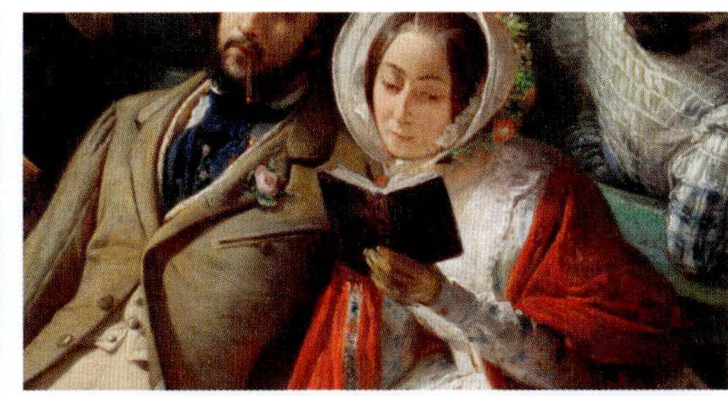

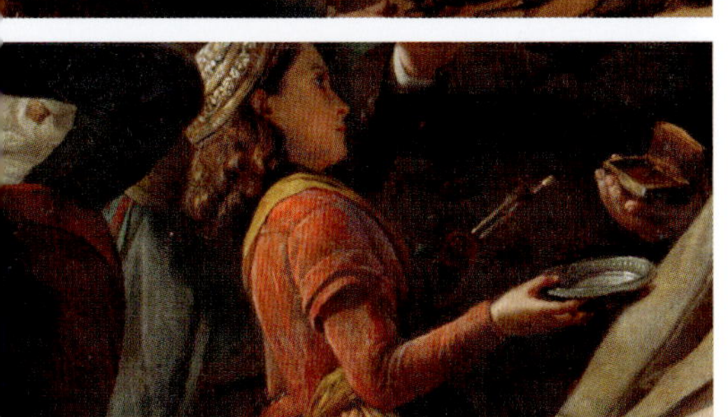

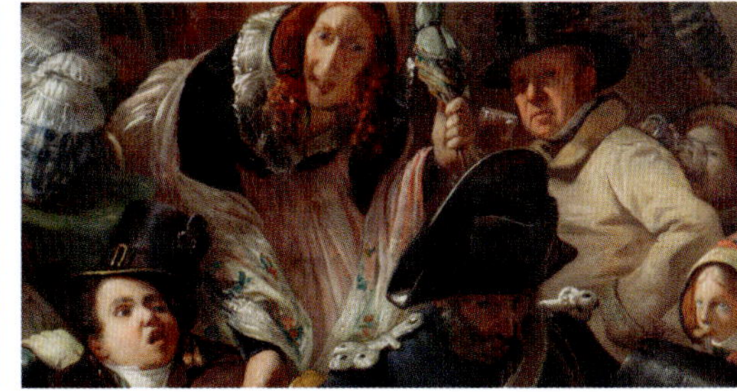

Romans, schmomans

Aah, the classic "stretch-your-cheeks-with-your-index-fingers" face—a classic among stupid faces. It's the go-to look for a five-year-old trying to annoy their little sibling. But this gentleman? Not exactly a toddler. His hair is thinning, his teeth are rotting, and he has the ears of an 80-year-old, making his childish gesture a bit creepy. He's even wearing armor, so he's probably some kind of soldier or knight. Hardly the kind of behavior you'd expect from an armed man on duty. Why is he acting like this? And who is the target of his mockery?

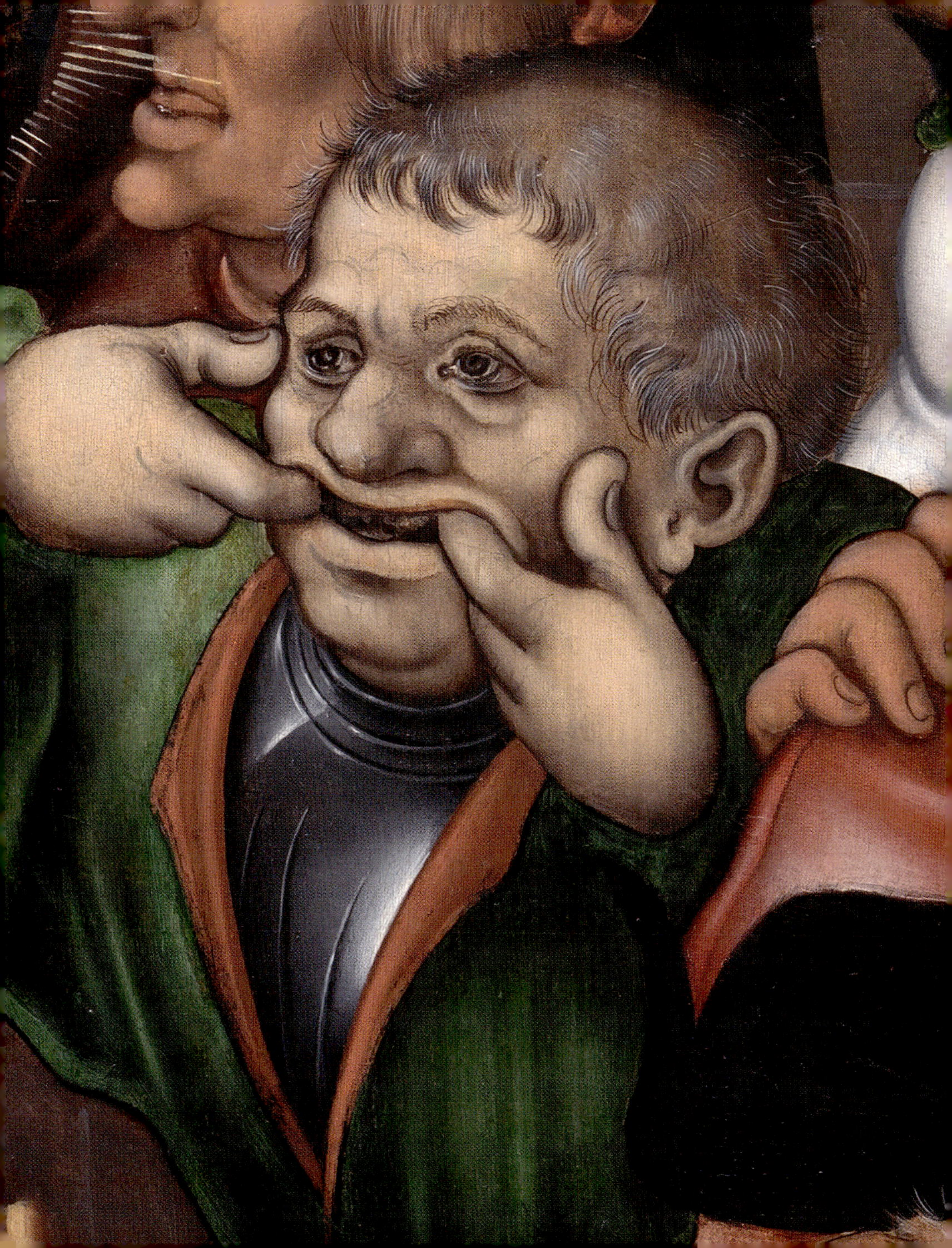

It's Jesus Christ, of course, and this time he's in bad shape. Jesus claimed to be the King of the Jews, a declaration that, as you probably know, didn't go down well with the authorities of the time. After being arrested and sentenced to crucifixion, Jesus endured waves of humiliation and suffering. As you can tell from this painting, Roman soldiers mockingly dressed him in a royal red robe. He gets pushed and prodded, and they're using a stick to force a crown of thorns deep into his scalp. His body shows bruises from whippings, and if all that isn't enough, they're also showing him an array of absurd faces. That'll teach "His Royal Highness."

But let's have a closer look at those weird faces, because they really stand out—not just for their silly expressions, but also because of how they're painted. These soldiers are caricatures, grotesque figures with swollen noses, exaggerated ears and big chunky hands. They border on the cartoonish but are still pretty horrific, if you ask me. Compared to his tormentors, Jesus's face looks much more delicate and naturalistic. His face isn't a caricature at all; it shows a suffering and defeated man with a sorrowful look in his eyes. He's surrounded by chaos, but remains heartbreakingly calm.

This stark contrast between Jesus and his tormentors wasn't an accident, but a deliberate choice by the artist. Because all those bizarre and ugly faces stand for the ugliness of human sin, and they clash wonderfully with the purity and grace of Christ's sorrowful gaze. So, as is often the case in art, we're looking at another good old battle between good and evil.

Master of the Pflock Altar, *Christ Crowned with Thorns*, c. 1520.

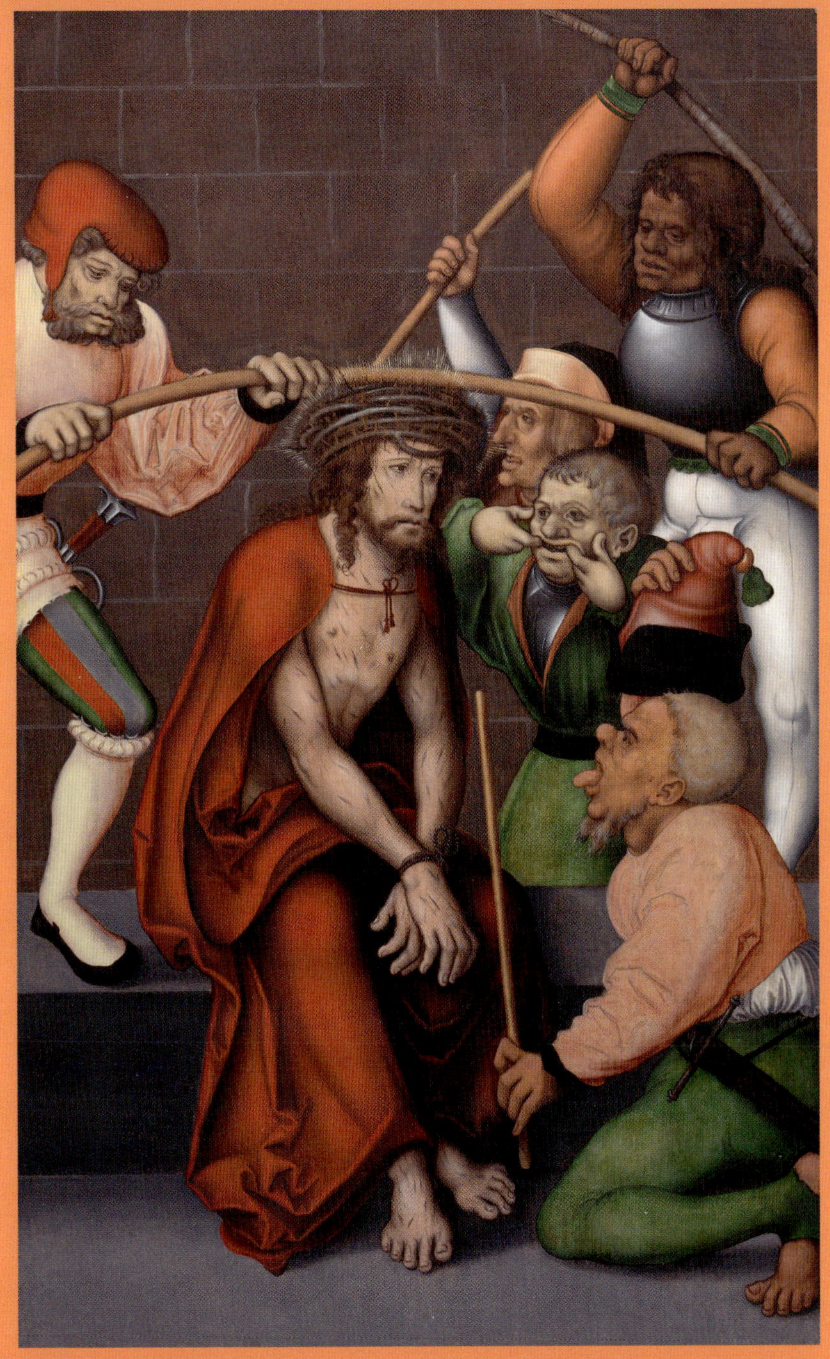

the postman from hell

Who needs drones to deliver your mail when you have a winged rat to do it for you? Judging by his expression and posture, this grotesque creature is clearly fed up with his job of delivering sealed documents. With his pointy claws, long, spindly arms and crooked, gaping mouth, he's as unnerving as they come.

This rat-like creature was created by the mysterious Dutch master Hieronymus Bosch. This man just loved mixing and matching different animals, creating monsters that represent the darker forces surrounding us . . . and within us. In this case, our little winged friend is a demon that probably represents temptation. Speaking of which, if someone waved this envelope in front of my face, I would be very tempted to break that seal and find out exactly what's inside—even if that person is in fact a rat-faced demon. Let's see who's at the receiving end of this mysterious piece of paper.

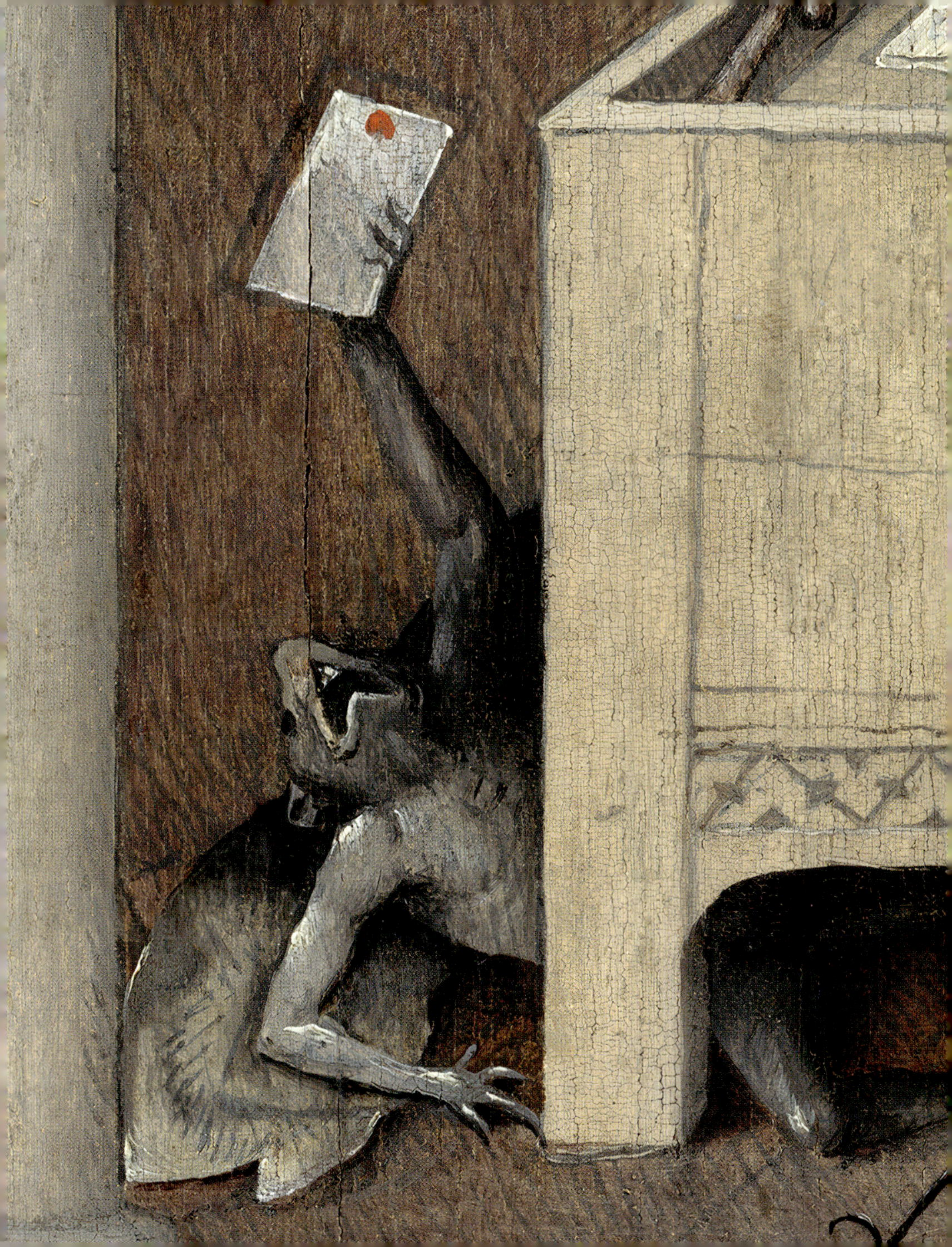

We can't exactly say what's inside the sealed envelope, but judging by this scene, it probably has something to do with money, because here we have our main character, tossing coins to another rat. This time, the creature sits comfortably in a chest, quietly feeding the old man's desires and gladly accepting his money. This little beast is all about greediness.

Which means our coin-throwing gentleman isn't just any old man, he's a man of greed. Despite his frailty, with a hunched back and leaning on his cane, his lust for gold remains strong. He certainly looks important, dressed in a green robe with a large key dangling from his waist (a symbol of authority)—perhaps even a religious authority. Because while he's throwing coins to the rat with one hand, he's also clutching his rosary with the other. This man is serving God and the devil at the same time. Something tells me this story isn't going to end well.

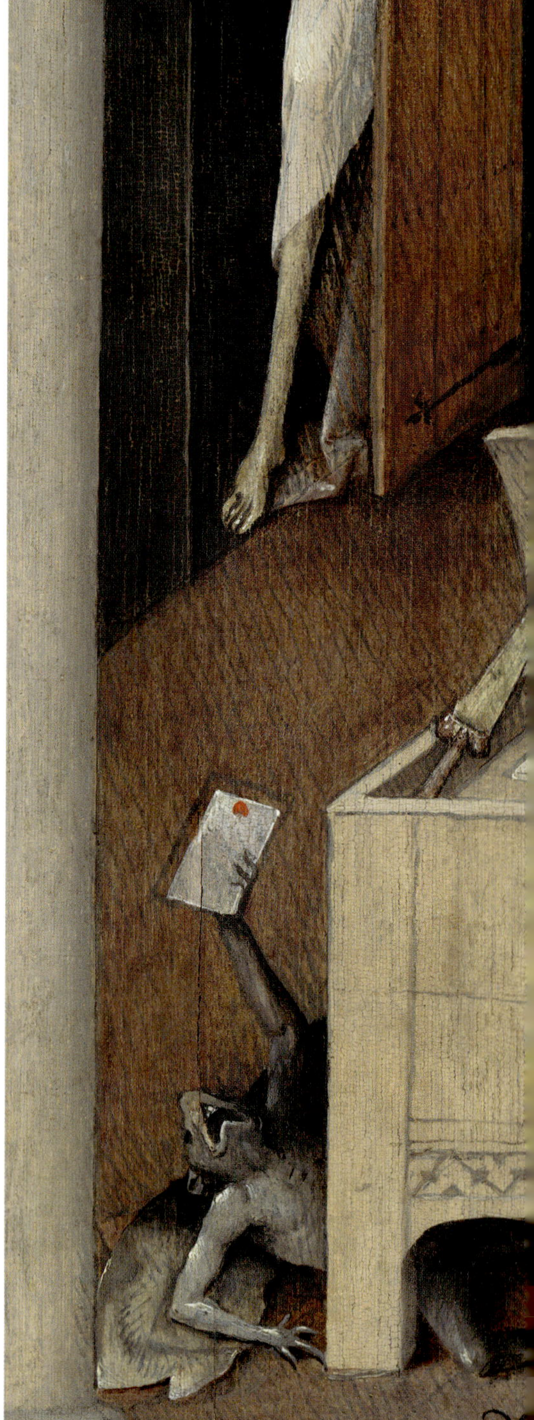

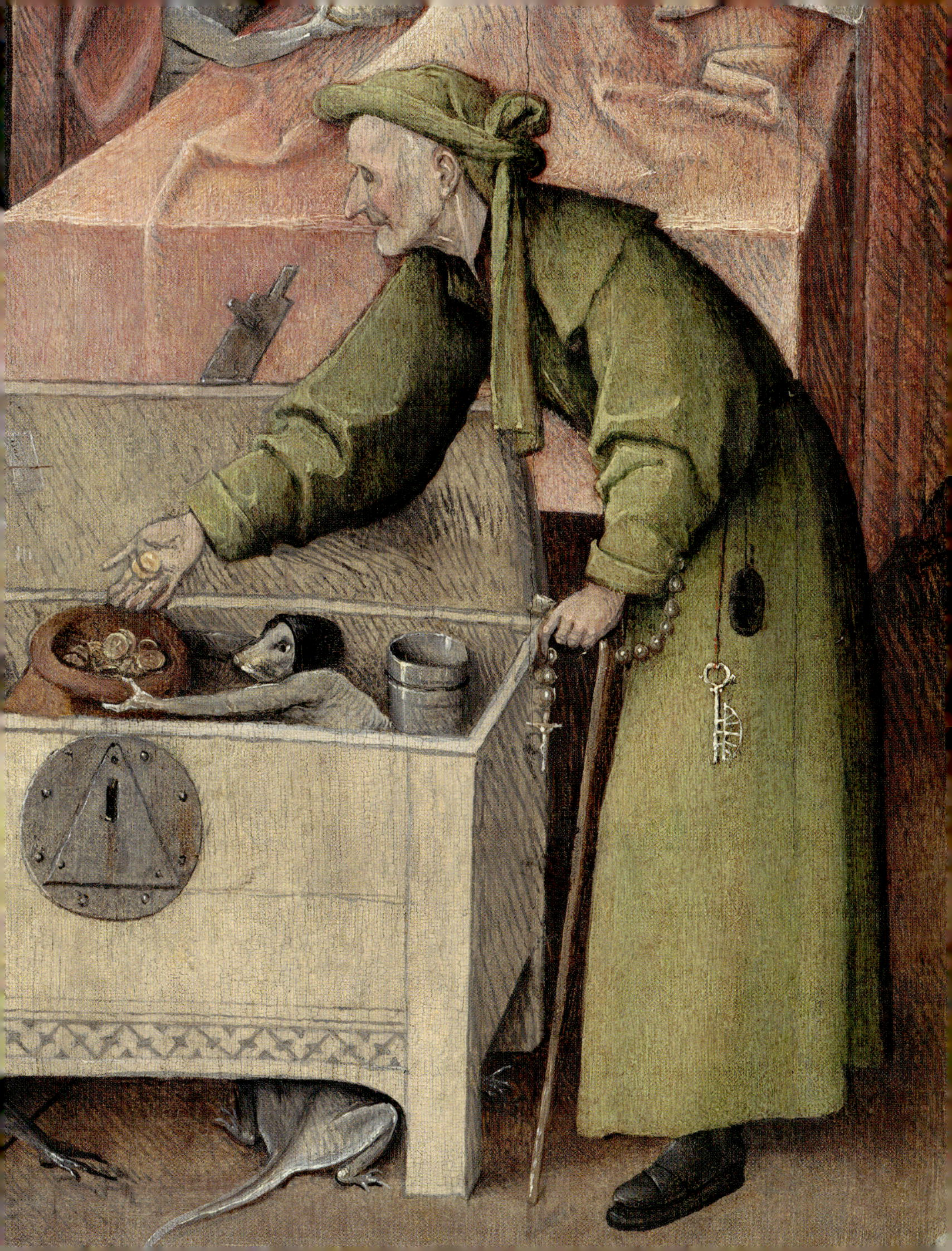

This is *Death and the Miser*, a painting that warns us about the consequences of living a life of greed. In the upper half of this haunting masterpiece, we see our main character much later in life. So late, in fact, that he's lying on his deathbed, facing a choice that will seal his fate forever. Death is literally knocking at his door, while a frightening little monster emerges from behind the curtains, offering him one last, tempting gift: a fat bag of cash. But there's also one single angel, desperately trying to convince the miser to give up his wealth and choose eternal salvation instead. It's a tough choice for a man of greed. With one hand, he reaches out for the money bag, while with the other he points weakly toward the glowing crucifix in the window. This painting is all about the *ars moriendi* or the "art of dying"—religious texts and illustrations intended to push Christians to choose Christ over cash, booze or other earthly delights.

Hieronymus Bosch, *Death and the Miser*, 1485–1490.

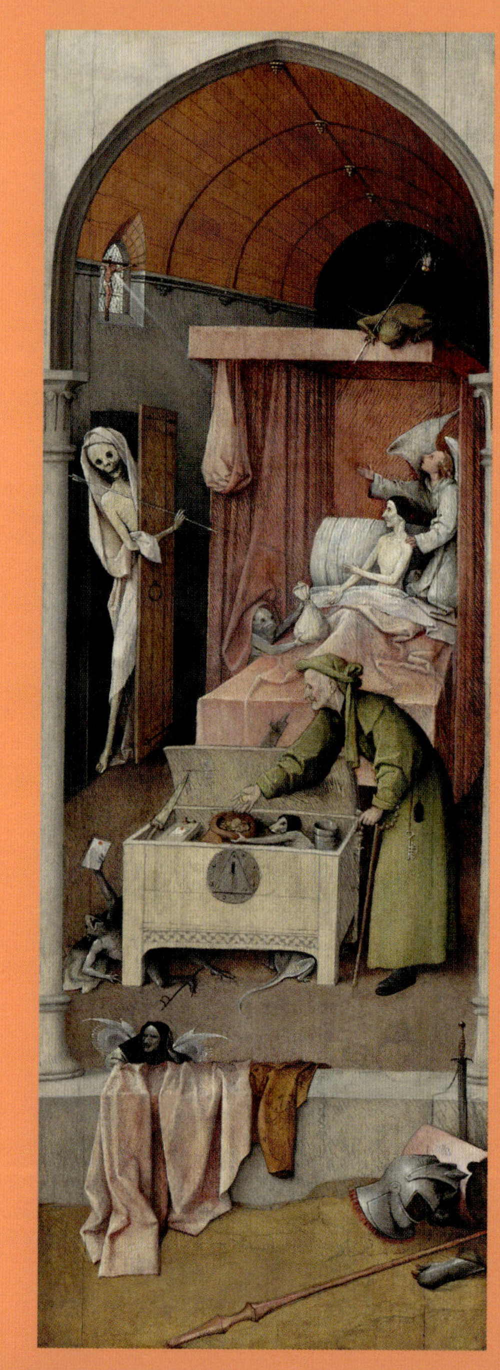

Indecisive to the very end, the dying man remains unsure of which path to choose. And that's where you come in, because you can decide how this story ends: with or without the bag of cash.

But beware, since after this man dies, there will be nothing he can buy or sell, because the only thing he'll be spending is eternity . . . in heaven . . . or hell.

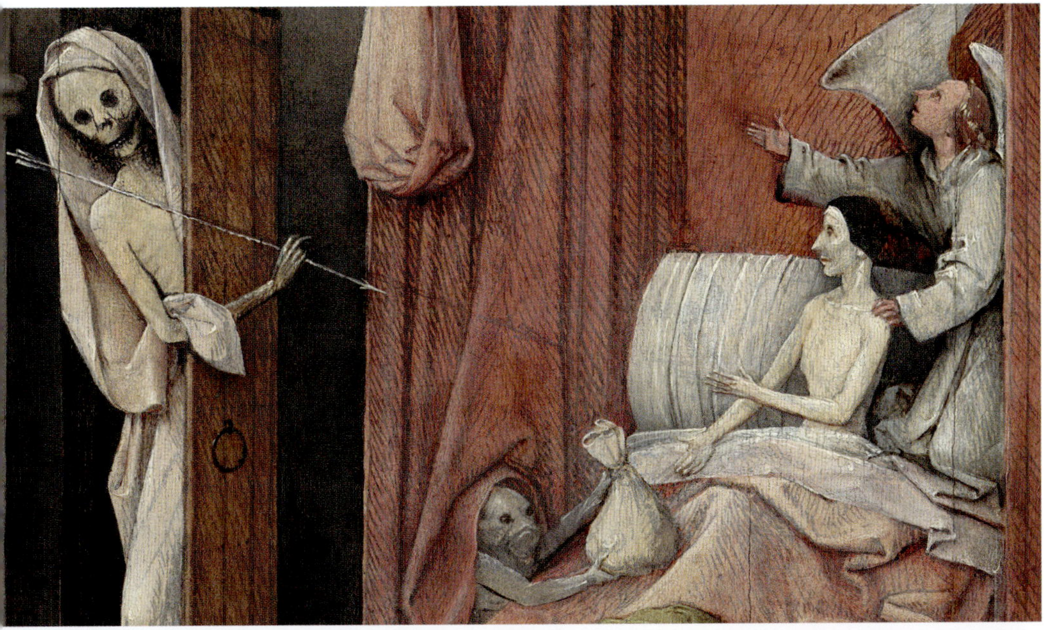

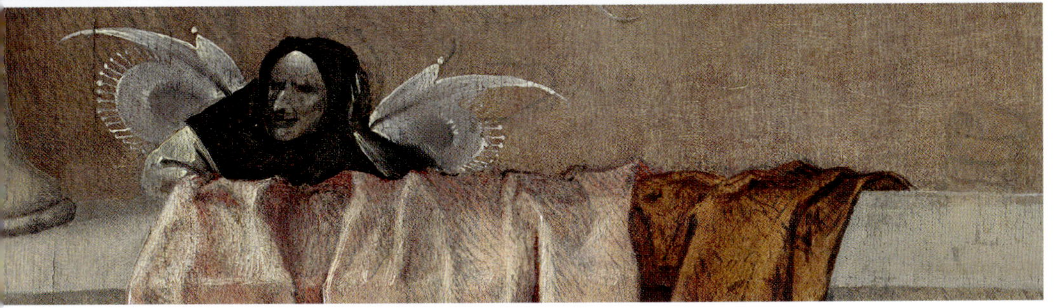

Japanese face carving

A twisted grimace. Eyes wide with terror. And a samurai sword slicing through a face like it's tofu. What you're looking at isn't a freeze-frame from a samurai horror film; it's part of a revenge fantasy. And as you may or may not know, revenge is best served cold and woodblock-printed.

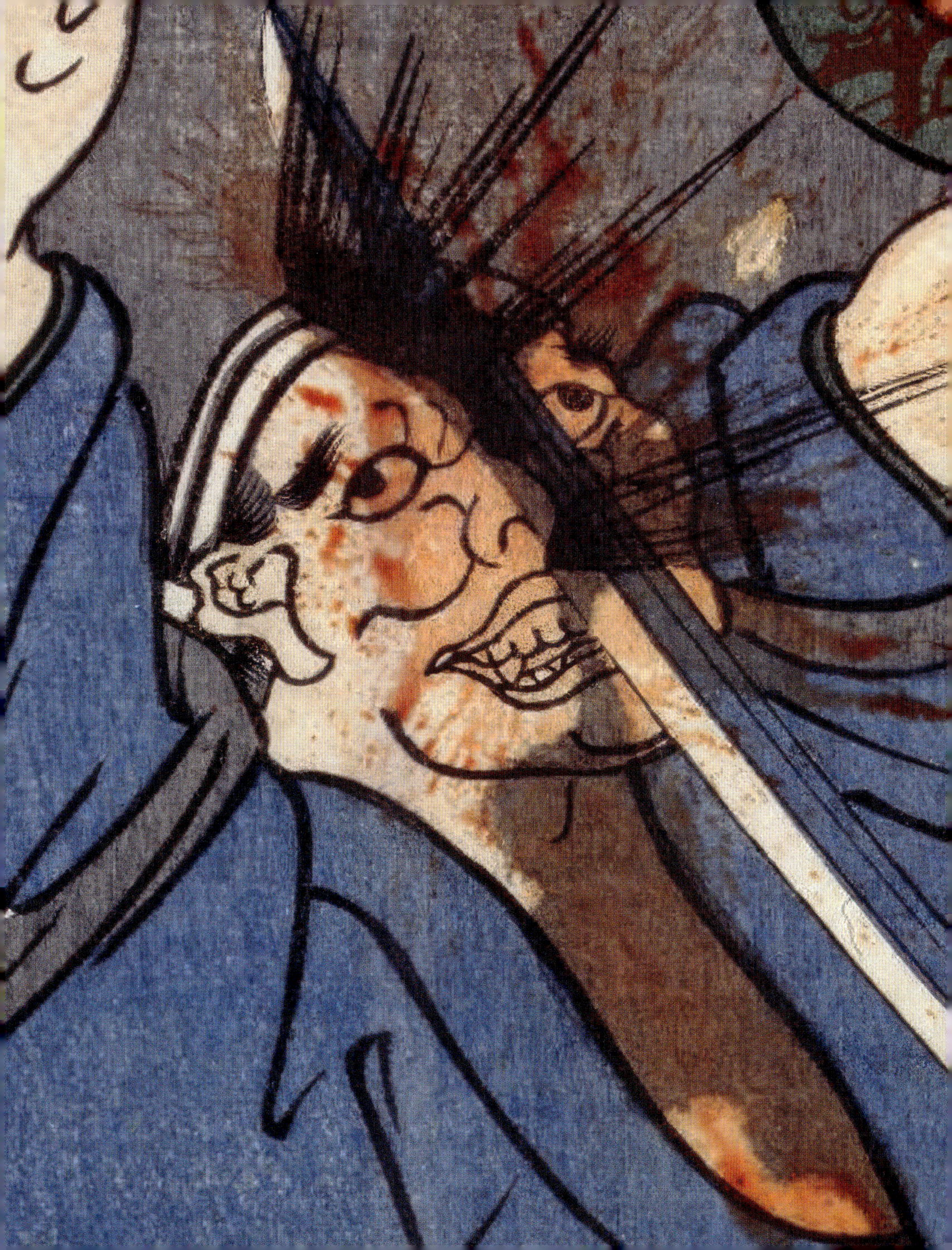

This is a print by Utagawa Kuniyoshi, a 19th-century Japanese artist who specialized in landscapes, battle scenes and evenly split faces. But he didn't create this artwork alone. Woodblock prints are team efforts: Kuniyoshi would design the image, and then highly skilled carvers and printers would translate it into blocks of wood, one for each color. So yes, someone's actual job was to carve that perfect geyser of blood. Lovingly. Painstakingly. By hand.

Utagawa Kuniyoshi, *Yatô Yomoshichi Norikane* from *Mirror of the True Loyalty of the Faithful Retainers*, 1857.

The warrior carving the face is Yatô Yomoshichi Norikane, one of the famous 47 ronin. They were a real group of samurai who avenged their lord's death with a meticulously planned assault on the residence of Kira Yoshinaka, the man they held responsible. The fighters spared women, children and innocent bystanders, but slaughtered everyone else who got in their way. One face at a time.

The ronin became instant legends, symbols of loyalty and honor, immortalized in countless artworks. This particular print is part of a series that turned each one into a heroic action figure, complete with a dramatic pose and designated syllable. Yatô was assigned the character み (*mi*), which—coincidentally—is the sound you might make when a samurai splits your face.

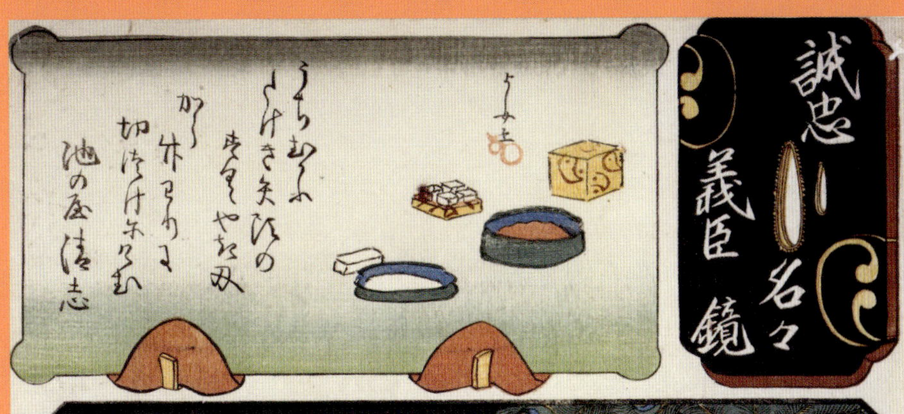
誠忠義臣名々鏡

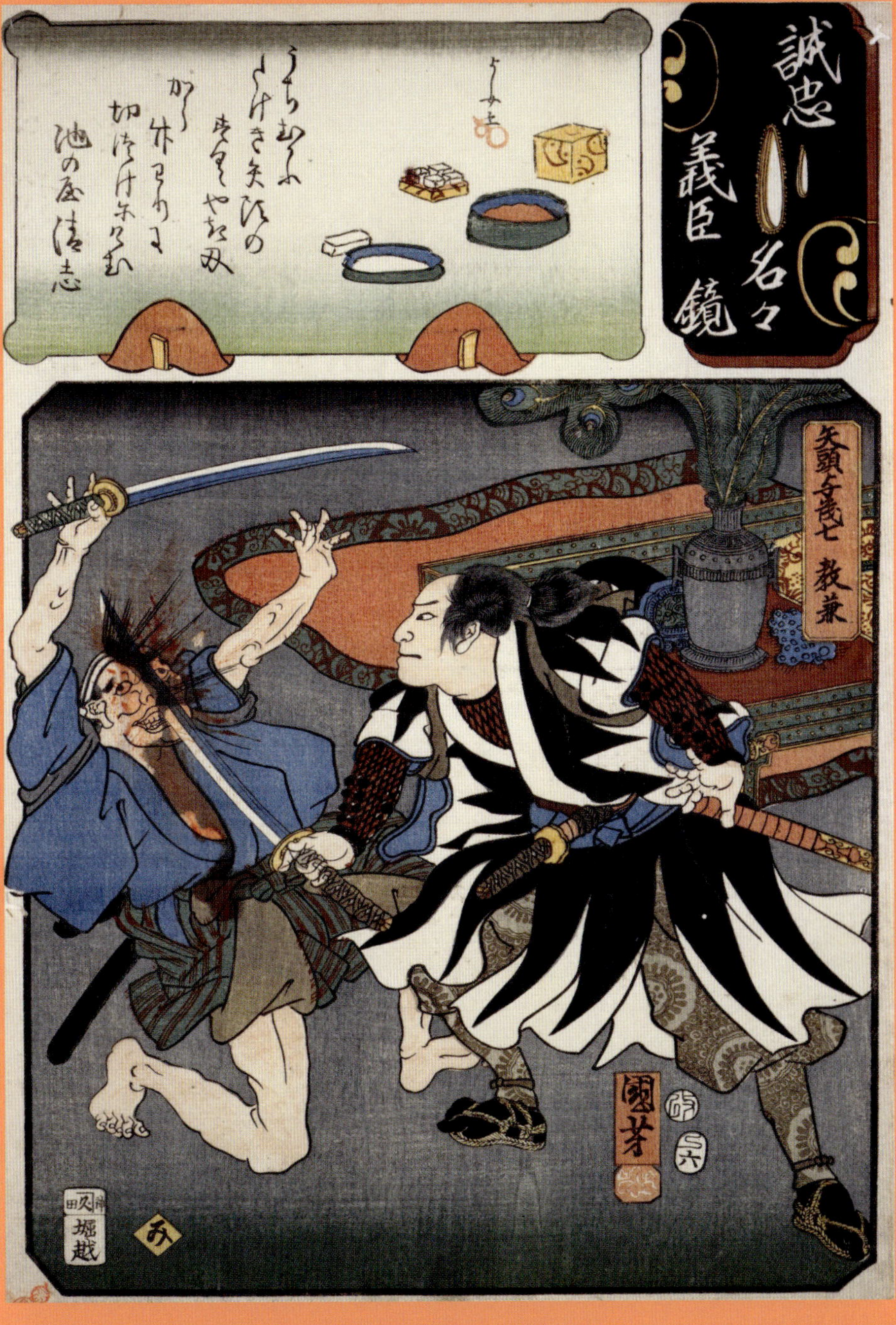

the furry phenomenon

These eyes are calm and steady, which is impressive, considering they're surrounded by a thick jungle of fur. This looks like a case of facial hair gone terribly wrong, but the owner doesn't seem bothered, staring at us as if to say, "What are you looking at?" Or as the great Star Wars hero Chewbacca once famously said: "GROOORR!"

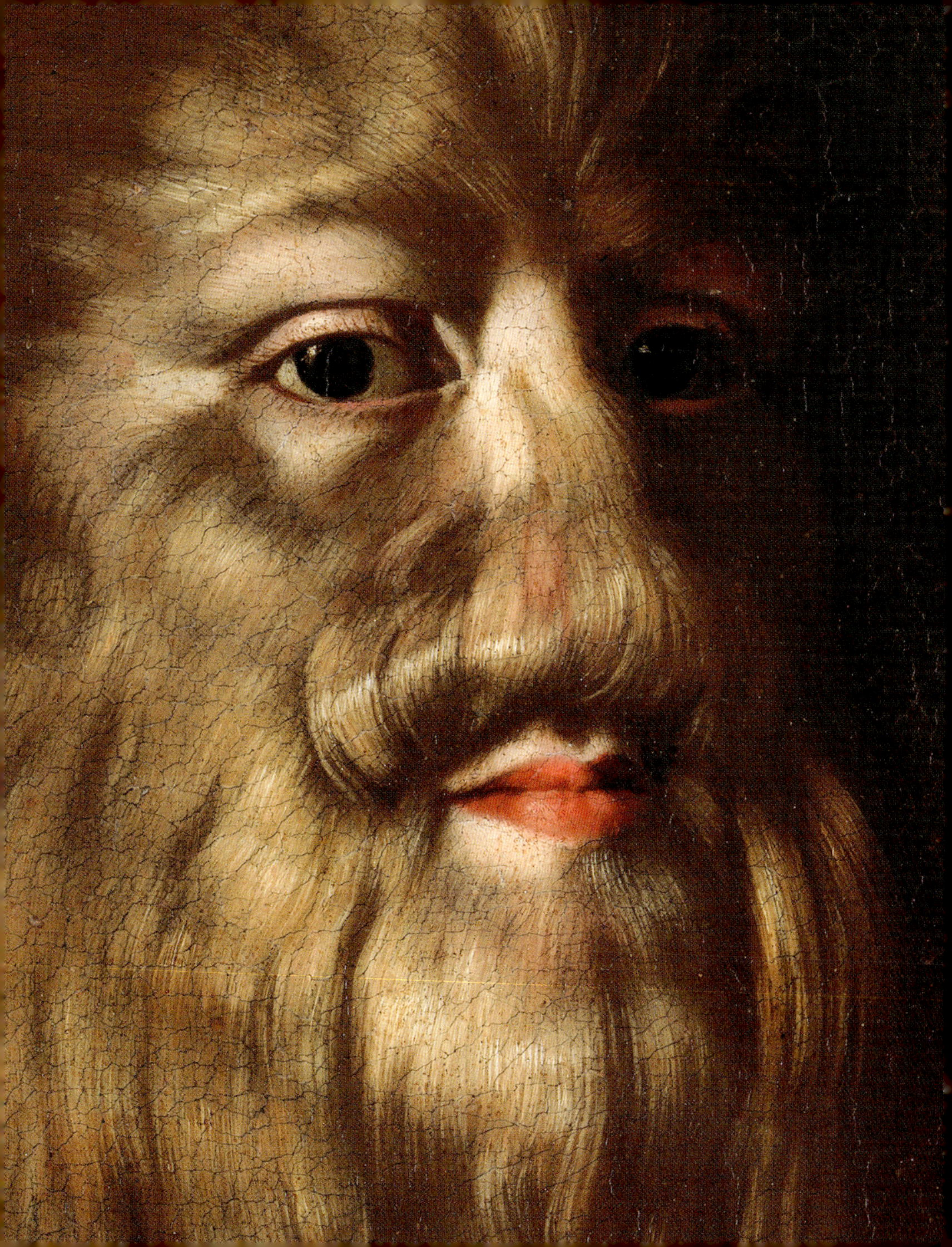

You probably didn't expect this, but our hairy protagonist is, in fact, a woman. It's none other than 17th-century German celebrity Barbara van Beck, to be precise. And she wasn't just any woman. Despite her rather unique condition, she had zero shame. No, Barbara knew exactly how to handle it—because she was a businesswoman.

Van Beck turned her furry appearance into a career, traveling across Europe, appearing in freak shows and dazzling crowds with her luxurious pelt and . . . her harpsichord skills. That's right. Barbara was part virtuoso, part furry phenomenon and full-time icon.

Unknown artist, *Portrait of Barbara van Beck*, c. 1650.

Her condition is called hypertrichosis, from the Greek words *hyper* (excess), *trikhos* (hair), and *-osis* (formation). It's also known by the slightly more dramatic and easier to remember name: Werewolf Syndrome. The condition looks wild but is otherwise harmless. And, apparently, also incredibly fascinating. Throughout history, there have been numerous cases of people with hypertrichosis, and many of them found their way into show business. Because let's face it—humans love the extraordinary. A fact that Barbara (and many others with hypertrichosis) fully embraced. After all, when life gives you fur, you might as well make it look fabulous.

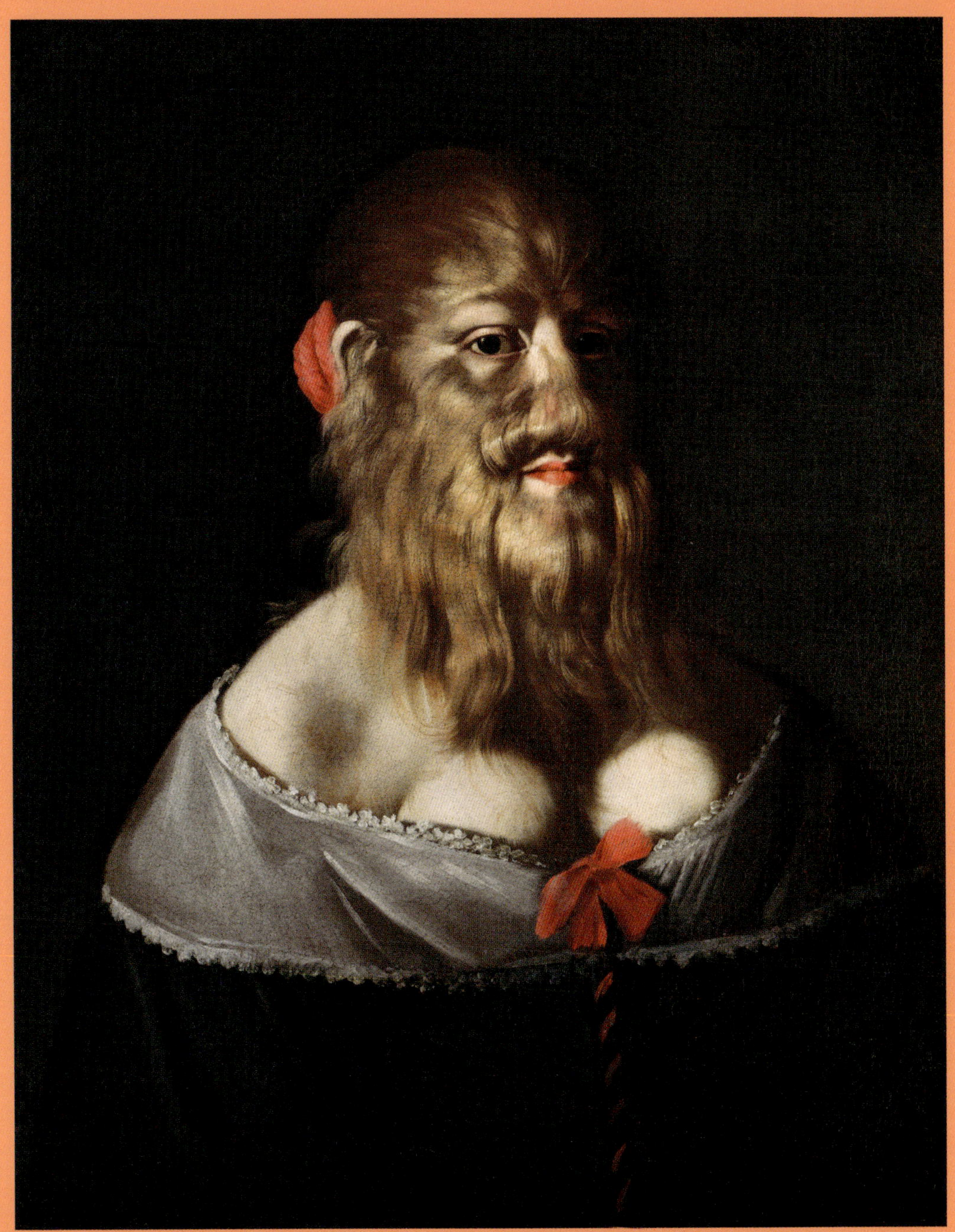

heads will roll

This poor man is undergoing his decapitation with what seems to be a fair amount of indifference—his expression neutral, his empty gaze drifting off into the distance. But this isn't indifference; it's the face of total surprise. This man didn't even get a chance to be afraid, as he was attacked in his sleep. I have to say, he does look a bit like Jesus, but as you probably know, Jesus died from crucifixion, not decapitation. More on that later in this book.

But anyway, this man isn't Jesus. He won't rise from the dead. Not just because he'll soon be lacking a head to properly do so, but mainly because he's a mere mortal. His name is Holofernes, an Assyrian general who picked the wrong fight with a determined Jewish lady named Judith. Let's see how Judith managed to pin down this awful man.

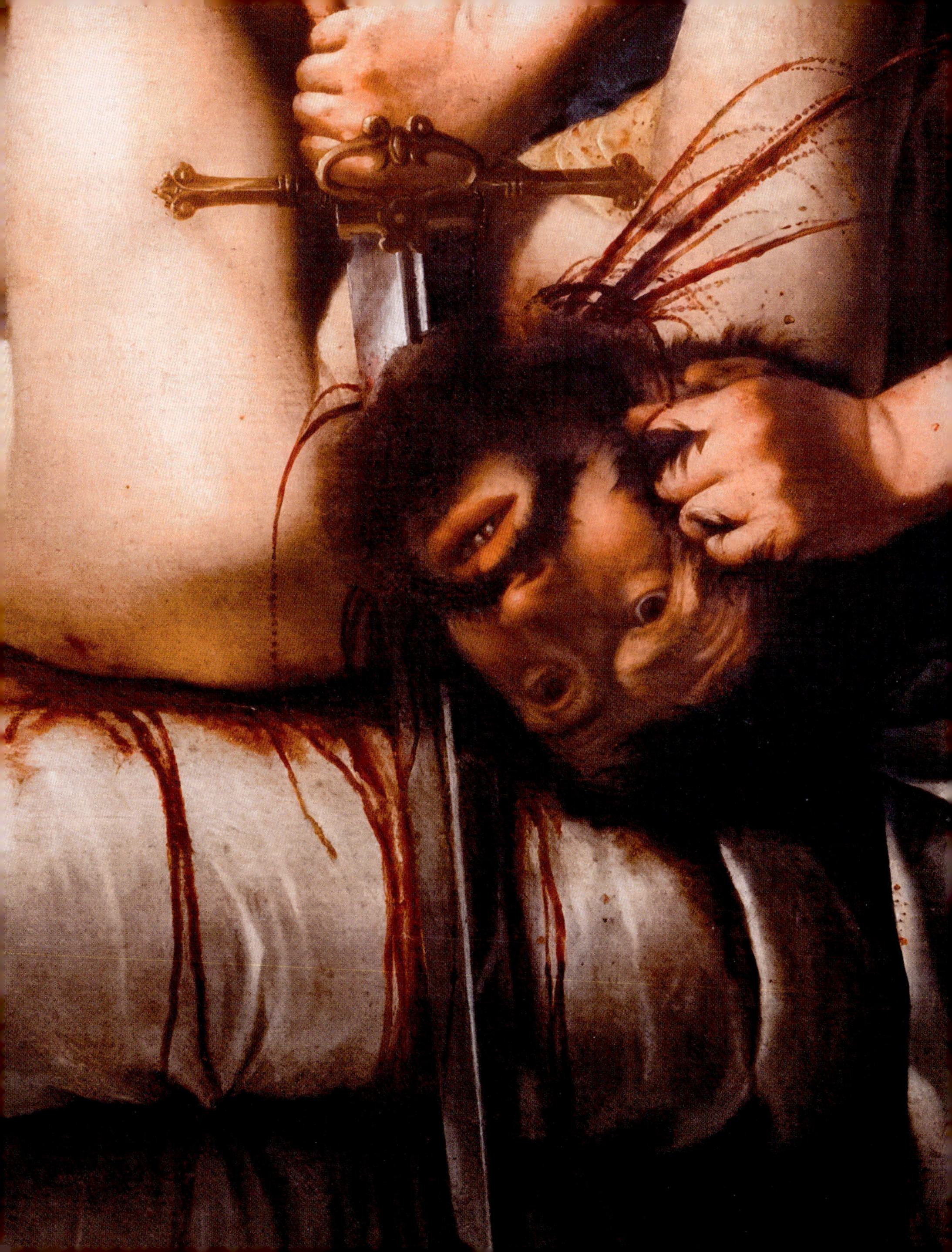

The full picture reveals that, despite his empty gaze, Holofernes is still putting up a fight. But he's losing, not only because Judith gets help from her loyal maid, Abra, but also because Holofernes is incredibly drunk.

The thing is, Judith has every reason to be furious with Holofernes. His army had besieged her hometown, Bethulia, leaving the Israelites in despair. Devout and determined as she is, Judith plans her revenge and devises a cunning plan. She visits Holofernes and seduces him, but before he can respond to her charms, he falls asleep, drunk with wine. And that's when Judith seizes her moment, planting a sword in his neck. Together, she and Abra finish the job and voilà: the head of the Assyrian army is now literally theirs.

It's no wonder that Artemisia Gentileschi chose this particular scene. She wasn't just a brilliant painter who defied the male-dominated Renaissance art world, she also triumphed over trauma. Because even though Holofernes might look like Jesus, art historians believe his face actually resembles that of Agostino Tassi, the artist who raped Artemisia in 1611. And what better way to avenge your rapist than by artistically beheading him, becoming an inspiration for female empowerment in the process. Bravissima, Artemisia.

Artemisia Gentileschi, *Judith Slaying Holofernes*, c. 1620.

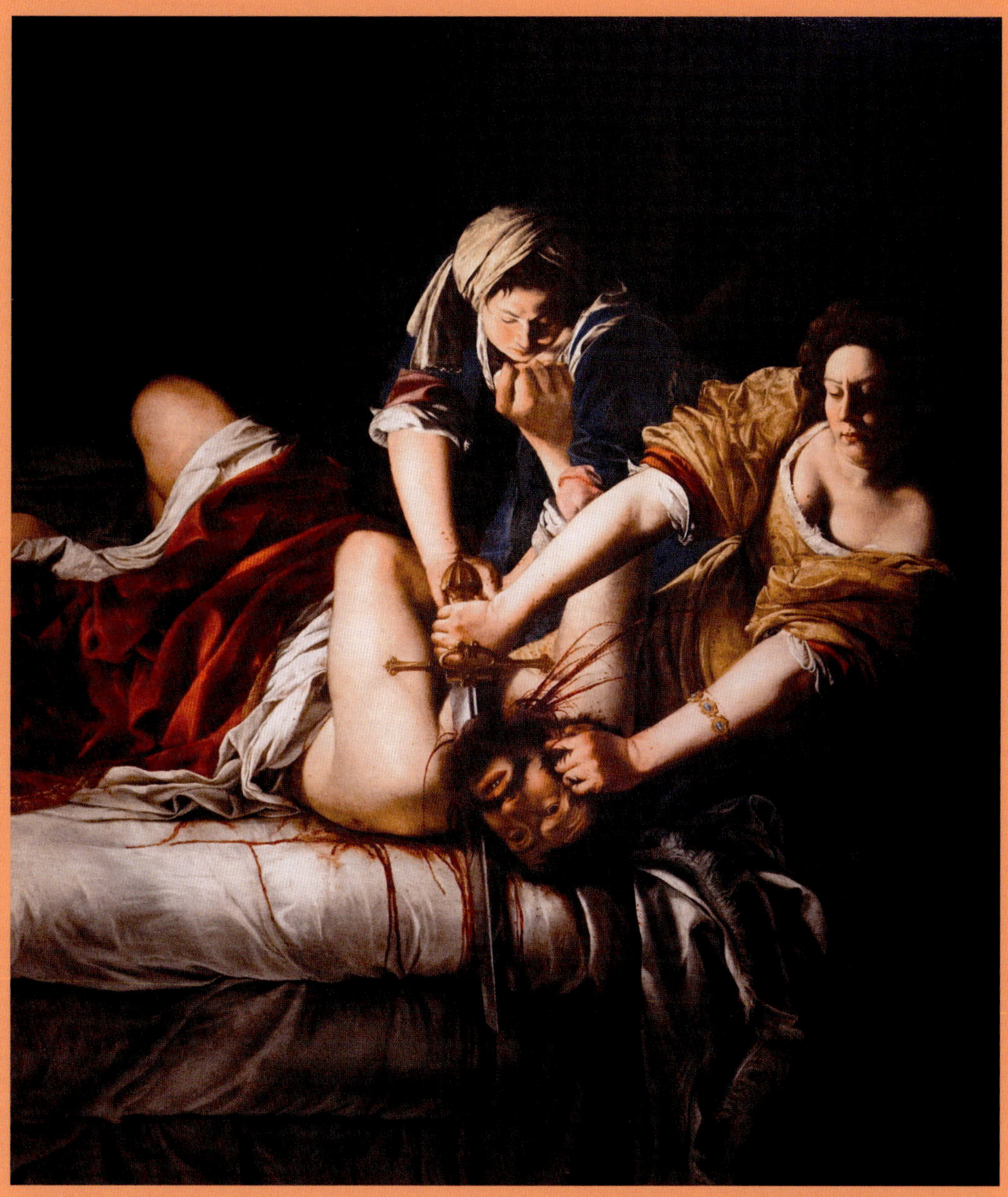

the hair makes the man

This is the bewildered face of someone who has just stumbled into a wild Bible story. His mouth is almost as wide as his mustache, and his bulging eyes are working hard to process the escalating chaos around him. And let's not forget the feathered hat—considering the sword, it's probably military. Which begs the question: What kind of war is going on here?

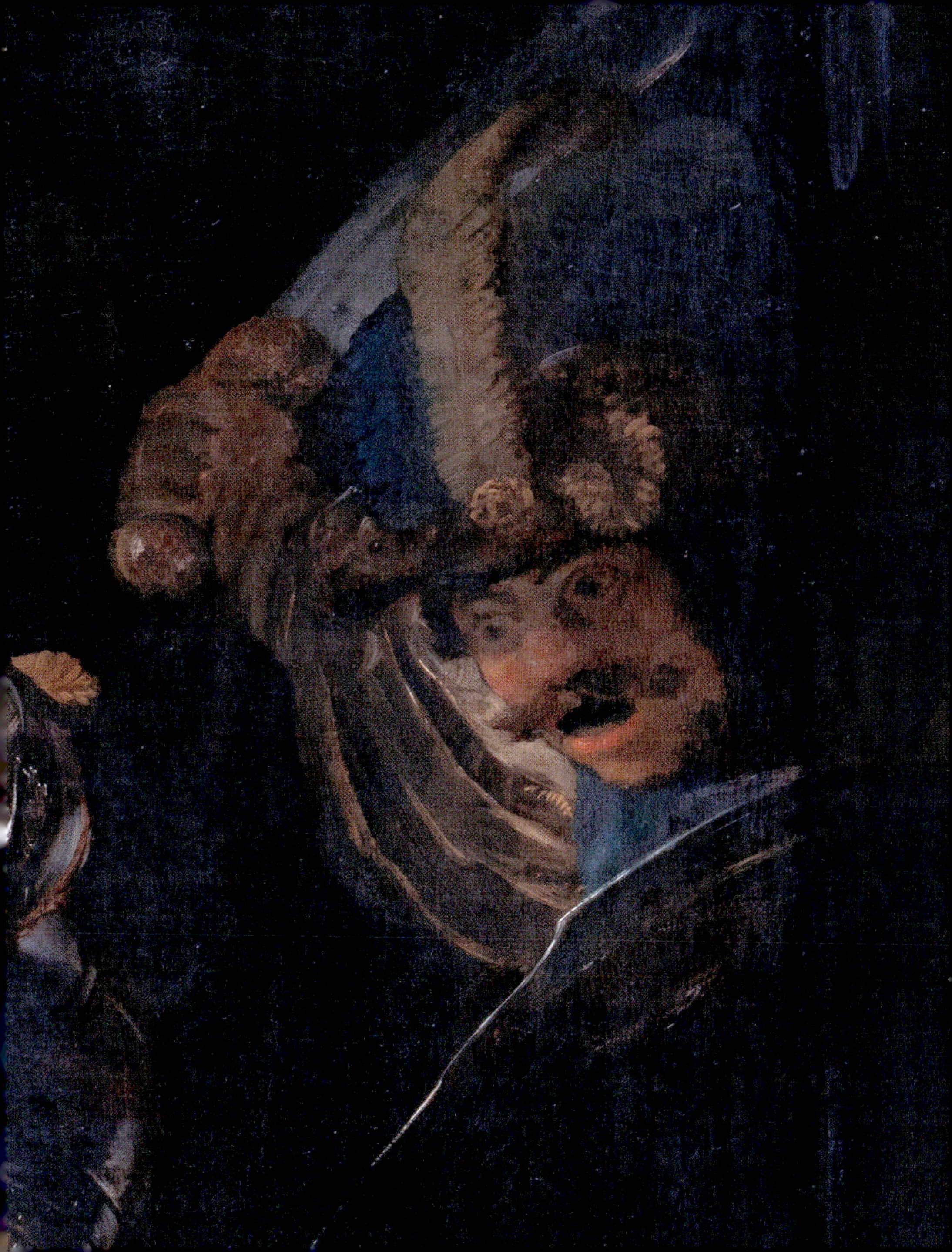

Zooming out a bit, we discover an interesting trio of warriors. Our bewildered soldier is joined by two other men who, unlike him, are less baffled. Their faces mean business—they're here to get a job done.

The warriors are arranged in a diagonal composition, intended to pull our gaze toward what seems to be a very unfortunate man. They're wrestling him and tightening chains around his wrist until it bleeds. It's as if they're struggling to pin down some larger-than-life force. Who exactly is this poor guy?

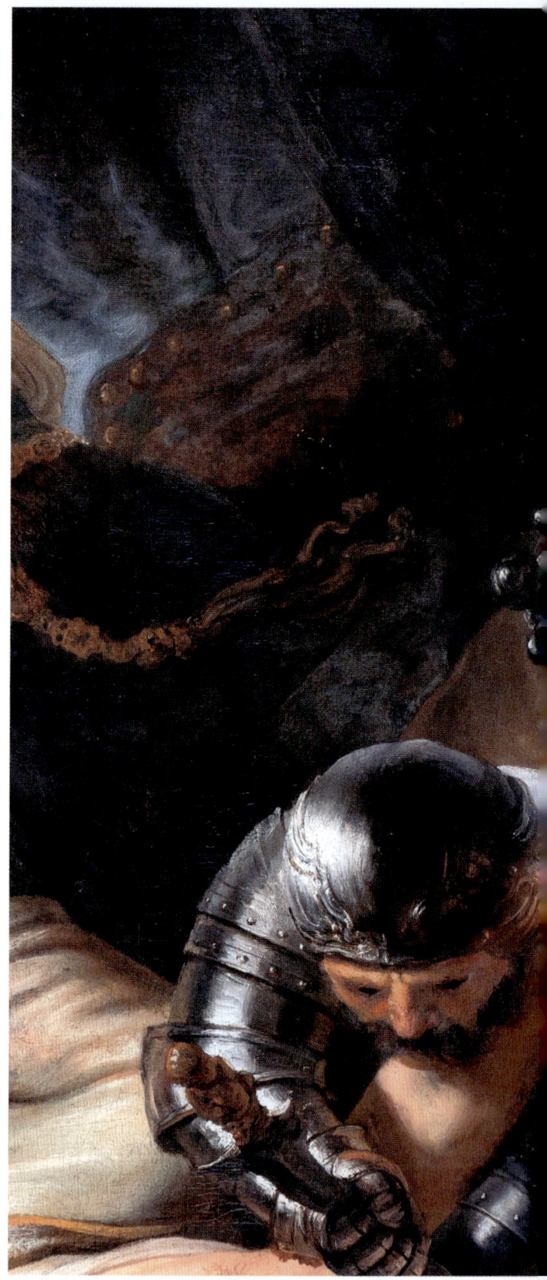

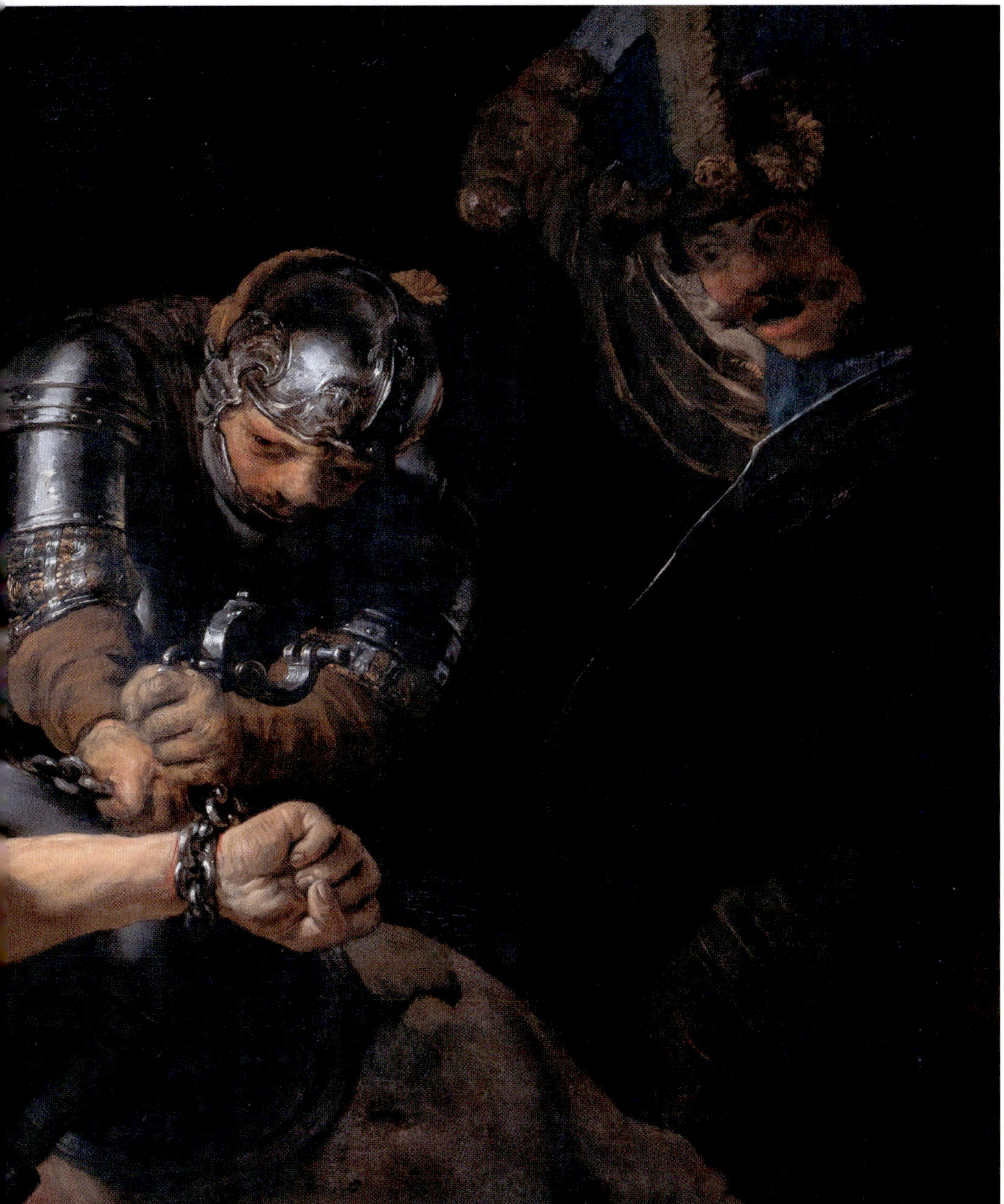

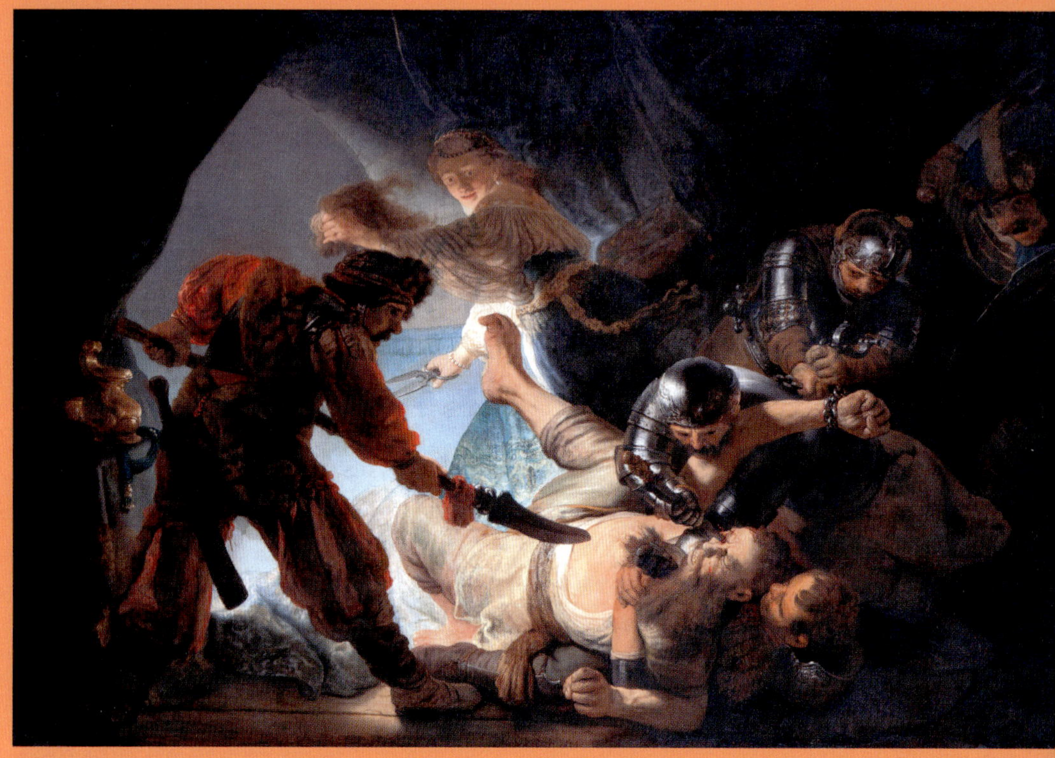

It's Samson—Judge Samson, to be precise—a biblical figure with superhuman powers that were granted to him by God to fight off his enemies. But there was one peculiar condition: Samson had to keep his beard and hair uncut. Lose the hair; lose the power—that was the deal.

And that's exactly the problem here, because the scissor-wielding lady at the center of this spectacular painting has just snipped off a big chunk of Samson's mane. She's his lover, Delilah—though "lover" is a bit generous, because she has a nasty hidden agenda. Delilah got bribed by Samson's enemies, the Philistines, to betray

Rembrandt Harmensz van Rijn, *The Blinding of Samson*, 1636.

her super-strong boyfriend. Which, as you can see, she's done quite successfully. But even though Samson's strength is slipping away, he still manages to put up a fierce fight. He might even have broken free, if not for that final, brutal blow, delivered straight into his eye—resulting in a grim little fountain of blood.

It's a wild scene. One that, the first time I saw it, left me just as stunned as our poor, wide-eyed soldier.

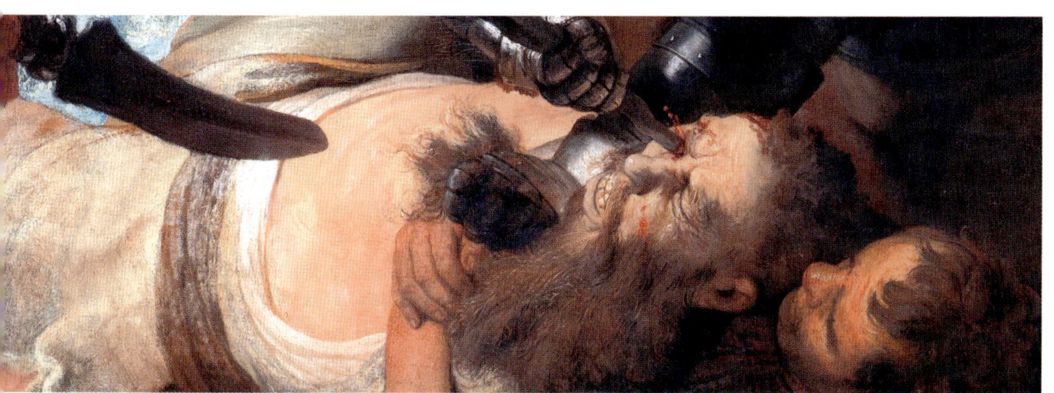

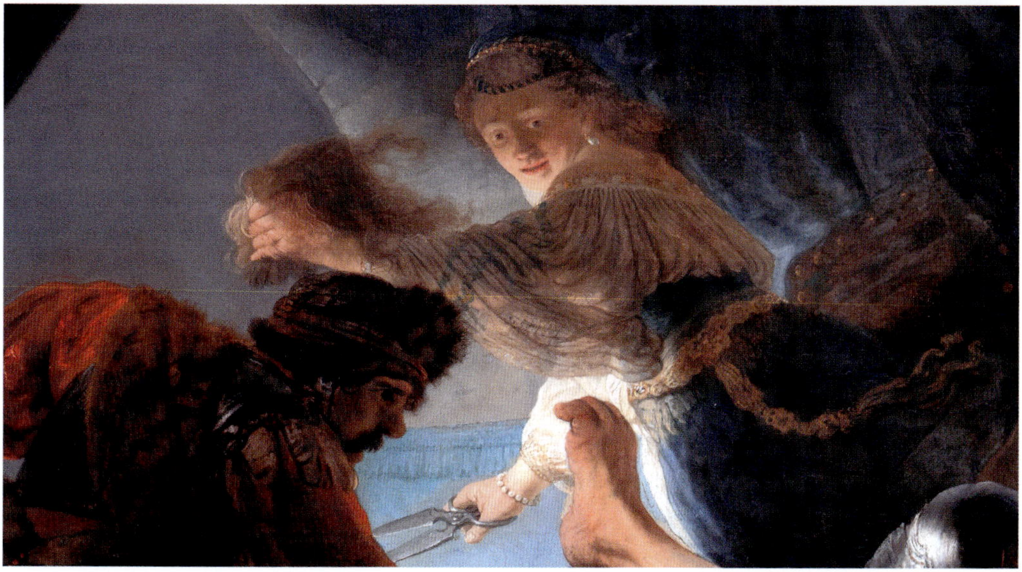

furball of confusion

When cats and humans collide, you end up with this furball of confusion. This creepy creature has the eyes, ears and whiskers of a cat, but for some reason, the artist gave this poor animal a human-like mouth and nose. In doing so, he transformed what should have been a cute little kitty cat into a horrendous cocktail of creatures.

And the cocktail seems to be in the middle of something, because he's fiddling with a mousetrap. However, the trapdoor is open and his lunch is about to escape, because the cat is distracted by something. Maybe it's the brave little caterpillar crawling over the flower stem on the right, raising its head in defiance. It's cute, but it's not why our main character is so distraught. So then, why is he yelling? And why does this animal have such a stupid face?

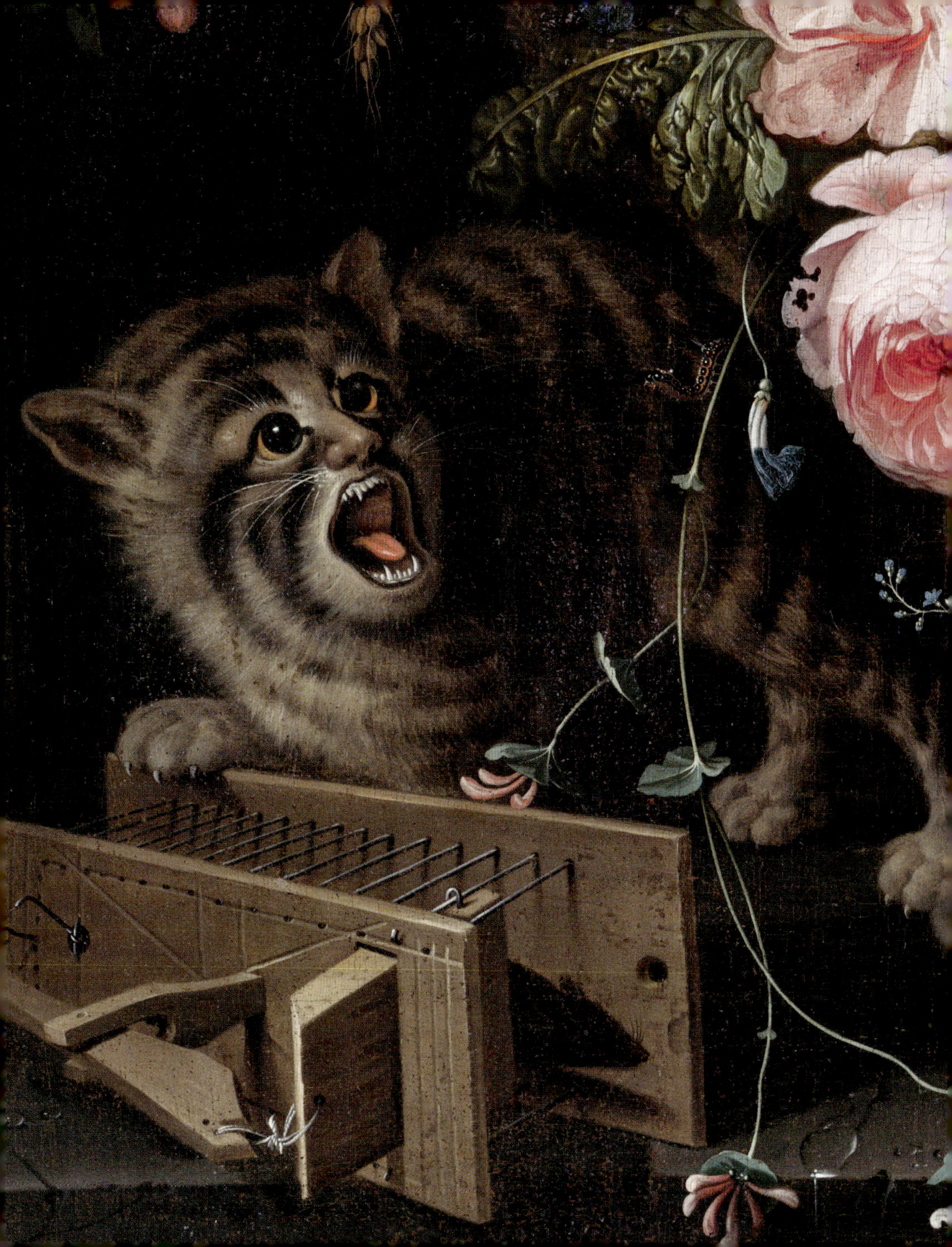

The cat is screaming at a huge vase filled with all kinds of stunning flowers. There are roses, peonies, poppies and many more, each rendered with incredible color and detail. But it's not just flowers—the artist also added plenty of little creatures like spiders, beetles and snails, creeping over the blossoms and leaves.

Yet all this beauty still doesn't answer our first question: Why is this humanoid cat screaming? Well, while playing with the trap, he seems to have accidentally bumped his rear into the vase. Maybe you haven't noticed yet—if you have, I salute your keen eye—but the vase is actually tipping over. You can tell by its diagonal position and also by the water spilling onto the stone table. So there you have it—our odd-looking cat is terrified because he just shoved a beautiful vase of flowers into oblivion.

Abraham Mignon, *Flower Piece with Cat and Mouse Trap*, undated.

And that leaves us with a second question: What's up with the human face? The artist clearly has the skill and talent to create insanely detailed flowers and beautiful, tiny animals, yet at the same time, he painted this cat with an incredibly silly face. Well, as so often in art, it's probably all about symbolism. You could interpret this face as a symbol for human foolishness, because just like cats hunting for mice, humans are prone to being clumsy and stupid, especially when they're blinded by their own stupid desires. So I guess the lesson learned is simple: If you want something in life, please go for it with all your power, but please: mind the freakin' flowers.

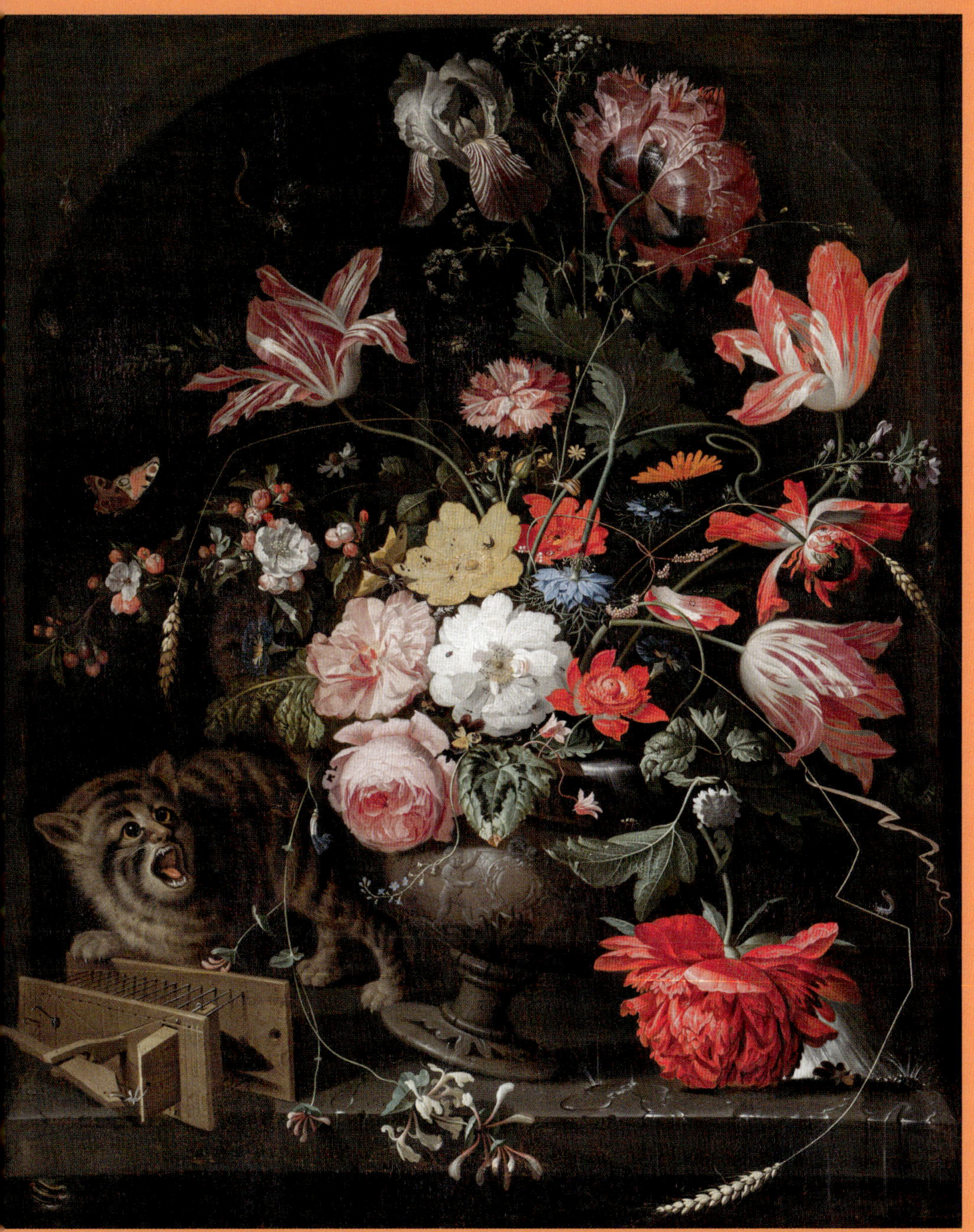

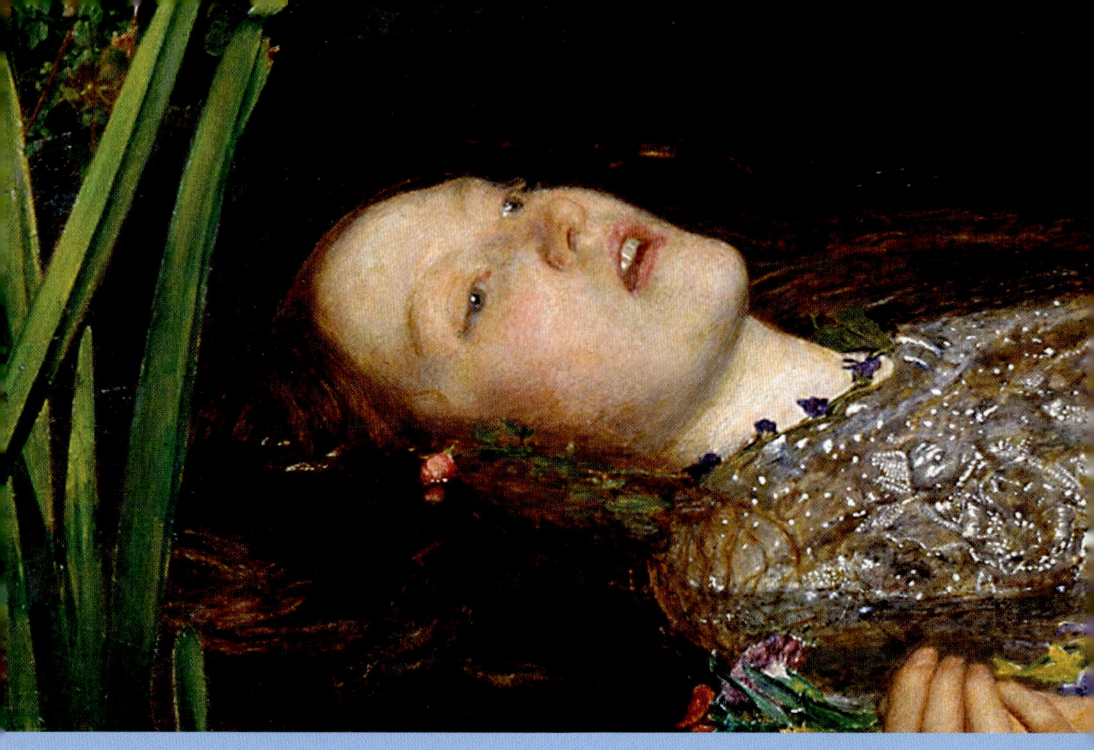

is she dead, alive, or both?

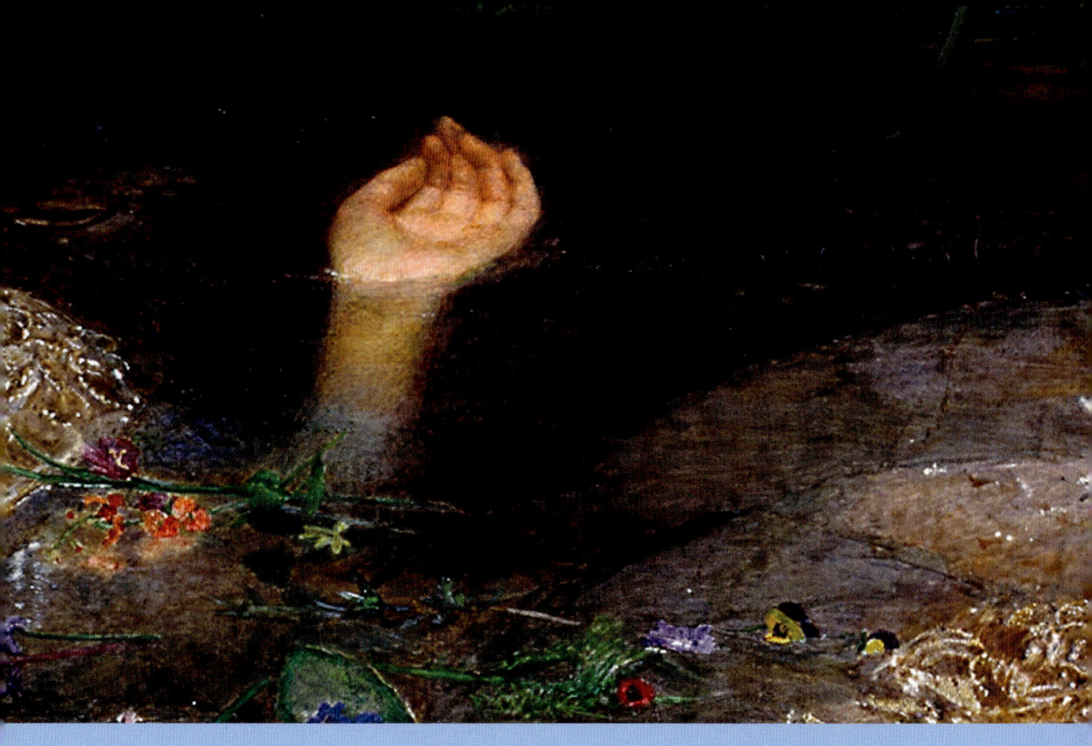

This girl looks like she's dead. Her eyes are open, but her gaze is empty. Her mouth is slack, and her facial muscles seem to be entirely relaxed as if all tension has left her body. The girl wears a necklace of delicate flowers, and a tiny rose rests beside her face, like she's been gently laid out for her loved ones to see, just before being buried. But then again, her cheeks still have a subtle blush, and her lips look shiny and alive. So she's probably fine.

Maybe she's just relaxing, lying in the grass on a Sunday afternoon, gazing up at the sky and wondering if that fluffy cloud looks more like an elephant or a rabbit. Whatever she's doing, it's obvious that this girl is completely detached from reality. What's going on inside that head? I'll tell you one thing—she's not dead, but very soon she will be.

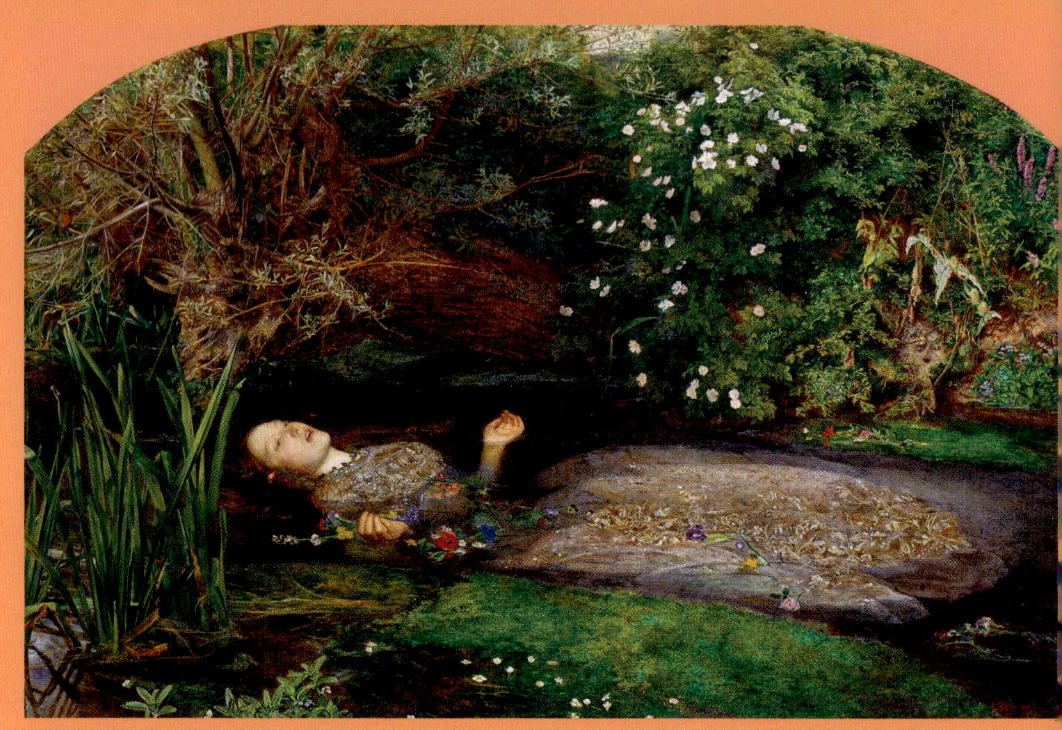

Our beautiful, buoyant lady is in fact two different people—one of them belongs to the world of fiction and the other is a person who really existed. The fictional character is Ophelia, and she appears in Shakespeare's tragedy *Hamlet*. Like in any good tragedy, she's spiraling toward her demise after a series of unfortunate events.

In the play, Ophelia is madly in love with Hamlet, but the prince—tormented by his own family's turmoil—doesn't return her love. And if that isn't tragic enough, Hamlet also accidentally stabs Ophelia's father to death, which is more than enough to push her over the edge. With a broken heart, she wanders into nature

Sir John Everett Millais, *Ophelia*, 1851–1852.

to gather wildflowers near the riverbank, when she suddenly slips and falls into the water. Numb with grief, she surrenders to the gentle pull of the river and starts singing, unaware of the danger she's in. When her dress starts to soak up the water, it pulls her down to what Shakespeare calls her "muddy death." Poor thing.

Knowing Ophelia's story, the expression on her face becomes all the more powerful. Her mouth is open because she is singing. Her gaze is empty because she is grieving. And her blush is subtle because the cold water is slowly pulling it away from her skin. The rest of the painting only adds to the tragedy. In the upper left corner, a little robin sits perched on a branch, maybe answering Ophelia's final song. The flowers in her hands and the deep green riverbank are stunning, but also unforgiving, as they were the cause of Ophelia's demise.

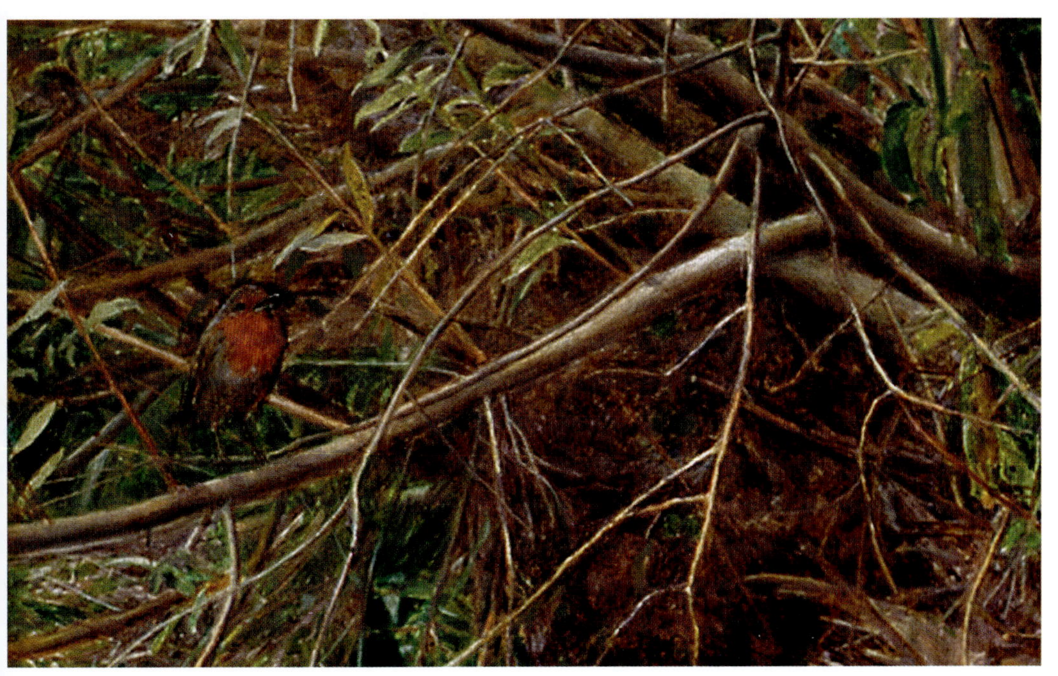

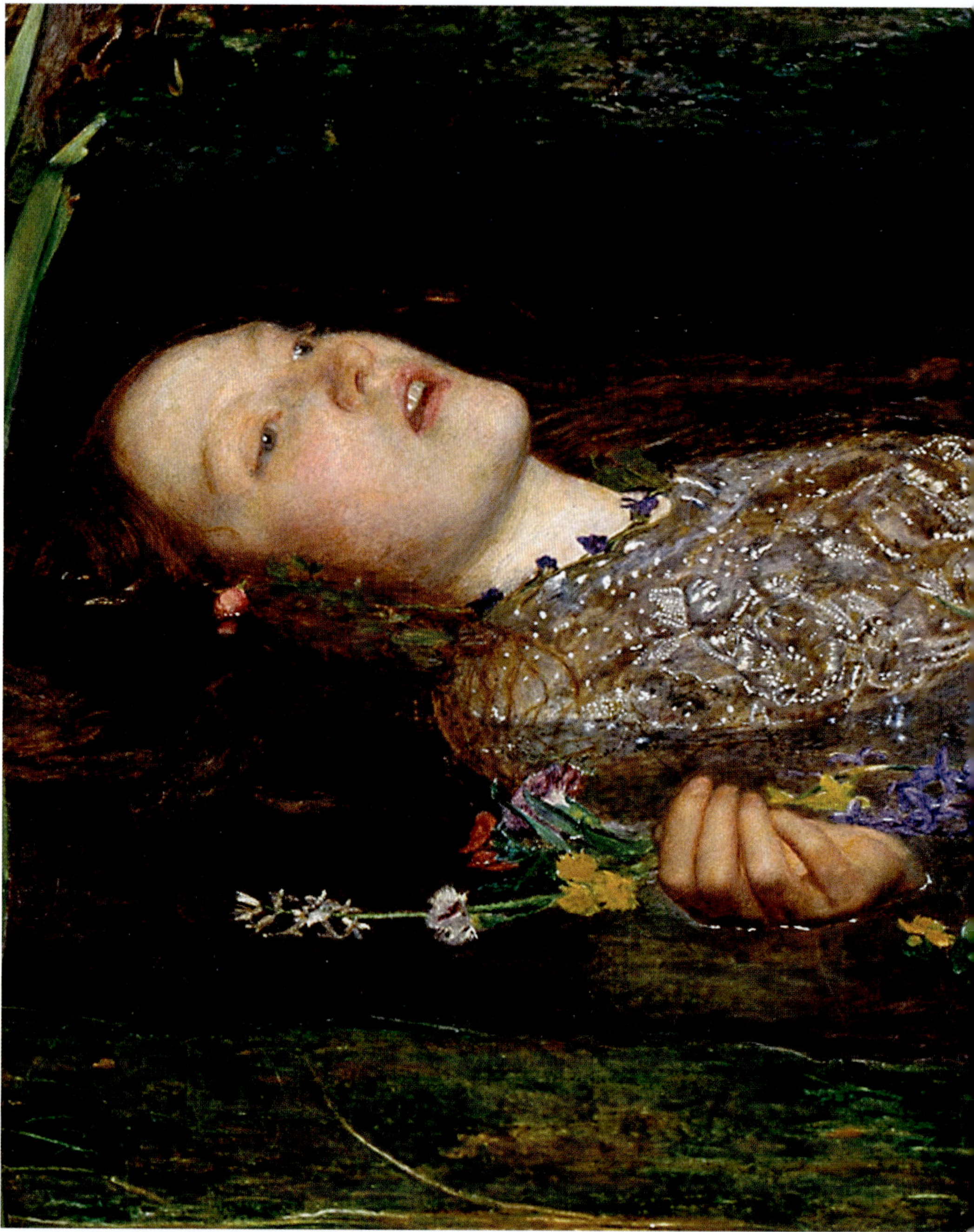

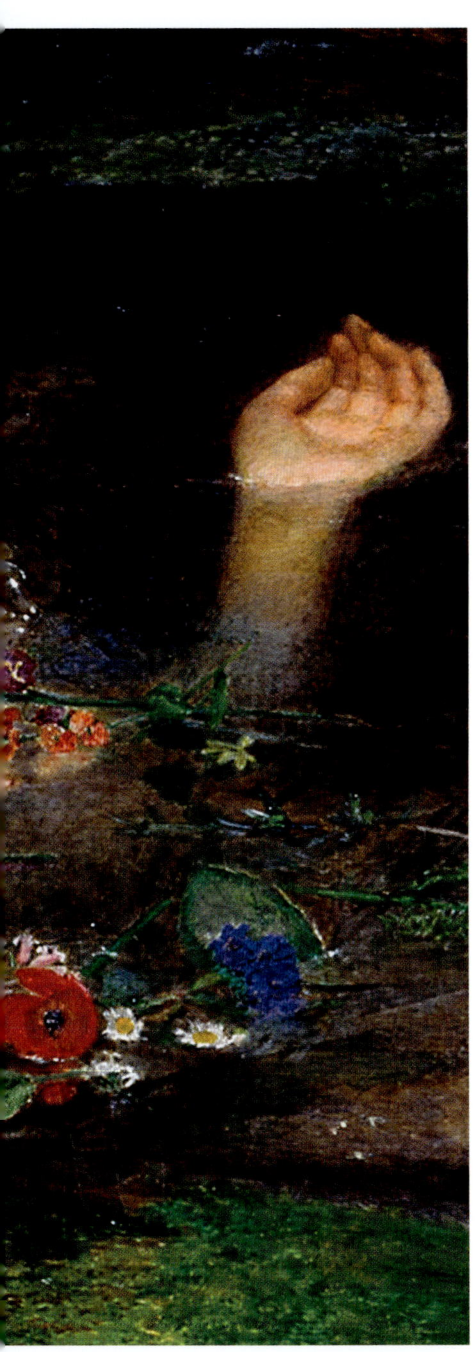

But Ophelia's beautiful face also belongs to someone else: Elizabeth Siddal, who modeled for this painting. Unlike Ophelia, Elizabeth didn't slowly float toward her death on a river; she slowly floated toward a severe case of hypothermia in a bathtub. Because Siddal, an artist herself, posed for hours in a water-filled tub while Sir John Everett Millais painted her. The oil lamps under the bathtub were meant to keep the water warm, but on one occasion they went out. Millais didn't notice and Siddal didn't complain, so they continued. The result? Elizabeth slowly cooled down and became severely ill with pneumonia. Luckily, she completely recovered, and Millais paid the doctor's bills to avoid legal action. And even though it's not exactly Shakespeare, I do think that's a pretty amazing story.

Amedeo Modigliani was a painter of faces—strange, elongated faces. They are often stretched and tilted, with long necks, vacant eyes, bent noses and single lines for brows. If a museum has a Modigliani (and huge galleries), you'll probably spot it from a mile away. And once you've seen a few of these uncanny faces, they're hard to forget. Especially this one, because the story behind this painting is heartbreaking.

why such a long face

The face you're looking at belongs to someone who was very special to Modigliani: Jeanne Hébuterne. They met in the spring of 1917, in the bohemian buzz of Montparnasse in Paris. He was a handsome Italian sculptor and painter and she, an elegant French artist and model. It was an obvious match. But it was also one that would end in tragedy.

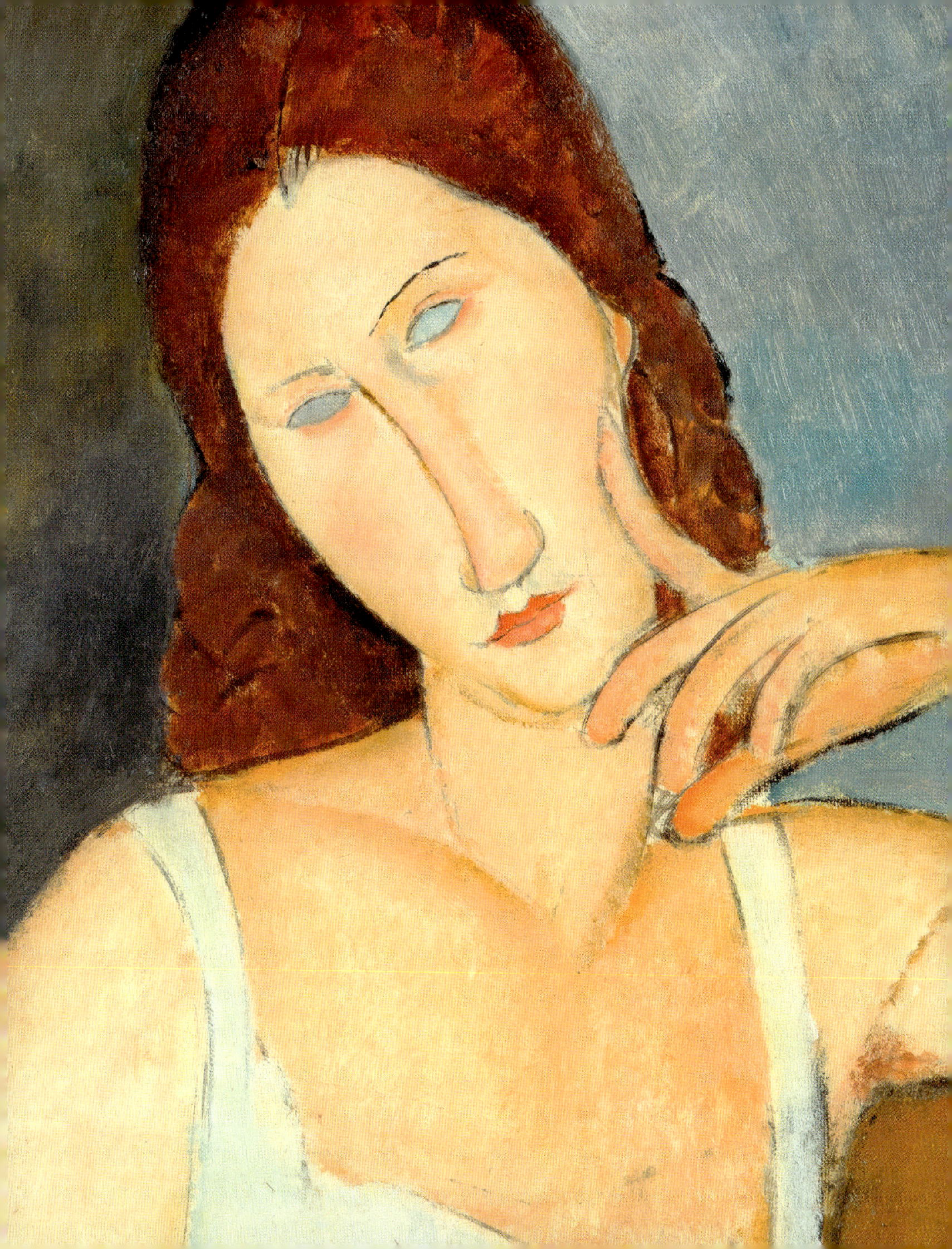

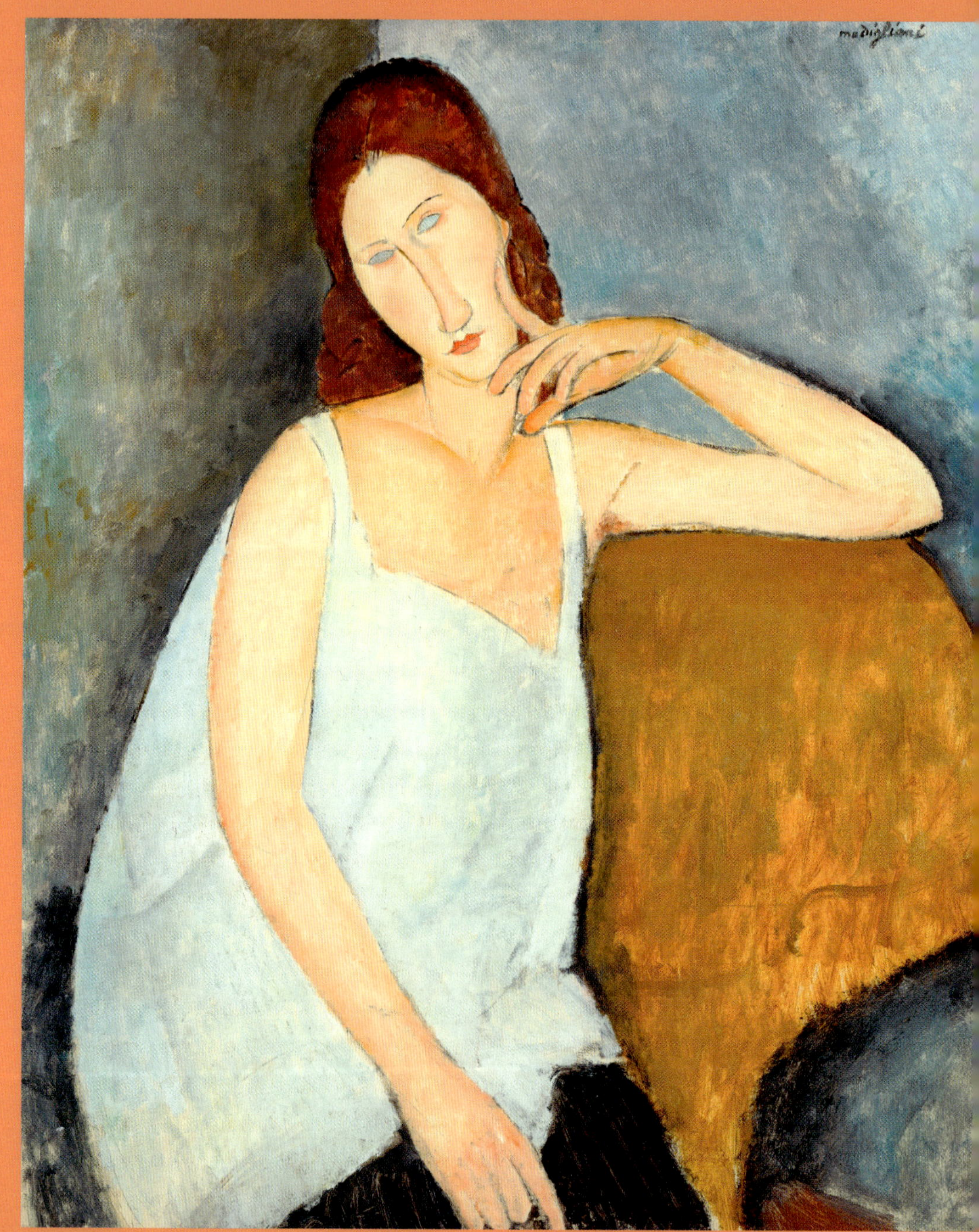
modigliani

Amedeo Modigliani, *Jeanne Hébuterne,* 1919.

It's striking that in some photographs of Jeanne, she actually *looks* like a Modigliani painting, which is no coincidence as she was a trained model. She knew how to adjust her posture and face so that it looked good in a photo or painting. But still, it's uncanny. In one of Jeanne's photos, her face is gently tilted to the side, showing her long neck, while she looks at us with an intense, empty gaze—all quintessential features of Modigliani portraits. No wonder he was drawn to her. Her face *had* to be painted. Which he did . . . 25 times, more than any other person Modigliani painted (and he painted a lot).

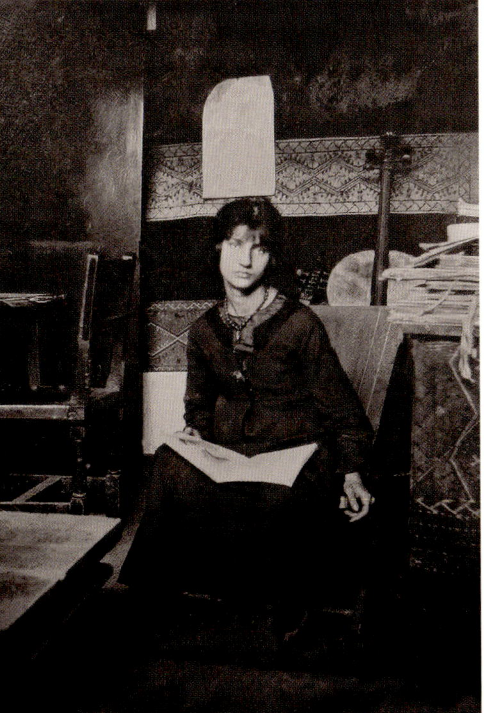

Unknown photographer, *Jeanne Hébuterne,* 1919.

And—surprise, surprise—they fell in love. They were Italian and French, so it was a passionate love. A year after they met, Jeanne got pregnant and in November 1918, she gave birth to their daughter, also named Jeanne.

Lovely. So far, so good. But let's go back to our portrait, because this love story isn't over. In 1919, Jeanne and Amedeo were expecting their second child. In the portrait you're looking at, Jeanne is wearing a casual and loose shirt, suggesting that this was painted during that second pregnancy. But this time, it wouldn't end well.

Modigliani was a heavy drinker, smoker and drug user, and his passions ignited his demise. His health deteriorated quickly, he got ill, and died in January 1920, at the age of 35. The young Jeanne, then 21 years young, couldn't handle this huge loss. Two days after Modigliani's death, she leapt off a building, killing both herself and their unborn son—and leaving behind their one-year-old daughter.

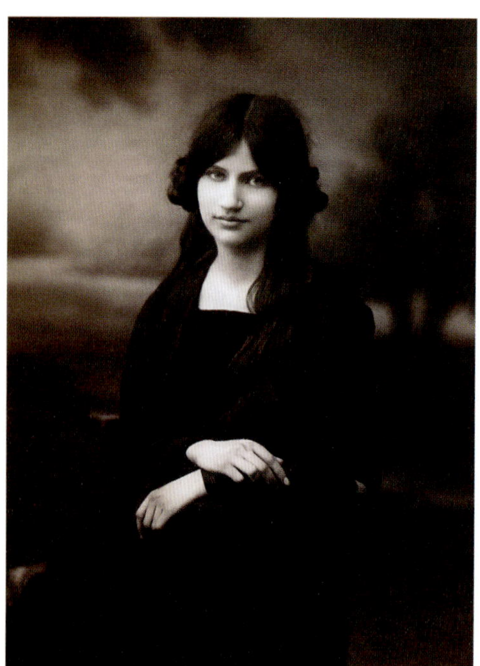

Luckily, the girl turned out all right. Jeanne was raised by Modigliani's parents in Italy, where she studied art history, became a researcher of her father's work, and later wrote his biography—which, all in all, is a great way to cope with such a tragic loss.

Unknown photographer, *Jeanne Hébuterne*, c. 1914–1919.

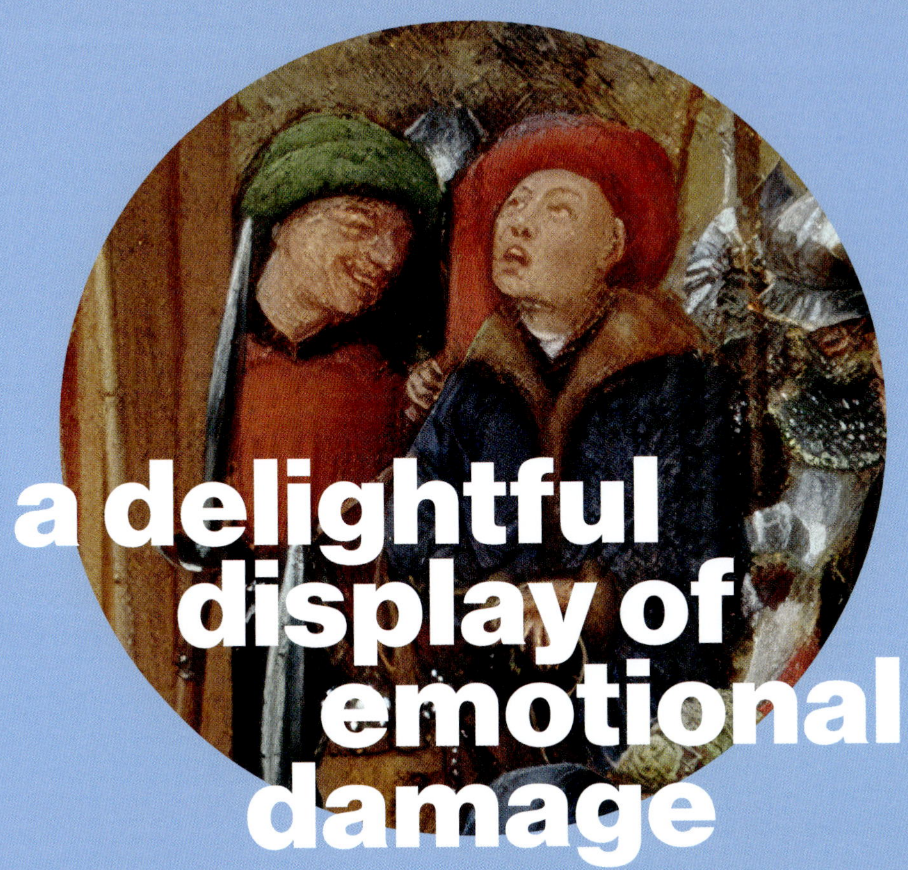

a delightful display of emotional damage

These two stupid faces show a wonderful clash of emotions: delight versus disgust, amusement versus amazement, laughter versus speechlessness. Whatever is happening before their eyes, it's clearly triggering a strong reaction.

The man with the green turban seems to be really enjoying it. His wide grin and squinting eyes betray his amusement. Is he mocking his friend? Or is he encouraging him to lighten up and join in the laughter? Because the man in the blue coat really seems absolutely overwhelmed. What is he witnessing? A bad weather front? His neighbors' Christmas decorations? Two copulating pigeons? Let's see what all the fuss is about.

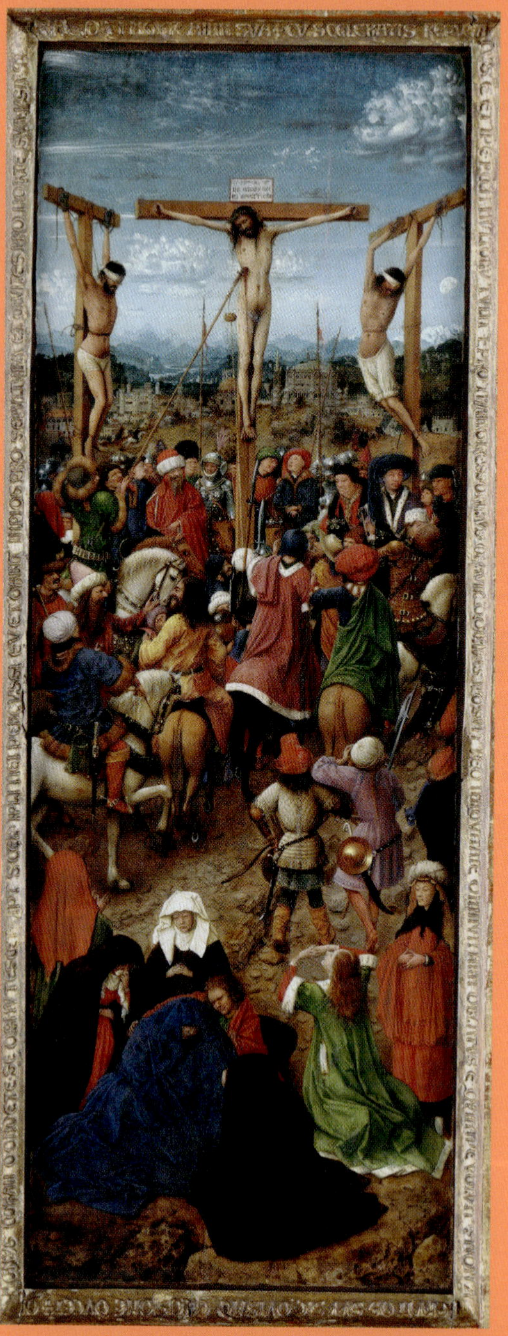

Oh. It's Jesus Christ again, and this time he's being crucified. This changes the mood. This incredibly detailed panel is one half of a small diptych by Jan van Eyck. Our two friends are standing among a chaotic crowd of soldiers, onlookers, friends and enemies of the (temporarily) deceased. Some of them turn away in disgust; some are sad; others are jeering; while a few seem amused or entirely unfazed. This group of people is deeply divided.

The painting shows the moment when a soldier pushes his lance into the side of Christ to check if he is dead. Just below the lance, you can see the vinegar-soaked sponge used to quench Christ's thirst. In the foreground, the Virgin Mary (in blue), Mary Magdalene (in green) and their entourage are mourning their loss.

Jan van Eyck, Left panel of the *Crucifixion and Last Judgement* diptych, c. 1436–1438.

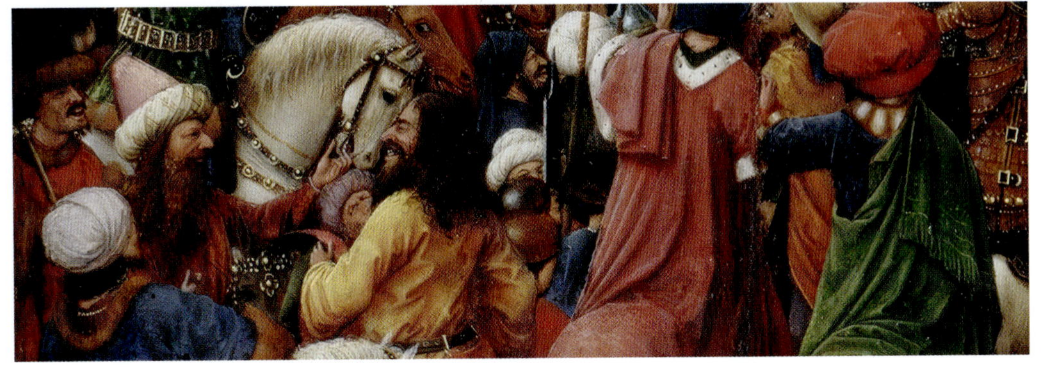

The dynamics between our jolly duo are clear now. The man with the green turban and the big grin? He seems genuinely delighted—maybe because that "stupid preaching son of God" finally got what was coming to him. His wide-eyed friend, however, appears like he has never seen a crucifixion before. Maybe he's one of Christ's followers, devastated by the idea that he will never see his savior again. Little does he know.

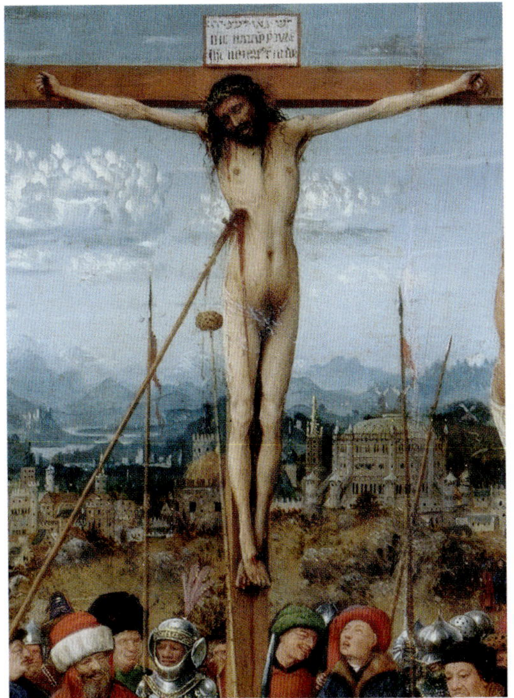

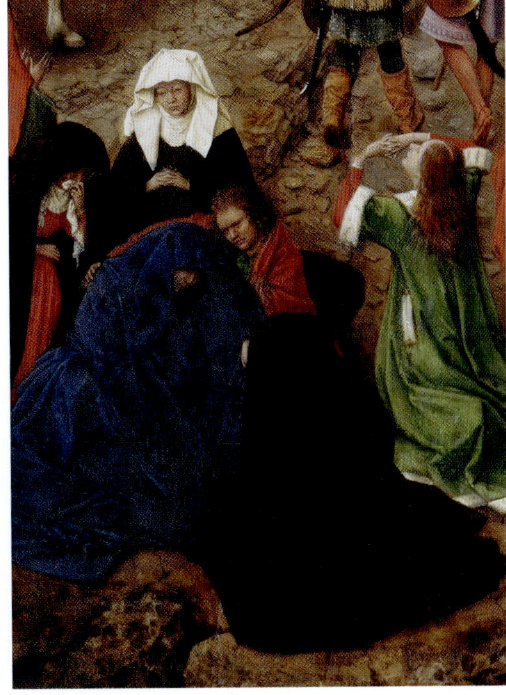

beautifully exposed child abuse

If paintings had sound effects, this one would be deafening. One of the loudest sounds would surely be the scream of this boy. His mouth is wide open, yelling in agony, and his eyes are darting sideways, desperately looking toward the owner of the big yanking hand. But his scream wouldn't be the only noise here. There would also be crying, yelling, gasping and laughing, because this painting is packed with colorful characters.

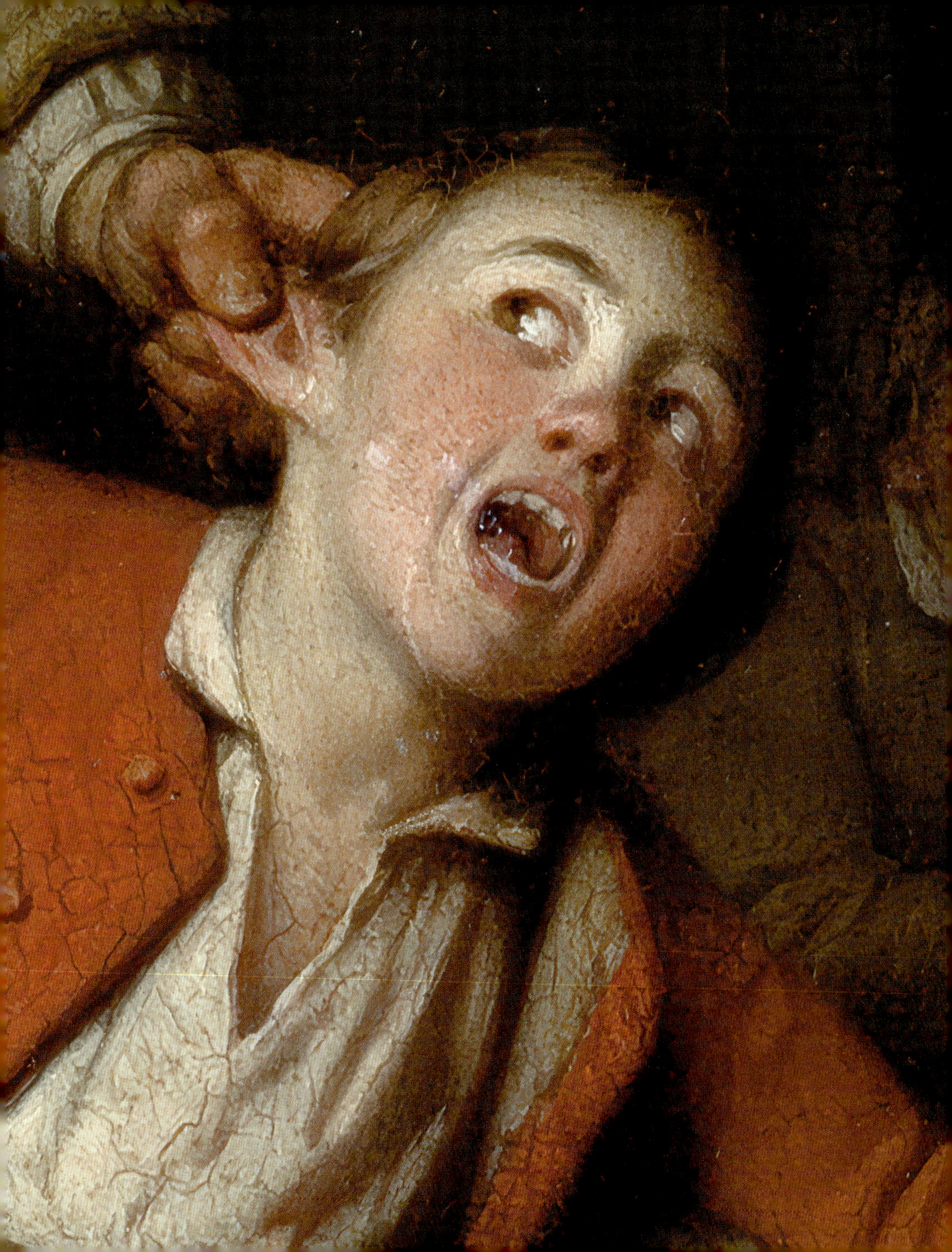

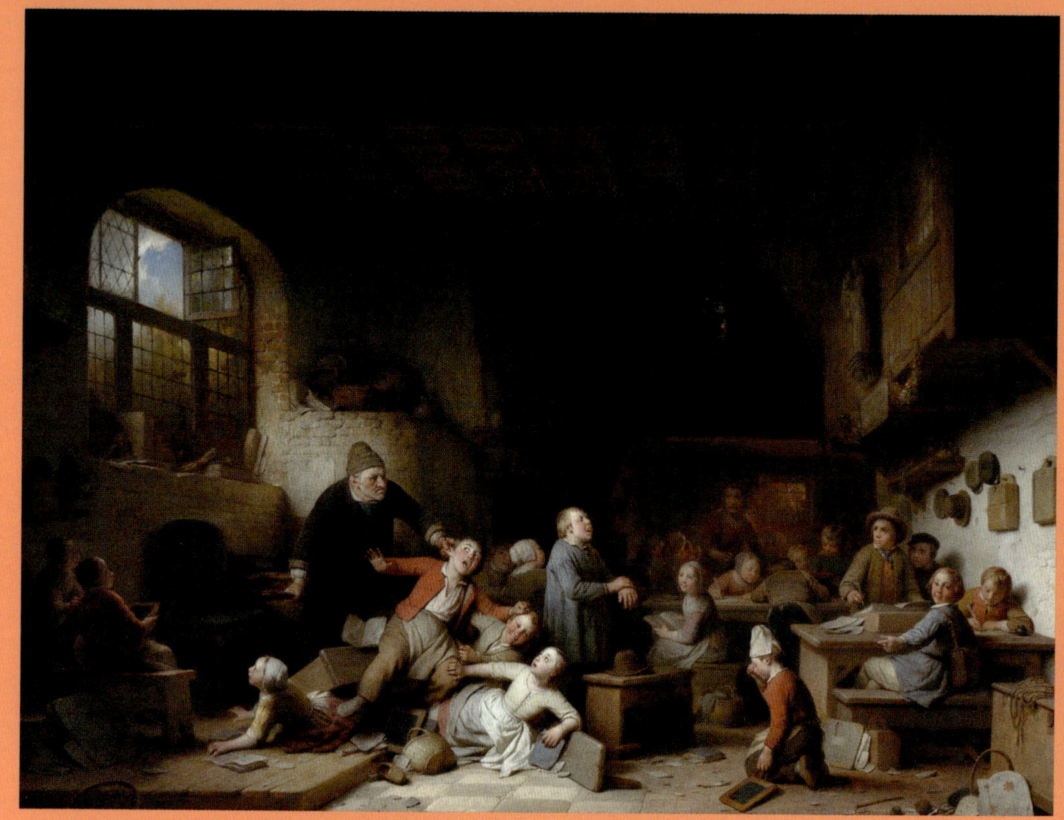

As you might have guessed, we're in a classroom—a very rowdy one, kept in line by a teacher who doesn't shy away from physical punishment. He's not just pulling ears; it looks like he's also smacked the hand of the crying boy in the blue shirt.

Ferdinand de Braekeleer, *The Village School*, 1854.

And in the middle of the chaos, next to the kid with the painful ear, we find a little rascal whose grin suggests he's enjoying the spectacle—even though his hair is getting yanked just as hard as his friend's ear. But let's be honest, is he really his friend? Because that joyful face hints at something more devious. Maybe he's the one behind all the trouble, happily letting his classmates take the blame for his mischief.

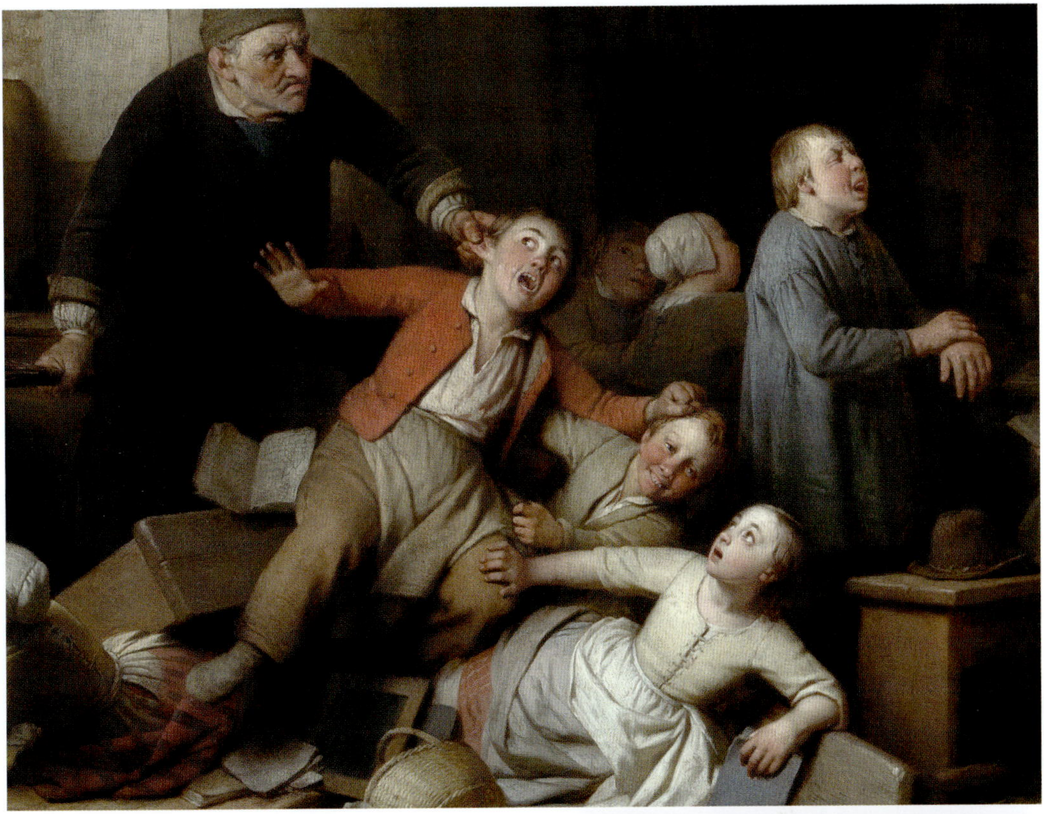

This is *The Village School* by the Flemish genre painter Ferdinand de Braekeleer, showing just how tough it was to keep a bunch of 19th-century schoolkids under control. This teacher really loves inflicting pain, because besides the ear-pulling and hand-smacking, there's also some painful kneeling involved. Just look at the crying kid in the red shirt, forced to bruise his knees on the hard stone floor while his classmate laughs at him.

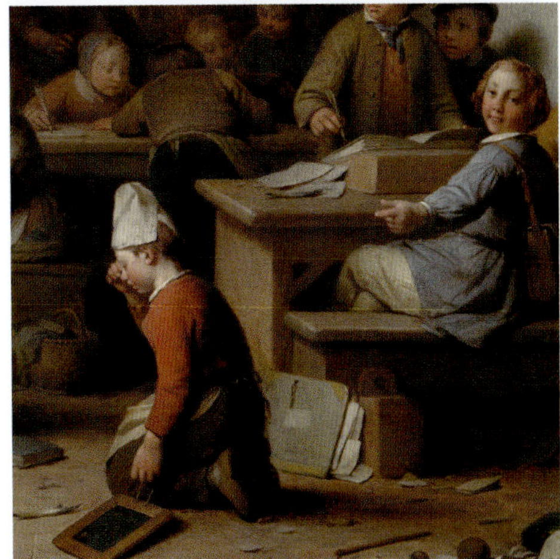

Cruelty aside, the detail in this painting is stunning. Notice the beautiful warm sunlight pouring through the window, illuminating the child abuse and adding an extra layer of drama to the chaos. In the darker background, there's another adult. She looks shocked by what she's witnessing. Meanwhile, the other kids in the back seem oblivious to the chaos unfolding right next to them. This painting is full of chaos, cruelty and just a touch of humor. The takeaway? Punishing kids by hurting them doesn't seem like the most efficient way to maintain peace in the classroom. But, then again, it does make for one incredible painting.

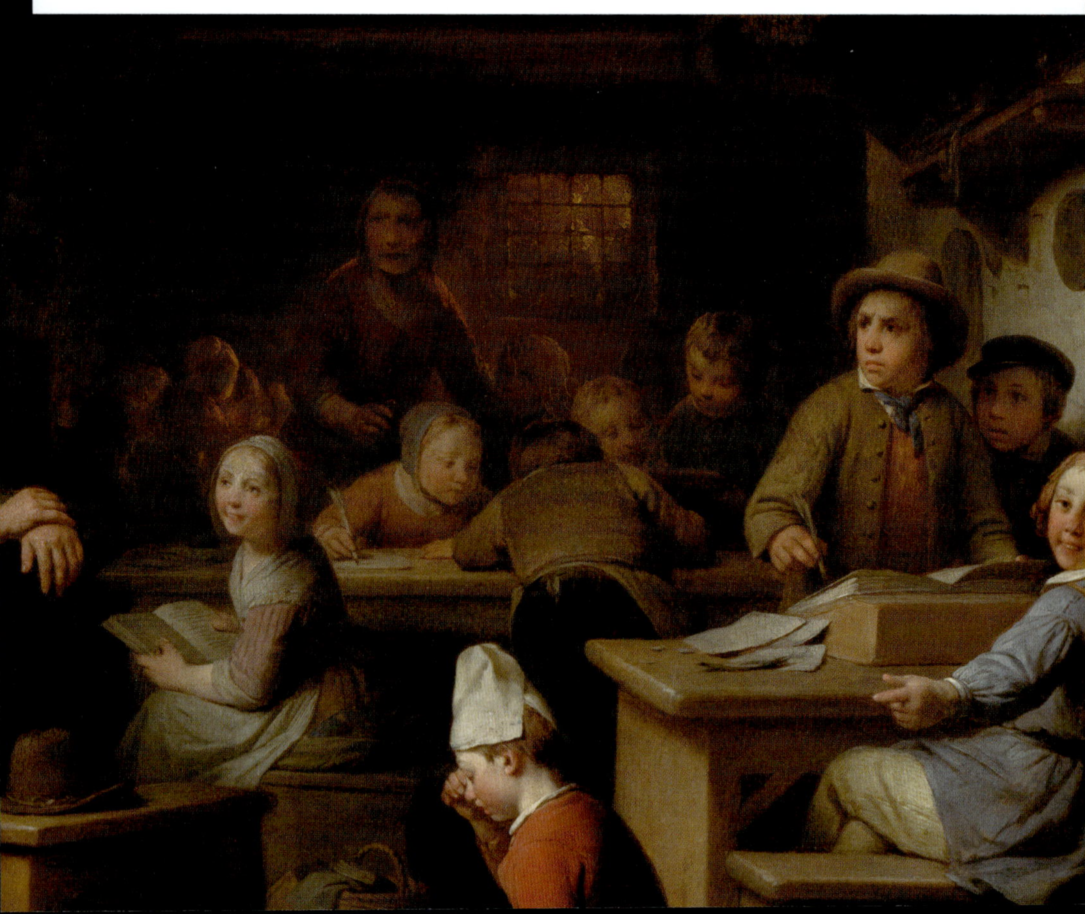

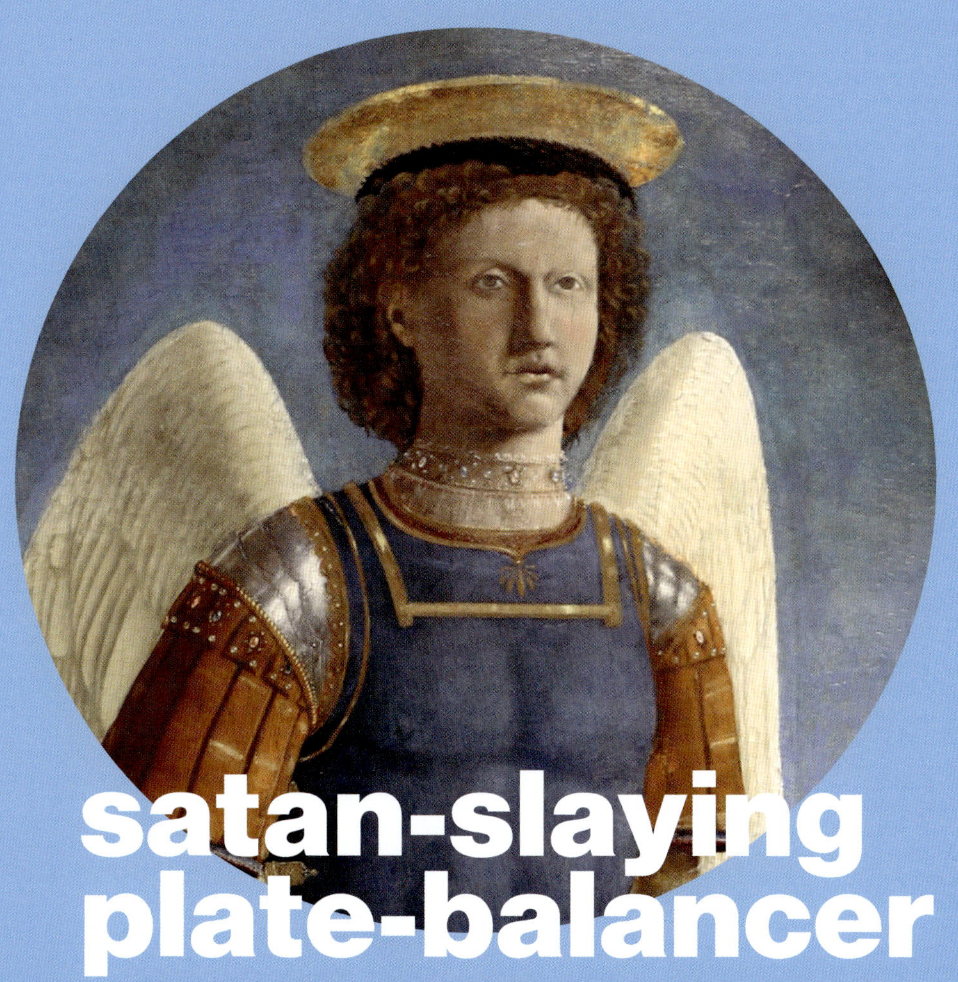

satan-slaying plate-balancer

I feel for this man, because balancing a plate on your head is super difficult. It might explain his facial expression, which falls somewhere between mild confusion and extreme concentration. Or maybe it doesn't, since the plate is obviously a golden halo, hovering awkwardly over his head.

So, we're dealing with an angel. And despite his slightly odd expression, I have to say he looks pretty good. His golden curls serve as the perfect cushion for his laurel wreath—a crown worn as a symbol of victory. He's also rocking a lovely lace choker, delicately decorated with blue and pink gemstones, peeking out from beneath his blue and gold body armor.

And my God, this angel must have a membership at Heaven's Gym, because his body looks ripped. His shirt clings tightly to his impressive chest and abs. His clenched fist shows that we're dealing with a very determined angel. Is he about to get into a fight? Or is he grabbing something?

You're looking at the awkward face and pose of the archangel Michael, painted by the 15th-century Renaissance master Piero della Francesca. He doesn't seem to fully grasp it yet, but Michael has just managed to slay Satan himself, who is represented here on Earth as a snake. It's a fresh kill—his tail is still wiggling—but Michael has it pinned down with his lovely red boots, clutching the severed head by its . . . ears?

Piero della Francesca, *Saint Michael*, 1469.

Yes, Piero gave this snake a small upgrade, because in reality, there's no snake on earth with ears like this. But this painting isn't about reality; it's about the story of an angel defeating Satan. Many medieval or Renaissance artists loved to mix and match animal features to create unsettling, otherworldly creatures. Adding a pair of ears was probably Piero's way of contributing to this tradition. And all the while, Michael still looks like he hasn't quite realized the monumental feat he just pulled off, or what exactly he's supposed to do next with Satan's head.

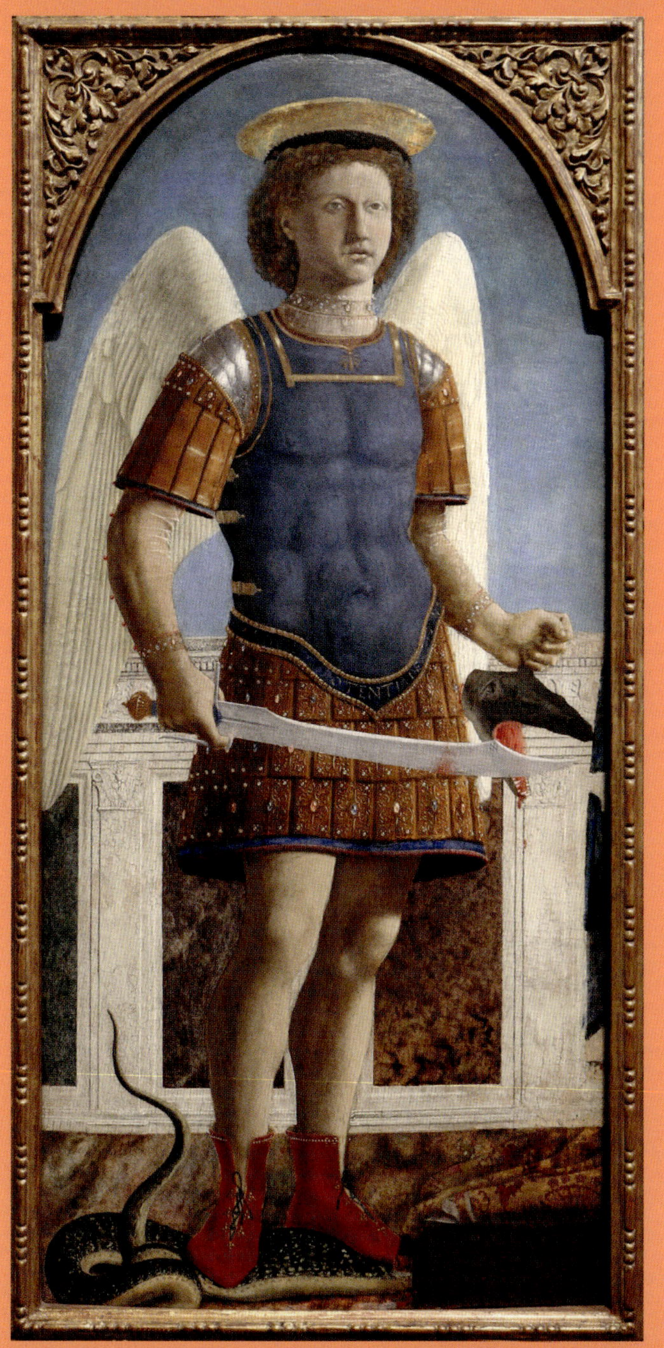

a face of divine stupidity

Any decent Renaissance painter should be able to render a good-looking sheep. And by good-looking I mean with normal eyes that are placed at the side of the head, as is the case with any healthy sheep. But the person who painted this sheep clearly can't. This specimen has oddly positioned, human-like eyes that are staring straight at us. By all means, it's a weird sheep, but still, this creature deserves our attention . . .

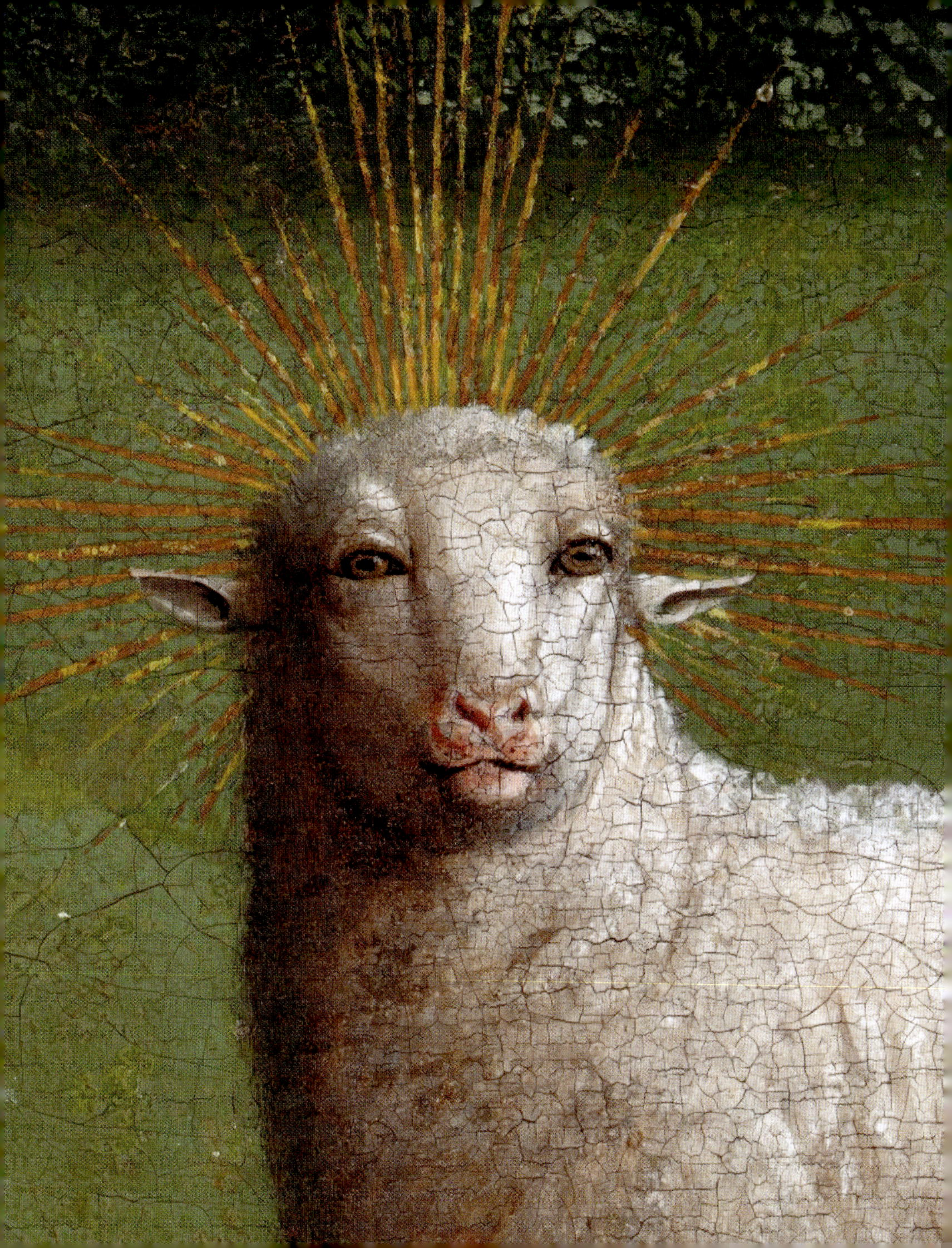

Our medical attention, it seems, because the poor thing is being sacrificed by a flock of fervent, bloodthirsty angels who've cut its side, creating a cute little fountain of blood. Animal cruelty taken aside, the artist behind this work did create a stunning scene. Just look at the animal's entourage. No less than 14 angels with colorful wings surround his altar—kneeling, praying and swinging their shiny censers in full devotion of a sheep with a very freaky face. But they're not alone.

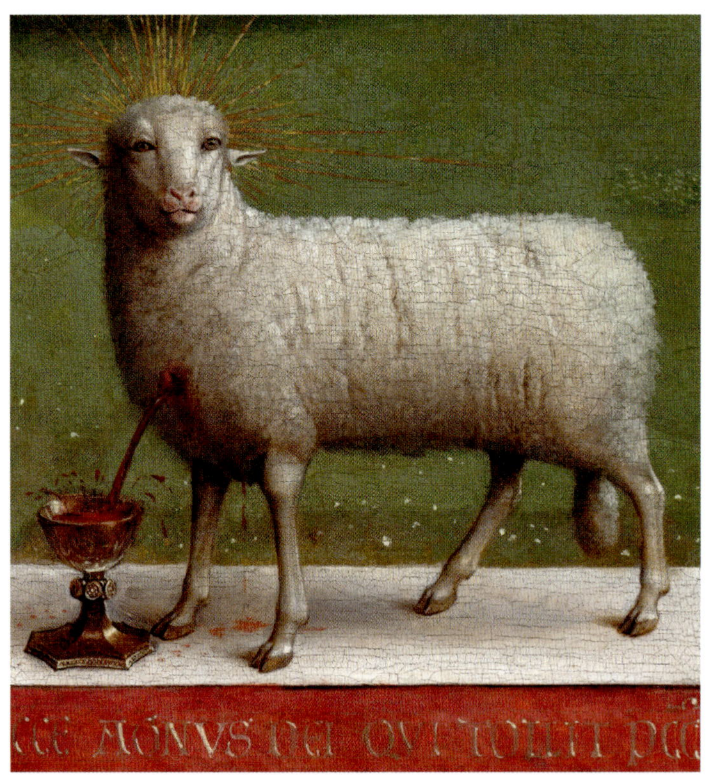

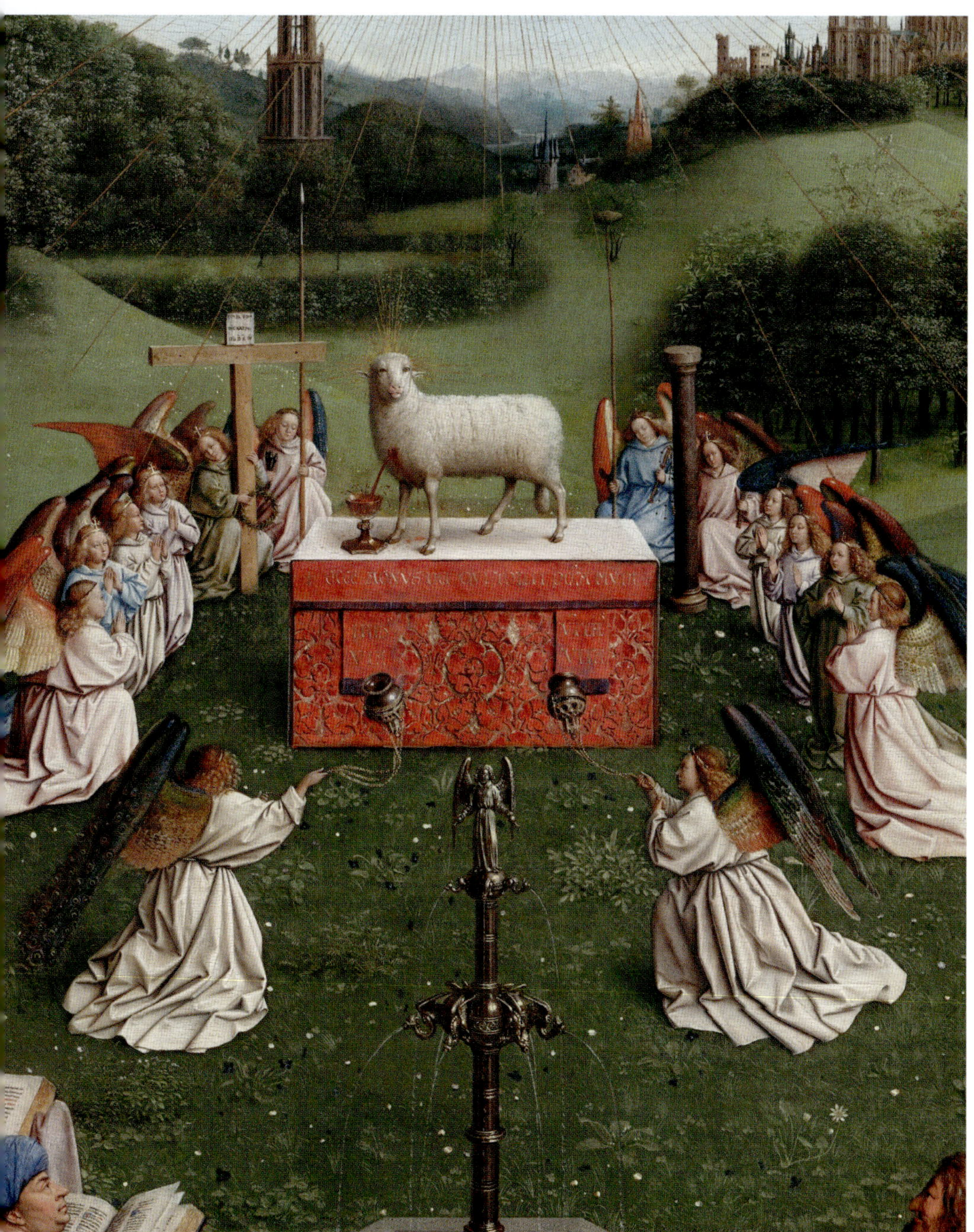

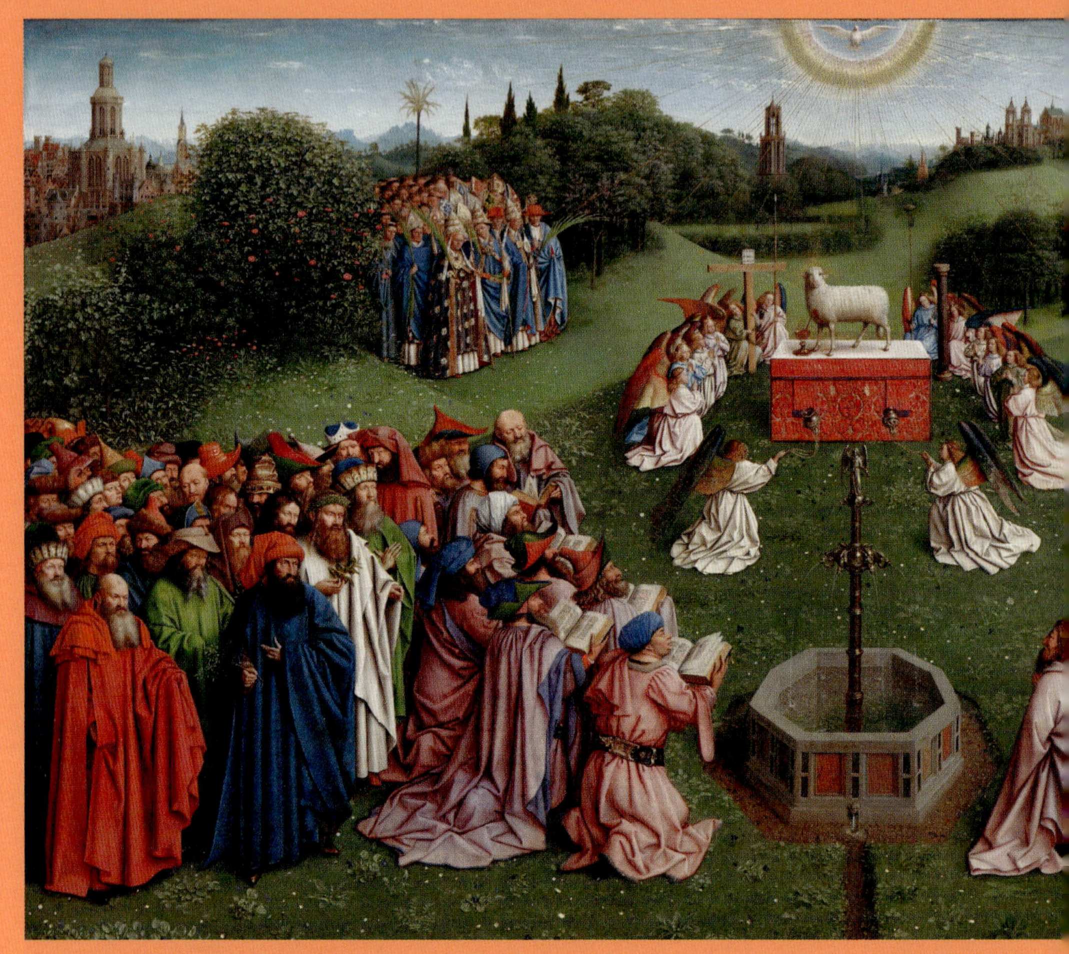

It gets busy. As we move away from the sheep, the crowd thickens with a band of martyrs, prophets and saints. This is the central panel of the incredible *Ghent Altarpiece* by Jan van Eyck. And Jan was a real sucker for detail. The buildings on the horizon, the flowers, the leaves: He gets every little detail right. But then why couldn't he paint a normal sheep?

Well, in fact, the sacrificed sheep is painted exactly as it should be, because it represents the person whose name I actually called out when I first saw our wooly friend's humanoid face: Jesus Christ. In that sense, the depiction is incredibly effective.

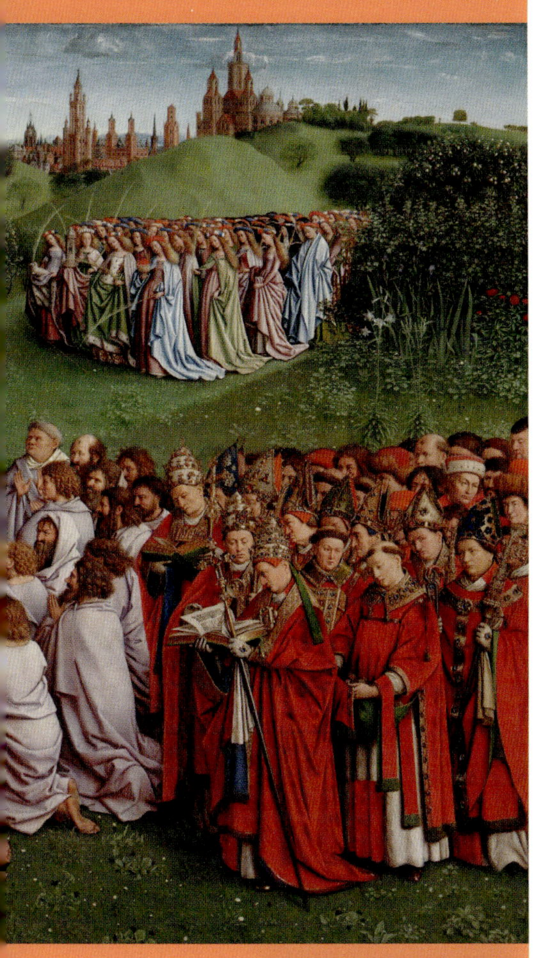

You see, in the Middle Ages it was common to represent the so-called Lamb of God with human-like eyes, staring right back at the viewer. And that's exactly what Jan van Eyck chose to do. Not everyone liked it though, because the face got painted over in the 16th century and was only uncovered during an extensive restoration. So I would like to say, well done Jan van Eyck, you're a very decent Renaissance painter. And just like all the other great painters of stupid faces in this book, you knew exactly what you were doing.

Jan van Eyck, *The Adoration of the Mystic Lamb* from *The Ghent Altarpiece,* 1432.

The overpainted version of the lamb, with one of the original ears still visible

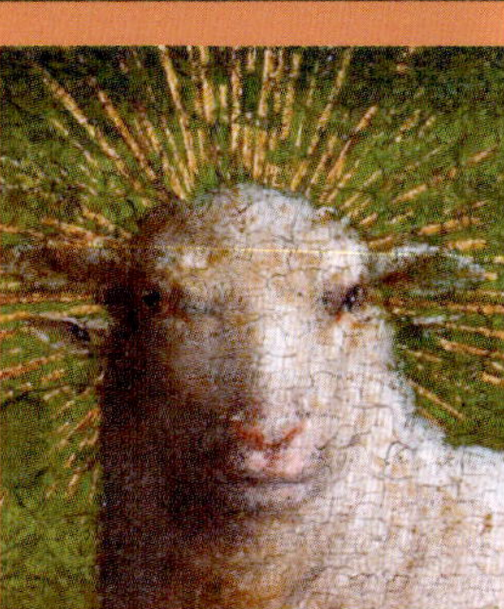

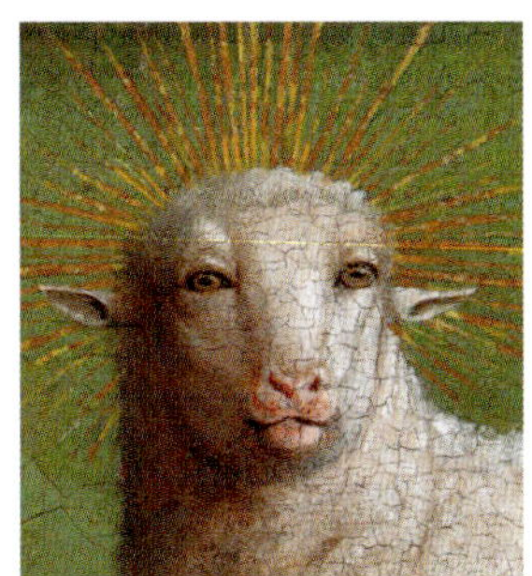

The lamb as Jan van Eyck painted it.

acknowledgments

I had an absolute blast writing this book, but this wasn't a solo undertaking by any means. Time to show some well-deserved gratitude.

First, to my wife, Hilke, an experienced reader of fiction who also proved to be an excellent proofreader of non-fiction: Thank you so much for your support. I love you. To my two kids, Rinus and Robin, whose crazy artworks I value more than any Van Gogh or Van Eyck: You two mean the world to me. My lovely parents, who dragged my five-year-old ass through the Galleria dell'Accademia in Florence: Thank you for giving me the core memory of seeing Michelangelo's *David* for the very first time. It left a mark. To my older brothers and sister, who are always in the first row supporting me: I will forever be your little brother, but at least you make me feel big.

To my publisher, Sam, who first contacted me back in 2023 to ask if I was interested in writing a book: Thank you for your enthusiasm, your insights and your keen eye. To my editors, Nils and Sadie: Thank you for combing through my text and guiding me through the process of publishing *Stupid Faces in Stunning Paintings*. Thank you to the amazingly skillful Gert Dooreman and Meg Baskis, who designed the cover and pages of this book. And of course, thank you to William and all the people at Page Street Publishing for your trust and support in bringing my work to an international audience.

And last but not least, thank you to all the people who support The Gaze. Thank you for reading this book. Thank you for watching my videos. Thank you for sending your comments and insights. In short, thank you so much for joining me on this journey. Without you, The Gaze simply would not exist, and this book would forever remain a figment of my imagination. I'm infinitely grateful.

about the author

Matthijs Van Mierlo is a writer and digital creator who has made it his mission to open up the world of art history with humor and a healthy dose of irreverence. He is the founder of The Gaze, a widely popular channel on Instagram, TikTok and YouTube, where millions of viewers discover that art isn't just beautiful, but also bizarre, messy, and filled with human stories.

Before diving into the art world he loves, Matthijs earned an MA in Theatre and Film Studies. He went on to work as a copywriter and content creator, honing the storytelling skills he now brings to both his videos and his writing. Since launching The Gaze in 2019, he has collaborated with major museums across Europe and the United States, from the Van Gogh Museum to the National Gallery of Art, creating content that bridges the gap between online audiences and centuries-old masterpieces.

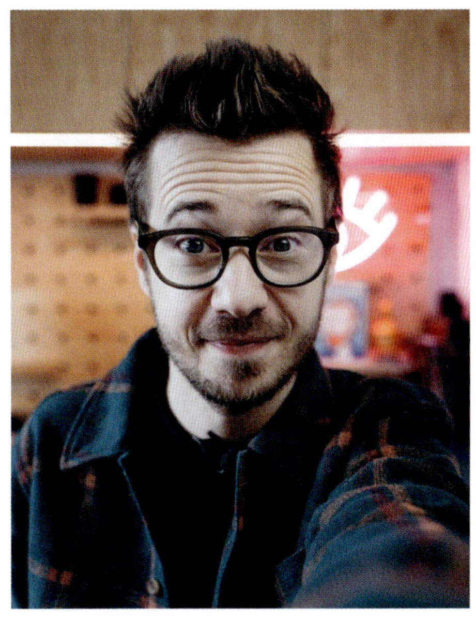

His debut book, *Stupid Faces in Stunning Paintings*, grew out of the same curiosity and playfulness that fuel his videos: a fascination with the overlooked details that make great art feel alive and relatable. Matthijs lives and works in Antwerp, Belgium.

image list

Alma-Tadema, Lawrence. *The Roses of Heliogabalus.* 1888, Private Collection. Oil on canvas, 52 x 84 in (132.1 x 213.7 cm). Wikipedia Commons. Licensed under CC0.

Arcimboldo, Giuseppe. *Vertumnus.* 1590–1591, Skokloster Castle, Sweden. Oil on panel, 27.5 x 22.8 in (70 x 58 cm). Wikipedia Commons. Licensed under CC0.

Bacon, Francis. *Self-Portrait with Injured Eye.* 1972, Private Collection. Oil on canvas, 14 x 12 in (35.5 x 30.5 cm). © The Estate of Francis Bacon / All rights reserved / Sabam, Bruxelles and DACS, London 2025.

Biard, François-Auguste. *Seasickness at the Ball, on Board an English Corvette.* c. 1860s, Dallas Museum of Art, Dallas. Oil on canvas, 38.6 x 51.6 in (98.1 x 131 cm). Wikipedia Commons. Licensed under CC0.

Bigallo Master. *Madonna of the Fiesole Cathedral.* c. 1215–1250, Fiesole Cathedral, Italy. Photo by Sailko. Wikipedia Commons. Licensed under CC3.0.

Blake, William. *Head of a Damned Soul in Dante's Inferno.* c. 1789, The British Museum, London. Engraving and etching on paper, 15 x 10.8 in (38.3 x 27.5 cm). © The Trustees of the British Museum.

Bloch, Carl. *In a Roman Osteria.* 1866, National Gallery of Denmark, Copenhagen. Oil on canvas, 58.5 x 69.9 in (148.5 x 177.5 cm). Wikipedia Commons. Licensed under CC0.

Boilly, Louis-Léopold. *The Art Connoisseurs.* 1823–1828, Metropolitan Museum of Art, New York. Lithograph with hand-coloring, 12.4 x 10 in (31.4 x 25.5 cm). Licensed under CC0.

Bosch, Hieronymus. *Cutting the Stone.* 1501–1505, Museo del Prado, Madrid. Oil on panel, 18.9 x 13.8 in (48 x 35 cm). Wikipedia Commons. Licensed under CC0.

Bosch, Hieronymus. *Death and the Miser.* c. 1485–1490, National Gallery of Art, Washington, D.C. Oil on wood, 36.6 x 12.2 in (93 x 31 cm). Wikipedia Commons. Licensed under CC0.

Botero, Fernando. *Monalisa.* 1978, Museo Botero, Bogotá. Oil on canvas, 65.4 x 72 in (166 x 183 cm).

Botticelli, Sandro. *Venus and Mars.* c. 1485, The National Gallery, London. Oil on panel, 27.2 x 68.1 in (69 x 173 cm). Wikipedia Commons. Licensed under CC0.

Bronzino. *An Allegory with Cupid and Venus.* c. 1545, National Gallery, London. Oil on wood, 57.5 x 45.7 in (146 x 116 cm). Wikipedia Commons. Licensed under CC0.

Brouwer, Adriaen. *The Bitter Potion.* c. 1635–1638, Städel Museum, Frankfurt. Oil on panel, 14 x 18.8 in (35.5 x 47.7 cm). Wikipedia Commons. Licensed under CC0.

Bruegel, Pieter the Elder. *The Peasant Wedding.* 1568, Kunsthistorisches Museum, Vienna. Oil on panel, 44.9 x 64.6 in (114 x 164 cm). Wikipedia Commons. Licensed under CC0.

De Braekeleer, Ferdinand. *The Village School.* 1854, Koninklijk Museum voor Schone Kunsten, Antwerp. Oil on panel, 35.6 x 43.1 in (90.5 x 109.5 cm). Licensed under CC0.

Dubreuil, Toussaint. *Henry IV as Hercules Slaying the Lernaean Hydra.* c. 1600, Musée du Louvre, Paris. Oil on canvas, 35.8 x 29.1 in (91 x 74 cm). Wikipedia Commons. Licensed under CC0.

Fragonard, Jean Honoré. *The Swing.* 1767, The Wallace Collection, London. Photo by Cassandra Parsons/The Wallace Collection. Oil on canvas, 31.9 x 25.3 in (81 x 64.2 cm). Wikipedia Commons. Licensed under CC4.0.

Gentileschi, Artemisia. *Judith Slaying Holofernes.* c. 1620, Uffizi Gallery, Florence. Oil on canvas, 78.3 x 63.9 in (199 x 162.5 cm). Wikipedia Commons. Licensed under CC0.

Goya, Francisco. *Saturn Devouring His Son.* 1820–1823, Museo del Prado, Madrid. Oil on plaster transferred to canvas, 56.6 x 32 in (143.5 x 81.4 cm). Wikipedia Commons. Licensed under CC0.

Kahlo, Frida. *Dressed up for Paradise (The Deceased Dimas Rosas at Three Years of Age).* 1937, Museo Dolores Olmedo Patiño, Mexico City. Oil on canvas, 18.9 x 12.2 in (48 x 31 cm). Licensed under CC0.

Kuniyoshi, Utagawa. *Yatô Yomoshichi Norikane* from *Mirror of the True Loyalty of the Faithful Retainers.* 1857. Woodblock print, 14 x 10 in (36 x 25.5 cm). GetArchive LLC. Licensed under CC0.

Maître à l'œillet et au brin de lavande de Baden et atelier. *Retable de la passion.* c. 1500. Musée des Beaux-Arts, Dijon. Oil on panel, 66.1 x 29.9 in (168 x 76 cm). Licensed under CC0.

Massys, Quinten. *An Old Woman (The Ugly Duchess).* c. 1513, National Gallery, London. Oil on oak, 24.6 x 17.9 in (62.4 x 45.5 cm). Wikipedia Commons. Licensed under CC0.

Master of the Pflock Altar. *Christ Crowned with Thorns.* c. 1520, Museum of Fine Arts, Ghent. Oil on panel, 64.2 x 37.8 in (163 x 96 cm). Licensed under CC0.

Mignon, Abraham. *Flower Piece with Cat and Mouse Trap.* Undated, Musée des Beaux-Arts, Lyon. Oil on canvas, 44.7 x 33.5 in (113.5 x 85 cm). Wikipedia Commons. Licensed under CC0.

Millais, John Everett. *Ophelia.* 1851–1852, Tate Britain, London. Oil on canvas, 29.9 x 44 in (76 x 112 cm). Wikipedia Commons. Licensed under CC0.

Modigliani, Amedeo. *Jeanne Hébuterne.* 1919, Metropolitan Museum of Art, New York. Oil on canvas, 36 x 28.7 in (91.4 x 73 cm). Licensed under CC0.

Monet, Claude. *Head of a Woman.* 1862–1863, Musée Marmottan Monet, Paris. Oil on canvas, 20.5 x 16.3 in (52 x 41.5 cm). Wikipedia Commons. Licensed under CC0.

Monet, Claude. *Woman with a Parasol.* 1875, National Gallery of Art, Washington. Oil on canvas, 39.4 x 31.9 in (100 x 81 cm). Wikipedia Commons. Licensed under CC0.

Picasso, Pablo. *Les Demoiselles d'Avignon.* 1907, Museum of Modern Art, New York. Oil on canvas, 96 x 92 in (243.9 x 233.7 cm). © Succession Picasso - Sabam Belgium 2025.

Piero della Francesca. *Saint Michael.* c. 1469, National Gallery, London. Oil on wood, 52.4 x 23.4 in (133 x 59.5 cm). Wikipedia Commons. Licensed under CC0.

Reichlich, Marx. *A Jester.* c. 1520, Yale University Art Gallery, New Haven. Tempera on panel, 17.5 x 13.3 in (44.5 x 33.7 cm). Licensed under CC0.

Rembrandt Harmensz van Rijn. *The Blinding of Samson.* 1636, Städel Museum, Frankfurt. Oil on canvas, 86.2 x 120.1 in (219 x 305 cm). Licensed under CC0.

Rombouts, Theodoor. *Prometheus.* c. 1623, Koninklijke Musea voor Schone Kunsten, Brussels. Oil on canvas, 60.6 x 87.6 in (154 x 222.5 cm). Wikipedia Commons. Licensed under CC0.

Rousseau, Henri. *Tiger in a Tropical Storm* or *Surprised!.* 1891, National Gallery, London. Oil on canvas, 50.8 x 63.8 in (129 x 162 cm). Wikipedia Commons. Licensed under CC0.

Rubens, Peter Paul. *The Hippopotamus and Crocodile Hunt.* c. 1615–1616, Alte Pinakothek, Munich. Oil on canvas, 97.6 x 126.4 in (248 x 321 cm). Licensed under CC0.

Rubens, Peter Paul. *The Miraculous Draught of Fishes.* c. 1618–1619, Church of Our Lady Across the River Dyle, Mechelen. Oil on canvas, 221.7 x 135.8 in (563 x 345 cm). Licensed under CC4.0, KIK-IRPA, Brussel, 21060.

Sanzio, Raffaello. *Portrait of Young Woman with Unicorn.* c. 1505-1506, Galleria Borghese, Rome. Oil on canvas, 26.4 x 22 in (67 x 56 cm). Wikipedia Commons. Licensed under CC0.

Sasse, Arthur. *Albert Einstein.* 1951. Image HQ. Wikipedia Commons. Licensed under CC0.

Unknown artist. *Head-Baker.* c. 1600–1630, Phoebus Foundation, Antwerp. Oil on copper, 18.3 x 13.4 in (46.5 x 34 cm). Licensed under CC0.

Unknown artist. *The Muse Urania*, from the house of Julia Felix, Pompeii. c. 79 AD, Musée du Louvre, Paris. Photo by Hervé Lewandowski. Fresco, 18.4 x 14.4 in (46.7 x 36.5 cm). Photo by Hervé Lewandowski. © GrandPalaisRmn.

Unknown artist. Illustration from *Livre de la Vigne.* 15th century, Bodleian Libraries, University of Oxford [2025]. Bodleian Library MS. Douce 134, folio 36r. Photo by Bodleian Libraries.

Unknown artist. *Portrait of Barbara van Beck.* c. 1650. Oil on canvas, 27.7 x 20 in (70.5 x 50.5 cm). Welcome Collection, London. Licensed under CC4.0.

Unknown artist. *The Virgin and Child with the Archangels Michael and Gabriel.* c. 1504–1505, J. Paul Getty Museum, Los Angeles. Tempera, 13.4 x 10.2 in (34 x 26 cm). Licensed under CC0.

Unknown photographer. *Jeanne Hébuterne.* c. 1914–1919. Licensed under CC0.

Unknown photographer. *Jeanne Hébuterne.* 1919. Licensed under CC0.

Van Eyck, Jan. *The Adoration of The Mystic Lamb* from *The Ghent Altarpiece.* 1432, Sint-Baafs Cathedral, Ghent. Oil on panel, 52.4 x 92.9 in (133 x 236 cm). Photo by Dominique Provost and Hugo Maertens, contractual limitations.

Van Eyck, Jan. *Crucifixion and Last Judgment Diptych.* c. 1436–1438, Metropolitan Museum of Art, New York. Oil on canvas, 22.2 x 7.7 in (56.5 x 19.5 cm). Wikipedia Commons. Licensed under CC0.

Van Eyck, Jan. *The Singing Angels* from *The Ghent Altarpiece.* 1432, Sint-Baafs Cathedral, Ghent. Oil on panel, 64.7 x 27.2 in (165.5 x 69.3 cm). Artinflanders.be. Photo by Dominique Provost and Hugo Maertens, contractual limitations.

Van Eyck, Jan. The upper panels of *The Ghent Altarpiece.* 1432, Sint-Baafs Cathedral, Ghent. Oil on panel, 83.46 × 204.72 in (212 x 520 cm). Artinflanders.be. Photo by Dominique Provost and Hugo Maertens, contractual limitations.

Van Gogh, Vincent. *Portrait of a Man.* 1889, Van Gogh Museum, Amsterdam (Vincent van Gogh Foundation). Oil on canvas, 12.8 x 9.3 in (32.5 x 23.5 cm). Wikipedia Commons. Licensed under CC0.

Van Gogh, Vincent. *Portrait of a One-Eyed Man.* 1889, Van Gogh Museum, Amsterdam (Vincent van Gogh Foundation). Oil on canvas, 22.2 x 14.4 in (56.5 x 36.6 cm). Wikipedia Commons. Licensed under CC0.

Van Gogh, Vincent. *Young Man with Cornflower.* 1890, Private Collection. Oil on canvas, 15.9 x 12.4 in (40.5 x 31.5 cm). Wikipedia Commons. Licensed under CC0.

Van Kessel, Jan. *Concert of Cats.* c. 1650, Phoebus Foundation, Antwerp. Oil on copper, 5.3 x 6.5 in (13.5 x 16.5 cm). Wikipedia Commons. Licensed under CC0.

Vermeer, Johannes. *The Girl with the Wine Glass.* c. 1659, Herzog Anton Ulrich-Museum, Braunschweig. Oil on canvas, 30.7 x 26.4 in (78 x 67 cm). Wikipedia Commons. Licensed under CC0.

index